#49.95
4/25/11

BADMEN, BANDITS, AND FOLK HEROES

BADMEN, BANDITS, AND FOLK HEROES

The Ambivalence of
Mexican American Identity
in Literature and Film

Juan J. Alonzo

The University of Arizona Press   Tucson

The University of Arizona Press
© 2009 The Arizona Board of Regents
All rights reserved

www.uapress.arizona.edu

Library of Congress Cataloging-in-Publication Data
Alonzo, Juan José.
 Badmen, bandits, and folk heroes : the ambivalence of Mexican American
 identity in literature and film / Juan José Alonzo.
  p. cm.
 Includes bibliographical references and index.
 ISBN 978-0-8165-2868-4 (cloth : alk. paper)—
  1. Mexican Americans in motion pictures. 2. Stereotypes (Social psychology) in motion pictures. 3. Motion pictures—United States—History—
 20th century. 4. Mexican Americans in literature. 5. Stereotypes (Social
 psychology) in literature. 6. American literature—History and criticism.
 I. Title.
PN1995.9.M49A46   2009
791.43'65296872073—dc22   2009008729

Publication of this book is made possible in part by the proceeds of a permanent
endowment created with the assistance of a Challenge Grant from the National
Endowment for the Humanities, a federal agency.

Manufactured in the United States of America on acid-free, archival-quality paper
and processed chlorine free.

14   13   12   11   6   5   4   3   2

Contents

Figures

BADMEN, BANDITS, AND FOLK HEROES

Introduction

Ambivalence and Contingency in the Representation of Mexican Identity

In an early scene from Jim Mendiola's independent Chicano/a production *Come and Take It Day* (2002), Miguel and Jesse, the two main characters of the story, rap about the meanings of cultural identity in the contemporary world.

MIGUEL: Alright, what does this mean: neo-hippie-*pachuco?*

JESSE: What?!

MIGUEL: Neo-hippie-pachuco?

JESSE: Let me guess, that high-Spanic college chick, right? . . . Neo-hippie-pachuco. Alright, you know what a pachuco is, right?

MIGUEL: Yeah, like Eddie Olmos in *Zoot Suit*. [Imitating Olmos] "*Órale!*"

JESSE: Yeah. And "neo" means new.

MIGUEL: Okay, like *nuevo*.

JESSE: And you probably had a flower behind your ear like you always do, *¿qué no?* Like a hippie?

MIGUEL: Yeah.

JESSE: *Pues, hay 'ta.* Neo-hippie-pachuco. The *ruca* was saying that you're mixing a Mexican style with an Anglo one.

MIGUEL: Ah, okay.

JESSE: It's all about hybridity, *¿tú sabes?*

As this scene suggests, Miguel and Jesse well represent the contingency of modern Mexican American identity, for these characters mix popular cultural styles to suit their expressive needs. They understand the particular meanings and malleability of images, and they rework and recombine them in self-conscious and ironic ways. This hybridizing of identity is nothing new for Chicanos/as, since *mestizaje* goes to the core of their existence. Provocatively, even the blending of Anglo elements is not necessarily new, for Miguel and Jesse remind us of an earlier incarnation of the *pachuco*, Louie Rodriguez in Jose Montoya's classic Chicano/a movement poem "El Louie." In the 1960s, Louie could be seen "sporting a dark topcoat / playing in his fantasy / the role of Bogart, Cagney / or Raft." Louie could also embody personas from Mexican popular culture and play them with high style. "He dug roles, man, / and names—like 'Blackie,' 'Little / Louie'" (334).

Together, Miguel, Jesse, and Louie stand as exemplary figures of hybridity and cultural exchange as they incorporate American and Mexican popular cultural forms to create mixed and multiple identities. Louie, for instance, celebrates the roles of his favorite actors and characters to make up the palette for his subjective formation, allowing him to live "like in the / mono [movie]." Louie, Miguel, and Jesse's ability to create contingent identities is indicative of the condition of Chicano/a culture in the United States.[1] Montoya's line, "He dug roles, man," and Jesse's line, "It's all about hybridity, ¿tú sabes?" demonstrate the pleasure to be derived at the site/sight of the subject's representation, even when that representation carries potentially negative determinations, as in the formation of stereotypes. "El Louie" and *Come and Take It Day* initiate a dialogue between American and Mexican identities on the one hand, and between film and literature on the other. The formation of identities and the productive intersection of film and literature in the articulation of said identities make up the principle concerns of this study.

Badmen, Bandits, and Folk Heroes argues that Mexican male identity representation in American culture may be productively read in terms of its ambivalent or contingent status. Acknowledging the importance and necessity of Chicano/a critiques of the stereotype begun in the sixties and seventies, I depart from the insistence that stereotypes only negatively determine subjectivity. For instance, Rosa Linda Fregoso, in her exemplary study of Chicano/a cinema, *The Bronze Screen*, takes as given that "[n]egative representations about Chicanos originated during the first moving pictures" (xvii). While this assessment is incontrovertible, to stop at the recognition of "negative" representations does not tell the whole story.[2] Drawing upon the psychoanalytic, postmodern, and postcolonial theories of subjectivity in the work of Homi Bhabha and others, I propose that rather than seeing images as "positive" or "negative," we should examine instead the ambivalent points of attraction and revulsion within representations of Mexican identity.

By emphasizing the ways in which the stereotype's anxious repetitions reveal the impossibility of a fixed or original identity, we begin to understand that the stereotype is a construct, part of a representational apparatus. The stereotype must repeat itself to establish certain "truths" about the ethnic subject, but its repetitions produce a multiplicity of meanings or truths, which cannot all equally stand within the stereotype's logic. Revealing the stereotype's multiplicity finally enables "a transgression of [its] limits" by the very subjects who are "at once the object[s] of desire and derision" (Bhabha, 67). Indeed, because the stereotype cannot reliably point to the subject's identity, it is possible to read it in a "contradictory way" (70). Interpreting the stereotype in a contradictory or resistant fashion permits the subjects of its determinations to escape its often derogatory reasoning.

My theoretical perspective reads cultural identity as emerging out of lived cultural practices and social conditions rather than from predetermined cultural essences. This is an insight that contemporary post–Chicano/a Movement thinkers have made.[3] Renato Rosaldo, for instance, has observed the "demise of self-enclosed, patriarchal, 'authentic' Chicano culture" accompanied by a playful "improvisation and recombination" of diverse traditions (149, 215). The unique contribution my project proposes is the notion that the contingency of Mexican American cultural identity is not a new phenomenon, as Rosaldo implies. In fact, we see its expressions in the early work of Américo Paredes, and even in the work of non-Mexican writers such as Stephen Crane. Thus, these writers respond to the ambivalence of ethnic representation by demonstrating that contingency is its complement. Contemporarily, cultural contingency is the dominant mode of expression for Chicano/a writers and filmmakers alike, as my discussion of Evangelina Vigil and Jim Mendiola demonstrates in the concluding chapter.

While my study comments upon Mexican American representation in its variety of forms, my analysis will focus on the production and contestation of Mexican masculinity as it appears in several significant cinematic and literary incarnations, namely, in the characters of the "greaser," bandit, revolutionary, "badman," and social deviant. The Mexican male as a villainous figure appears as early as 1840s conquest fiction, but his enduring presence is owed to the concurrent emergence of the cinema in the United States at the turn of the century, to the consequent wholesale adaptation of previous literary stereotypes, and to the eruption of the Mexican Revolution in 1910. The Mexican Revolution, in particular, constitutes an important historical and aesthetic conjuncture, and it will allow a dialogue between film and literature and lead to alternative readings of film stereotypes. The historical causes of the revolution, as James Cockcroft has argued, include the continuance of a dependent, neo-colonial relationship between U.S. business interests and the government of Mexico (85–114). Due to its failures, the revolution exacerbated the relationship of dominance and subordination between Anglo-American culture and Mexican culture on both sides of the border. This relation of dominance, as José Limón recognizes, "bears some similarities to classic examples of world colonialism" ("Tex-Sex-Mex," 614), and this colonial relation is borne out in the ways that stereotypes are used to pejoratively define the Mexican threat.[4] In the realm of popular culture, the revolution and its figures form the iconic material from which cinematic stereotypes of greasers, bandits, and revolutionaries take their inspiration. Contrary to expectations, however, my examination of the Mexican Revolution and the stereotypical deployments of its figures does not merely decry the deprecatory subjectification of the Mexican, though this does not escape notice. Instead, it focuses on contradictions and slippages in the depiction of the Mexican male. Beginning with turn-of-the-century adventure stories and silent Westerns, I challenge accepted assumptions that early representations of the Mexican are simply stereotypically "negative." My recognition of ambivalence makes way for the re-imagination of a previously elided Mexican—and, by extension, Mexican American—history and identity.

As I lay out the theoretical framework of my study in the next several pages, it is also necessary to explain my focus on masculinity. The Anglo-American production of stereotypes often presents Mexican men and women in very different lights, with the Mexican male receiving the brunt of the denigrating depictions and the woman frequently cast as the object of erotic attraction. While the representation of Mexican women is by no means always positive, it is certainly true that depictions of women are often framed within overt feelings of desire. For instance, in his cataloguing of the six basic Latino/a stereotypes in American movies, Charles Ramírez Berg lists *el bandido*, the male buffoon, and the Latin lover among the male stereotypes, while he notes the harlot, the female clown, and the dark lady among the female stereotypes (*Latino Images*, 66–77). Among the Latina stereotypes, even the most negative one—the harlot—is tinged with a manifest desire for the female Other that is not present in male stereotypes. As for the most positive male stereotype, that of the Latin lover, it is overdetermined with anxiety, fear, and jealousy.

Yet a close examination of the construction of Mexican masculinities reveals that even in the case of the Mexican male, who stands as among the most derided objects of literary and popular cultural representation, we witness latent admiration, desire, and even identification. *Badmen, Bandits, and Folk Heroes* focuses on the multivalent ways in which desire emerges through seemingly negative representations of Mexican male identity. Furthermore, by comparing the construction of Mexican masculinity with that of Anglo-American masculinity, we will see the complex similarities and instances of identification between these two cultural constructions. To be sure, I will not ignore the importance of Mexican female representation as part of a triangle of stereotypical relations. The Mexican female often constitutes a point of attraction in literary and cinematic texts that influences the forms Mexican male depictions take.

In "The Other Question" in his book *The Location of Culture*, Homi Bhabha introduces the idea of ambivalence in his discussion of the production of the stereotype in colonial discourse. He argues that if "[t]he object of colonial discourse is to construe the colonized as a population of degenerate types on the basis of racial origin, in order to justify conquest and to establish systems of administration and instruction" (70), then the stereotype is a key apparatus of dominance utilized by the colonial administration. Bhabha undermines the now conventional understanding of the stereotype as it has been conceptualized since Gordon Allport in *The Nature of Prejudice* (1954). This view holds that stereotypes "are primarily images within a category invoked by the individual to justify either love-prejudice or hate-prejudice" (189). Allport's view, in other words, gives the stereotype a strict binary quality: it is either an exaggeration of all that is deemed "positive" in an object or, in our contemporary way of understanding the stereotype, it is a representation of all that is "negative" in an object.

The stereotype contains within it a sense of "fixity," which is an under-standing clearly present in Allport's either/or construction. In order to sustain dominance, the colonial discourse is dependent "on the concept of 'fixity' in the ideological construction of otherness" (66). "Fixity" is a form of represen-tation that permits the Manichaean oppositions between the white Self and the colored Other: the colonizer is awarded the qualities of good and the colonized the qualities of evil, and this construction demands that the polar-ity between Self and Other remain fixed in place. Because the appearance of movement or variance in the representation of Self and Other can only subvert the possibility of colonial domination, fixity becomes an obsession. While "fixity" implies rigidity and static qualities, it also implies a fix-ation or fear that must be repeated over and over in order to reassure itself, and it is in its repetition that fixity marks its impossibility: "[f]ixity, as the sign of cultural/historical/racial difference in the discourse of colonialism, is a paradoxical mode of representation: it connotes rigidity and an unchanging order as well as disorder, degeneracy and daemonic repetition" (66). Thus, we may draw a homology between the idea of fixity and the idea of the stereotype: both concepts move between "what is 'in place', what is already known, and something that must anxiously be repeated." Therefore, the stereotype, as a form of knowledge that must continuously be repeated, "can never really, in discourse, be proved" (66). And it is here, in its impossible fixity, that we are able to see the stereotype as an ambivalent and vacillating form of discourse.

What is most useful in Bhabha's analysis of the stereotype is that it opens the possibility for a reading of a *"productive* ambivalence" in "that 'otherness' which is at once an object of desire and derision" (67). Bhabhan ambivalence operates in two ways. Initially, it "is the force of ambivalence that gives the colonial stereotype its currency: ensures its repeatability in changing historical conjunctures; informs its strategies of individuation and marginalization" (66), and thus makes possible the subjectification of the colonized Other. In its ambi-valence, ambivalence makes possible continuously changing representations of a supposedly unchanging, fixed Other. But ambivalence also contains an internally subverting function, signaled here by the use of the modifier "productive": we may read in the stereotype a *"productive* ambivalence" because "such a reading reveals . . . the boundaries of colonial discourse and it enables a transgression of these limits from the space of that otherness" (67).

A productive reading of the stereotype's ambivalence marks the point from which to initiate a conversation on Mexican stereotypes in Anglo-American cultural production. In my analysis, I employ the term "stereotype" without necessarily implying that it contains a derogatory connotation, though it often does. Stereotypes, as Allport recognizes, may be "positive" or "negative." Nevertheless, it is necessary to move away from the notion that stereotypes are either positive or negative because such judgments presuppose established standards of positivity or negativity, a "real" reality against which to compare stereotypes. I agree with Bhabha when he notes that the "analytic of ambivalence questions dogmatic and moralistic positions on the meaning of oppression and discrimination. . . . [T]he point of intervention should shift from the ready recognition of images as positive or negative, to an understanding of the *processes of subjectification* made possible (and plausible) through stereotypical discourse" (67). The question of *plausible processes of subjectification* is an important one because it asks the Chicano/a spectator to judge images not against an essential and unwavering past identification, but in the context of present (but also possibly past), changing, and future subjective formations.

To judge the stereotype in relation to a presupposed Chicano/a reality or "truth" sets up a binary between positive/negative, real/unreal images that inverts the original Manichaean dialectic of the stereotype. If, initially, white equals good and colored equals evil, then the inverted dialectic states that white equals evil and colored equals good. Like the original dialectic, the inverted dialectic depends on "fixed" notions of identity, and these notions are locked in unchanging past traditions. While a reference to past traditions has specific tactical purposes, past traditions cannot entirely account for present and future articulations of subjectivity. If tradition is necessarily renewed by the present circumstances of culture, then the polar and insistent negation of the stereotype fails to make this renewal possible. To negate the stereotype against a transcendent realist standard does nothing more than reproduce the stereotype, albeit in an inverted form—we simplistically move from "hate-prejudice" to "love-prejudice." As Bhabha illustrates, the stereotype, "as the primary point of subjectification . . . for both colonizer and colonized, is the scene of a similar fantasy and defence—the desire for an originality which is again threatened by the differences of race, colour and culture" (75). My argument, then, is that both colonizer and colonized are subjectified within the stereotype's "desire for an originality," perhaps especially more so when we resort to underdeveloped arguments about positive or negative stereotypes.

The positive or negative reading of stereotypical images, what Ella Shohat and Robert Stam call "stereotypes and distortions" analysis (178) or "image" analysis (220), demonstrates a marked preoccupation with a demand for realism. Shohat and Stam thus support the position that a reductive reading of positivity/negativity within stereotypes produces limited insights in the analysis of media images such as film. "Much of the work on ethnic/racial and colonial representation in the media has been 'corrective,' devoted to demonstrating that certain films, in some respect or other, 'got something wrong' on historical, biographical, or other grounds of accuracy. While these 'stereotypes and distortions' analyses pose legitimate questions about social plausibility and mimetic accuracy, about negative and positive images, they are often premised on an exclusive allegiance to an esthetic of verisimilitude" (178). The demand for realism is understandable, for as critics and viewers we also expect truth or authenticity based on our experiences, but too strict a demand for realism assumes that the experiential perspective from which a realist critique is launched is itself "unproblematic, transparent, and easily accessible" (178). Strict expectations of realism confuse realism as a cinematic strategy allied with particular genres operating with the aim of producing realism as an effect—for instance, the standard Hollywood drama—with realism as a critical goal of the cinema, wherein "realism" does not exist within the film's diegesis but only as a result of the film's critical operations.

We witness these alternative (i.e., nonrealistic) modes of representation in the ideological production or contestation of the real, for instance, in the films of Guillermo Gómez-Peña, the contemporary Mexican/Chicano performance artist. Gómez-Peña's cinematic style sets aside all pretense of "realism" in order to make his critiques of American cultural attitudes towards the Other all the more biting and all the more "real." An unnuanced insistence on the image as positive or negative, as realistic or unrealistic, overlooks other possible analyses of a film, especially ones in which the stereotype is read otherwise, or in which a stereotype is used to reflexively call attention to a particular theme or idea related to identity formation.

Moving beyond a thumbs-up/thumbs-down perspective on the question of realism allows us to develop the possibility for a dialogical analysis of film in which the "naïve faith in 'truth' and 'reality'" are supplanted by a critical and all-encompassing relationship with cultural expression. Shohat and Stam argue that "consciousness and artistic practice . . . do not come into contact with the 'real' directly but rather through the medium of the surrounding ideological world. Literature, and by extension, cinema, do not so much refer to or call up the world as represent its languages and discourses" (180). By moving away from an analysis of purely positive and negative images to an analysis of ambivalence within stereotypical images, in this study I propose a similar discursive move. Additionally, by putting literature and film in dialogue with one another, I show how one allows us to critically read the other, and how both mediums provide an understanding of the subject in question—Mexican male identity—that is far more nuanced than what each medium could provide on its own.

One of the aims of *Badmen, Bandits, and Folk Heroes* is to open a conversation about U.S. film and literature that critiques the "traditional reliance on the stereotype as offering, *at any one time*, a *secure* point of identification," and to examine the possibility that *"at other times and places*, the same stereotype may be read in a contradictory way, or, indeed, misread" (Bhabha, 69–70). By offering contradictory readings of Mexican American stereotypes, we may articulate Mexican American identity formations that are not limited—as in the inverted dialectic—by an absolute negation of Whiteness, nor, for that matter, by essentialist or strictly realist conceptions of Mexicanness.

Having proposed the possibility of reading the stereotype in an ambivalent fashion, there yet remains the necessity of delineating oppositional strategies for subverting it. In the discussion that follows, I theorize upon and supply practical examples of such contradictory and subversive readings. As I have noted, Bhabha suggests "in a very preliminary way, that the stereotype is a complex, ambivalent, contradictory mode of representation, as anxious as it is assertive, and demands not only that we extend our critical and political objectives but that we change the object of analysis as well" (70). A close investigation of "The Other Question" and other essays reveals a set of related psychoanalytic concepts that open a space for subverting stereotypical representation. Because the stereotype is an "arrested, fixated form of representation" (75), it locates the subject in an impossible fixed point of origin that may be so identified because it seems timeless—even as it subtly changes over time. A reading of the ambivalence within the stereotype is a reading that destabilizes the stereotype's ability to deprecatorily define the objects of its derision. Significantly, the contradictory reading is applied by precisely those subjects who have been "fixed" by the stereotype.[5] Although there is a long history of resistance to stereotypical representations, stereotypical subversions as forms of resistance are less well documented.[6]

Stereotypical subversion is made possible by the psychic process of subjective "splitting," a central concept in Bhabha's analysis of colonial relations. Splitting, in Freudian and Lacanian psychoanalysis, is the site of the subject's coming to conscious being and individuation by way of a primal separation from the mother that is deepened by the incest prohibition and enforced by the father or other authority figure. "In Lacanian calculus, '$' designates the split subject produced by primal repression. Never identical with itself, the faulty subject is haunted by an unknowable Other. An 'outside' that is 'inside,' this Other hollows out the place of desire" (M. Taylor, 101). Splitting marks a crucial moment in subjective self-awareness, a problematic yet unavoidable moment of pain and separation that leads to individual self-formation.

Bhabha draws an analogy between subjective splitting at the psychic level and a similar process at the levels of social authority and power. His reading of Frantz Fanon's *Black Skin, White Masks* (1952) uncovers the splitting of the ethnic subject in sites of colonialist racial differentiation and discrimination. In one of these "myths of origin of the marking of the subject within the racist practices and discourses of a colonial culture," Bhabha recounts the instance when a "white girl fixes Fanon in a look and word as she turns to identify with her mother. It is a scene which echoes endlessly through his essay 'The fact of blackness': 'Look, a Negro . . . Mama, see the Negro! I'm frightened.' 'What else could it be for me,' Fanon concludes, 'but an amputation, an excision, a haemorrhage that spattered my whole body with black blood'" (qtd. in Bhabha, 75–76). Like the moment of psychic splitting, the instance of colonial splitting draws the subject apart, but in a more violent manner. In another instance of splitting that is yet more significant for the objectives of my study, we learn of a moment in Fanon when "the child encounters racial and cultural stereotypes in children's fictions, where white heroes and black demons are proffered as points of ideological and psychical identification" (76). The example of splitting occurs in the precise encounter between the colonized Other and cultural representation. The Other is given a complex choice: identify with the "black demon" whose physiognomy is like yours, or, more likely and problematically, reject blackness—hence yourself—and identify with the "white hero," whom you definitely do not resemble. Either choice splits the colonial subject.

We see a strong analogy between, in the first instance, subjective splitting at the scene of maternal separation and sexual prohibition, and, in the second instance, colonial splitting at the scene of racial discrimination and stereotype production. This analogy links the concepts of gender and race in a manner that may richly complicate our readings of stereotypes, as I argue in my reading of *Viva Villa!* (1934) in chapter four, where the narrative feminizes an already raced Pancho Villa in order to make the differences between the superior Anglo characters and the weaker Mexican characters seemingly natural. The return, over and over, to markers of difference such as race and sex—while at the same time claiming equality among Mexicans and Anglos—constitutes a form of fetishism within the film's narrative. As the negation of difference, fetishism is the "repetitious scene around the subject of castration"; furthermore, fetishism is "always a 'play' or vacillation between the archaic affirmation of wholeness/similarity . . . and the anxiety associated with lack and difference" (Bhabha, 74). This oscillation between affirmation and negation of sexual/racial difference produces "multiple and contradictory belief" and makes "that threatened division" or splitting all the more powerful (75). As I will claim, the critical process of exposing the gaps between affirmation and negation, sameness and difference, presents the possibility of empowering the ethnic subject, returning a partial wholeness.

My argument, to clarify, is that splitting opens the way for the strategy of subversive reading by way of the fetish. If the "role of fetishistic [and stereotypical] identification . . . is to provide a process of splitting," it also then provides *"multiple/contradictory belief at the point of enunciation and subjectification"* (80, emphasis mine). The above statement is a key connection between the process of splitting and the possibility of contradictorily and subversively reading the stereotype, for splitting is not just a sundering of the subject; it is also a doubling, a multiplying of the subject. The idea of enunciation is central here because, as Robert Young argues, "the question of enunciation demonstrates the operation of a subject already" (*White Mythologies*, 142). In other words, the "point of enunciation and subjectification" implies the presence of a possibly active and resistant subject. I argue throughout my project that the subject of discourses of power—the Mexican male as a stereotypical "bandit revolutionary" in an example that follows—is a conflicted, split subject, and its splitting contains the possibility of multiple enunciatory positions (in this case, by way of performance) that demarcate the possibility of an agential subject.

Undeniably, the stereotype's easy categorizations and alignments of, for example, white/colored and good/evil, are "disturbed by the representation of splitting in the discourse" (Bhabha, 81). This disturbance is apparent in one particular instance in *The Fact of Blackness: Frantz Fanon and Visual Representation* (Read, 1996), a collection of essays and dialogues among artists and cultural theorists. In one of these dialogues, participants discuss the Hottentot Venus, the nineteenth-century African woman who was put on display throughout England in order to "prove" the essential animality of Africans. Renée Green, a visual artist whose art comments on the Hottentot Venus, provides a rationale for her work.

> I was trying to figure out the way in which a body could be visualized, especially a black female body, yet address the complexity of reading that presence without relinquishing pleasure or history. I used a clinical engraved image of the Hottentot Venus, a combination of texts by critics of Josephine Baker and a nineteenth-century traveler's text. . . . These elements in combination were intended to stimulate viewers into imagining in-between spaces: in-between what is said and what is not said and ways of being that didn't quite fit into what seemed to be the designated categories. (146)

This appropriation of the Hottentot Venus's image performs as a strategy of subversive reading and historical reclamation. Green takes the iconic text of the Hottentot Venus and through a series of re-articulations alters the possible understandings of this particular black body.

In similar fashion, another artist, Lyle Ashton Harris, uses the image of the Venus's body to subvert expectations about its significations. Harris's work, in collaboration with Renée Valerie Cox, sees in the Venus's image a "way of exploring my psychic identification with the image at the level of spectacle. I am playing with what it means to be an African diasporic artist producing and selling work in a culture that is by and large narcissistically mired in the debasement and objectification of blackness" (150). Harris and Cox read the image of the Hottentot Venus against the grain of conventional stereotype analysis, which would simply dismiss this image. As a repository of colonialist stereotypes of the Other, the Hottentot Venus demonstrates a certain "fixity," but she also demonstrates ambivalence. In an interview with W.J.T. Mitchell, Homi Bhabha argues that "there are certain regimes of sense, discourse, governmentality, and polity that function in and through the ambivalent social relations created in the social and discursive act of splitting" (W.J.T. Mitchell, 82). Through splitting, both colonizer and colonized come into being, but the "split doesn't fall at the same point" for these subjects. Crucially, this differential split "allows . . . the colonized the strategy of attempting to disarticulate the voice of authority at the point of splitting" (82). In my analysis of Mexican identity representation, the moment of disarticulation is coterminous with the moment when the Other recognizes him-or herself in the stereotype, then subverts it. In subverting the stereotype's ambivalence, a new understanding takes place, and it brings with it a new subjective formation, which is what Green is after when she imagines "ways of being that didn't quite fit into what seemed to be the designated categories." Significantly, the Other's histories and knowledges are not ignored, but taken and renovated through creative juxtapositions. What begins as a negative moment of splitting moves to recognition, subversion, and finally, renewal.

Stuart Hall calls cultural renewal an "imaginative rediscovery" of cultural memory and identity. Green's cultural reclamations are forms of "imaginative rediscovery" because in any "re-telling of the past," there is necessarily a creative act that involves a "production of identity" (222). Hall contrasts the idea of imaginative rediscovery with the realist tendency that concerns itself with tracing back exact essences or origins; this tendency seeks to un-cover the "real" cultural formations that the stereotype has missed. Imaginative rediscovery differs from the kind of activity that attempts to "excavate, bring to light, and express" (221), in a reflexive fashion, "true" and "authentic" cultural formations. Imaginative rediscovery contains an active sense that the search for authenticity does not; it represents a sense in which cultural identity "is a matter of 'becoming' as well as 'being.'" Hall acknowledges that "[c]ultural identities come from somewhere, have histories" (223). At the same time, however, "like everything which is historical, they undergo constant transformation. Far from being eternally fixed in some essentialized past, they are subject to the continuous 'play' of history, culture, and power. Far from being grounded in a mere 'recovery' of the past, which is waiting to be found and which, when found, will secure our sense of ourselves into eternity, identities are the names we give to the different ways we are positioned by, and position ourselves within, the narratives of the past" (223).

Hall's statement is important for two reasons. First, "rediscovery" and "reclamation" do not signal the recovery of an essential identity that exists in the past; they acknowledge the mediating role of history, as well as the possibility of transforming those past identity formations that seem essential and unchanging. Second, Hall's statement succinctly calls attention to anti-essentialist notions of culture. If, in Bhabha, "productive ambivalence" helps us unhinge the "fixity" of the stereotype, then Hall's "imaginative rediscovery" gives us access to dispersed, and sometimes obliterated, marginal histories that we may adapt to present circumstances.

I self-consciously use the pronouns "us" and "we" to signal an array of subject positions: "us" and "we" as ethnic subjects, critical spectators, cultural critics, and artistic producers. Our subject positions depend, in part, upon "our positions of *enunciation* . . . though we speak . . . of ourselves and from our own experience, nevertheless, who speaks and the subject who is spoken of are never exactly in the same place" (Hall, 220). This displaced positionality intensifies when someone else speaks for us, as in the Hollywood narratives that speak for the Mexican. This is the subject position we recognize as "the space of that otherness" (Bhabha, 67). The series of related concepts I have thus far introduced allow us, as those Other spectators, to speak precisely from a space of Otherness in transformative ways. Like the literature and film I place side by side, the critical spectator is another member of the broad constellation of discursive exchanges that allow us to think about Mexican American subjective formation. It is our initial response to stereotypes that may allow us to "look beyond caricatural representations to see the oppressed performing self," while subsequent viewings may permit us, "in a kind of double consciousness," an enjoyment despite what we "know to be misrepresentations" (Shohat and Stam, 182). This enjoyment recalls the pleasure in Louie's appropriations of cinematic representations in "El Louie," or Miguel's self-caricature as a "hippie-pachuco" in *Come and Take It Day*. Through a double-consciousness and critical enjoyment, we see the stereotype's ambivalence and tip the balance to articulate positive subjectivities.

We can now place the spectator's subversive readings and subsequent cultural renovations of Mexican identity representations in relation to contemporary identity formations. My first example of subversive reading derives from a private context—although representation, we should remember, is always public. I vividly recall as a child spending Saturday afternoons watching American Westerns with my father. As is well known, it was a usual practice in the movies to use Mexican actors to play Native American characters, perhaps because by that time there were very few Native Americans in urban California, perhaps because there was a cheaply available workforce of aspiring Mexican actors to play bit parts. My father and I watched these films, and upon the first appearance of the Indian, my father would customarily say, "*Él es mexicano*"—"He is a Mexican." The statement was usually uttered in a nonjudgmental, purely observational tone, but the consistency of its utterance served as a positive reminder of the Mexican presence, specifically in Hollywood, and more generally, in U.S. society and culture. While affirming this disguised Mexican presence behind the stereotyped image of the Indian may seem naïve, I think my father was pointing less to the representation than to the corporeal presence of the Mexican actor. My father well understood that in the Hollywood Western, the Mexican appears as bandit or fool, so pointing to the Mexican "Indian" was a way for him to note that Mexicans could play other roles, albeit similarly denigrated ones. A Mexican playing an Indian was proof of the quality of Mexicans' acting skills. My father was saying, in other words, that *mexicanos* are not the content of their stereotyped images, that they could play other, roles not customarily assigned to them.

At the deepest levels of unconscious identification, my father's affirming of the Indian on the screen was perhaps an affirmation of the Mexican's oftentimes repressed indigenous identity. While the stereotyped image of the Indian "splits" the Native American spectator, my father, because of his own repressed Native American identity, was split differently, and he was somewhat able to distance himself from the Indian. Yet instead of disavowal, these images produced a kind of affirmation. The recognition of the Mexican beneath the image of the Indian contains a double and reversing avowal that points to an even greater possibility for Hall's "imaginative rediscovery" of subjectivity: the deeply repressed Indian subject appears on the surface of the screen while the Mexican subject is recognized beneath the surface, on the body of the actor. Reading the Mexican in the Indian, then, allowed my Mexican father to imaginatively reclaim an indigenous heritage while making a claim for his Mexican subjectivity in U.S. culture.

The above anecdotal history of reception demonstrates the myriad private ways in which public representations of Otherness may be read. My father was taking his resistant knowledge of the Mexican stereotype, re-reading the stereotype of the Native American, and affirming the fleeting presence of his Mexicanness, beyond the stereotypes of the Mexican bandit and of the Indian that were given him. This was one way my father "misread" the stereotype; another way he did so was by taking the side of the Indian, no matter how un-heroic his representation. My father's critical stance contained a "different historical and (mass) cultural vision" of his place in American culture. This vision is one that creates a "space for an alternative narrative of what can now be called the ethno-racialized cultures of displacement" (J. Saldívar, *Border Matters*, 7). My father's own displacement, of course, occurred in his immigration to the United States, and a second displacement occurred when he found himself relatively erased on the Western's screen. His subversion of the stereotype, therefore, provided the means by which he could reinscribe his particular and alternative vision within dominant American discourses.

Contradictory readings may take on yet other forms. My father's are those of the Other's encounter with the stereotype's "fixity," and another example of subversion begins from the point of enunciation, when the Other is forced to enunciate itself in a deprecating fashion. This occurs in John Huston's *The Treasure of the Sierra Madre* (1948), in which the Mexican revolutionary appears. *Treasure's* subversions serve as a second introductory example of my object, theory, and method. By the time the image of the bandit appears in this film, its stereotype in American cinema has already undergone several alterations. The image of the bandit first appears in silent "greaser" films and continues in Westerns of the 1960s and beyond. After the Mexican Revolution of 1910–20, the stereotypical bandit iconography as we understand it today begins to dominate: the bandit is recognizable by "the unkempt appearance, the weaponry and *bandolero* bullet belts, the funny-looking sombrero, the sneering look" (Ramírez Berg, *Latino Images*, 8). What occurs in some Westerns set in the 1800s is the "historically inaccurate and anachronistic" (9) insertion of an image whose historical origin is the 1910s. More to the point, this is an image whose revolutionary import is completely evacuated by the negatively valenced criminal stereotype of the Mexican *bandido*.

The bandit revolutionary makes a cameo appearance in *Treasure*, and he comes at us with full stereotypical—and actual—guns blazing. He shows up, predictably, to take all he can, whether it be money, gold, or guns. In the most memorable scene of the film, Gold Hat (Antonio Bedoya) and his band of cutthroats stumble upon Fred C. Dobbs (Humphrey Bogart) and company as they prospect for gold in the mountains of Mexico. Initially, Gold Hat claims he and his group are the *federales*, the Mexican army, in search of vaguely alluded-to insurgents. When Dobbs asks to see their badges, Gold Hat scowls and famously responds, "Badges? We ain't got no badges. We don't need no badges. I don't have to show you any stinkin' badges!" And with this, the shooting starts.

The film uses the stand-off for comic relief, and the stereotype of the bandit is the joke's central core. While I agree that *Treasure* is not merely "another Hollywood foray into stereotypical Mexico" because it contains "a critique of U.S. imperialism" (Ramírez Berg, 101), the notion of the bandit as comic buffoon persists, for by 1948 his image is burdened with its stereotype's negative baggage.[7] In fact, one reason the bandit stereotype persists is that, like most stereotypes, it possesses a "narrative economy" that "require[s] little or no introduction or explanation" (46). In *Treasure*, the implication of the stereotype's narrative economy is that the viewer already knows the bandit's story, already knows that he is treacherous, unintelligent, and a buffoon. In other words, the bandit is the joke we are already in on. Therefore, he serves as a quick and convenient instrument of filmic humor. Gold Hat is shown in close-up for full comic effect, with a sweaty, dirty brow, a large sombrero, and a full mustache. He grimaces, he laughs loudly, he opens his mouth wide and leans back (fig. 1). His features and actions are distorted. He wears a bandoleer. Humorously, Gold Hat is shot through his hat, an action that in Freudian terms symbolizes castration, another instance of subjective splitting.

The stereotype's persistence—its continuing "fixity"—contains, at the same time, a countervailing impulse, an ambivalence. What fascinates me in the bandit's appearance is that his stereotype builds and builds until it can no longer sustain its distortions. In part, Bedoya's individual performance (and perhaps John Huston's ironic sense of humor) reveals the ambivalence. Ramírez Berg sees actors such as Lupe Velez and Gilbert Roland as examples of Latinos "who have resisted stereotyping, resisted as much as they could while being caught within the grip of Hollywood's stereotypical filmmaking conventions" (102).[8] Bedoya's acting produces similar results, but I would add that it is the spectator's ability to critically read the stereotype that makes the circuit of subversion complete. In the film, the bandit is not merely a mean, grotesque, and comic figure. This bandit stares straight at the camera and defies the signifying system's attempt to fix him as an inferior figure. His laughter is especially subversive, for it seems aimed at the very audience who may be comfortable with his fixed inferior status. If "in the objectification of the scopic drive there is always the threatened return of the look," and if "in the identification of the Imaginary relation there is always an alienating other (or mirror) which crucially returns its image to the subject" (Bhabha, 81), then Gold Hat returns the colonial gaze in his close-ups, and his laughter is as defiant as it is comical. In the scene at issue, three separate subversions occur. First, the Mexican actor's ability to inhabit himself outside the stereotype starts the circuit of critique. Then, the Mexican spectator's recognition of Mexican subjectivity outside the stereotype's fixity furthers it. Finally, the destabilizing stare of the Mexican subject escapes colonialism's administrative apparatus, creating a space for "creative rediscovery."

Gold Hat's anti-colonial posture also has its correlate in contemporary Mexican American social movements, in which we see a transformation of the bandit's comic speech. The unforgettable "We don't need no stinkin' badges"—as Mel Brooks famously riffs on the line in *Blazing Saddles*—was

FIGURE 1. Antonio Bedoya as Gold Hat in *The Treasure of the Sierra Madre* (Warner Bros.,1948) (DVD frame enlargement).

recently taken up as a slogan by civil rights groups in California in their protest against anti-immigration measures. In response to the government's demands for "proper" identification from all Latinos/as, American citizens included, the group held up signs that read, "We don't need no stinkin' badges." The phrase, therefore, uttered by a comical, stereotyped figure, acquires political dimensions through a complicated series of re-readings.[9]

As these examples show, my study agrees with the goals of contemporary Chicano/a cultural studies scholars, who, in the words of José David Saldívar, seek to "place greater research emphasis on the ways in which our lived memory and popular culture are linked—on how the postmodern shocks of electronic mass media create a crisis of 'absolutist' paradigms of national culture and [how] collective memory frames the production and reception of commercial culture." And "while new technologies certainly lend themselves to new forms of exploitation and oppression . . . , they also have utopian uses as new forms of resistance and struggle" (35). As Chicanos/as and as Americans, our identities come to be formed through our participation in the production and consumption of popular cultural forms. *Badmen, Bandits, and Folk Heroes* seeks to expand our understanding of how we use new (and old) technologies, and how we are used by them, for we must be ever watchful of the ways in which dominant cultural products can both imprison us and set us free. The production of ethnic stereotypes, for example, continues to define Mexican Americans in denigrating ways. But because these dominant cultural productions exploit us, they may also be reworked and used, if not to liberate us, then certainly to demonstrate our irrepressible presence in and redefinition of American culture.

In the chapters that follow, I read the ambivalence of film stereotypes and recover forms of memory and identity that are empowering for Mexican Americans. My proposed practice is important because the stereotype gives us entry into literary and cinematic texts in ways that permit critique, but also in ways that allow us to reclaim the images and overlay them with more productive readings. I also bring Mexican American and Anglo-American literature—what we can now call Greater Mexican literature[10]—into dialogue with film; I see in such a dialogue yet another possibility for the production of cultural memory. Delineating the interactions between film and literature permits an un-fixing of the stereotype. If the stereotype is an iconic shorthand for the repressed and disfigured histories of the ethnic subject, then the dialogues between film and literature may help us rewrite these erased histories so as to allow us to imagine a more complicated Mexican subjectivity. Literature, as a form of cultural memory, can help us counter the stereotype's fix-ations. The following chapter outline describes the ways in which I bring film and literature together in order to fully theorize the ambivalent character of stereotypes and the contingent quality of Mexican American identity.

The issue of adaptation forms a central part of my project because the film medium has always relied upon literary texts for its stories, and at the turn of the twentieth century, the borrowing of narrative and stereotypical tropes from popular literature was particularly prevalent. Therefore, an assessment of early film requires a comparison with its literary antecedents. The study begins, then, with turn-of-the-century adventure stories and silent Westerns, in which I challenge accepted assumptions that these depictions of the Mexican are simply stereotypical and "negative." Chapter one, "The Greaser in Stephen Crane's Mexican Stories and D. W. Griffith's Early Westerns," argues that the Mexican is a subject of ambivalent admiration in Crane's short stories and a subject of derision and desire in Griffith's earliest Westerns. Crane's adventure stories have been critiqued for reproducing the worst of the nineteenth-century Western adventure novel traditions. In contradistinction, I suggest that that it is the Anglo-American whom Crane disavows, and the Mexican whom he embraces. Crane's inversion of the adventure novel provides a critical lens with which to view Griffith's Westerns. In *The Greaser's Gauntlet* (1908), Griffith presents a subject who is at once villainous and heroic. Unlike his unremitting assaults upon African Americans in *The Birth of a Nation* (1915), Griffith's Western makes room for the greaser's redemption. The movie, however, is not without its contradictory ideological practices, as the Mexican must be repatriated to his country in order to make space for the Anglo-American hero in the West, and as another ethnic character, the Chinese American, becomes the narrative's scapegoat.

In chapter two, "Greasers, Bandits, and Revolutionaries: The Conflation of Mexican Identity Representation," I link the United States' response to the Mexican Revolution and the consolidation of the Western film genre as determinant events in the hardening of stereotypical discourse during the period from 1910 to 1920. Though the revolution inspired many writers to reassess Mexican character—witness Jack London's exaltation of the revolutionary in "The Mexican"—the revolution's vilification by the Hearst media conglomerate and industries with business interests in Mexico ensured that the Mexican male would appear as a villainous bandit. During this period, the emergence of the Western hero in film required the creation of a character against whom this hero could fight, and the Mexican revolutionary became the Western hero's nemesis. The period of the Mexican Revolution thus sees the melding of greasers, bandits, and revolutionaries to create the ultimate villain in the American Western.

Notwithstanding the hardening of the Mexican's representation that I have described, in chapter three, "The Western's Ambivalence and the Mexican Badman," I argue that the period after the Mexican Revolution evidences a contradictory relation to the Mexican subject as the character features of the Western's cowboy come to mimic those of an earlier Mexican *vaquero*. Like the previous two chapters, "The Western's Ambivalence" relies on rarely studied archival sources to delineate the figure of the "badman." This character makes his first appearance in the earliest American movies and culminates in *The Bad Man* (1923), a film based on Porter Emerson Browne's successful Broadway play (1921). *The Bad Man* was subsequently filmed two more times, in 1930 and 1941. The play and films are loosely based on the life of Francisco "Pancho" Villa and play upon perceptions of the Mexican's violent nature and good-heartedness. Yet delving deeper into film archives, we find that the Mexican revolutionary is not the first character to play the badman. During the 1910s, such film stars as Broncho Billy Anderson and William S. Hart became famous playing just such a character. Furthermore, these "original" Anglo badmen from the 1910s resemble Mexican badmen that were depicted in movies during the previous decade. The presence of both Mexican and Anglo badmen suggests that American cinema has disavowed the strong parallel between the Anglo and the Mexican, even as U.S. cinema has relied upon the vaquero's iconography to construct the figure of the heroic Anglo cowboy.

Chapter four, "Stereotype, Idealism, and Contingency in the Revolutionary's Depiction," examines the films *Viva Villa!* (1934) and *Viva Zapata!* (1952), submitting that the "bandit revolutionary" signals, yet again, repulsion and attraction, depending on the ideological needs of American political discourse. From the perspective of Mexican American literature, Américo Paredes's novella *The Shadow* (1955) responds to the easy categorizations of Mexican identity by displaying deep distrust for the Mexican hero of the revolution. Instead of offering such categorizations, Paredes proposes that we cannot rely on the myth of a transcendent, heroic subject of history, since the revolution's failures make this subject untenable. Furthermore, *The Shadow* represents its revolutionary subject as an effect of capitalist modernity's production of a "mimic man," a subject so profoundly shaped by the discourses of American modernity that its revolutionary potential is eviscerated. Though Paredes's novella is a ghost story, it is grounded in bitter realism, and he creates a questioning, haunted, and contingent Mexican identity that destabilizes the idealism of Kazan's *Viva Zapata!*

Chapter five, "Gregorio Cortez in the Chicano/a Imaginary and American Popular Culture," examines the published and unpublished writings of Américo Paredes, folklorist and author of *"With His Pistol in His Hand": A Border Ballad and its Hero* (1958). Paredes's landmark study on the *corrido* was among the first to challenge long-propagated stereotypes about the Mexican American, and it was later adapted for the screen as *The Ballad of Gregorio Cortez* (1982). Yet Paredes's unpublished writings reveal a critique of what he saw as the depiction of a "scared little peon" in the character of Gregorio Cortez. In Paredes's eyes, such characterization symbolically lessened Cortez's heroic stance, as well as his agency. Paredes's response brings us, yet again, to one of the principle concerns of my study, which has to do with the production and contestation of various American masculinities. The chapter will thus explore Paredes's intervention within an ongoing debate over the features of American and Mexican masculine identity. Paredes's study of the Gregorio Cortez story and its folk ballad has been so far reaching that it inspired not only a film, but a popular Western novel as well. In the final section of chapter five, I compare *"With His Pistol in His Hand"* with just that novel—Elmer Kelton's *Manhunters* (1974)—a work that recapitulates the story of Gregorio Cortez from the perspective of the Anglo Texas Ranger. *"With His Pistol in*

His Hand" and its adaptations show us that late into the twentieth century, the exact contours of Mexican identity are still under intense debate at the levels of ideology and representation.

Chapter six, "Reformulating Hybrid Identities and Re-inscribing History in Contemporary Chicano/a Literature and Film," concludes the study and highlights the welcome entry of Chicano/a independent cinema production in debates over representation and identity. In this chapter, I fast-forward to the contemporary moment of Chicano/a self-representation in Jim Mendiola's *Come and Take It Day* (2002) and Angelina Vigil's *Thirty an' Seen a Lot* (1982). Unlike the Chicano/a cinema of the sixties and seventies, with its concerns for defining an essentialist identity in resistance to Anglo-American cultural dominance, and unlike much of the eighties cinema, with its interest in participating in mainstream culture, *Come and Take It Day* proposes contingency and hybridity as the defining elements of Chicano/a identity. This film critiques contemporary media images of ethnic male deviance—the present-day equivalents of bandido stereotypes—but it does not posit the transcendent Chicano/a hero as antidote. Instead, *Come and Take It Day* intertextualizes Paredes's *"With His Pistol in His Hand"*—again demonstrating this work's profound influence on debates about identity representation—and imagines a Chicano/a unburdened by the demand to uphold a cultural essence but still capable of contesting discourses that deprecatorily define the culture. I bring together my analysis of *Come and Take It Day* with an examination of the poetry of Evangelina Vigil, a Chicana writer concerned with preserving Mexican American cultural memory in San Antonio while challenging and redefining Chicano masculinity. Like Mendiola, Vigil examines how dominant discourses and power structures frame Chicano/a identity and proposes strategies for contructing critical subjectivities from the standpoint of the present. Throughout *Badmen, Bandits, and Folk Heroes*, the theoretical perspectives of ambivalence and contingency inform my reading of key literary and cinematic texts. These texts exemplify the importance of seeing beyond the potential one-dimensionality of ethnic and racial representation—whether in a "negative" or "positive" sense—to the presence of complex and contradictory understandings of culture. Placing literature and film in comparative dialogue further amplifies the discursive field and at the same time acknowledges that different representational forms are always in conversation and open to the possibilities of alternative readings and empowering uses.

The Greaser in Stephen Crane's Mexican Stories and D. W. Griffith's Early Westerns

During perhaps the most climactic and disturbing moment in D. W. Griffith's *The Greaser's Gauntlet* (1908), the narrative presents the lynching of the central character, the "greaser" in the film's title. A member of the lynch party ties a noose around the Mexican's neck and another secures the rope to the branch of a tree. In the next horrific instant, the mob raises the Mexican, and he is left hanging from the tree. Because of its verisimilitude, the scene is shocking even to modern-day viewers. Fortunately for the Mexican, a woman intervenes on his behalf, and he is saved from a fate that befell many innocent real-life Mexicans on the western frontier.[1] *The Greaser's Gauntlet* seemingly confirms the critical consensus on the Mexican's representation in early American film: that the Mexican, like his nineteenth-century dime-novel predecessors, "remains a subject . . . to be killed or mocked, seduced or redeemed by Saxon protagonists" (Pettit, 132). This approach to Mexican stereotypes contains the binary quality that sees stereotypes as only positive or negative, yet the conclusion of *The Greaser's Gauntlet* challenges such a binary critique in an important way. The greaser is not vanquished; instead, he performs the story's most heroic deed. How can we account, then, for the contradictory moments in film when the Mexican is spared total denigration, when film narrative simultaneously expresses repulsion for and attraction toward the Mexican subject? In short, how do we explain the ambivalence of stereotypical representation?

This chapter draws upon the analytic of ambivalence for a reading of Mexican identity representation in two short stories by Stephen Crane and in several early films by D. W. Griffith. Rather than contending that representations of the Mexican in Crane and Griffith are merely stereotypical and derogatory, I read in their depictions a wavering, sometimes derisive, sometimes admiring attitude toward the Mexican subject. Crane's turn-of-the-century stories demonstrate an indirect regard for the Mexican in their refusal to make the Anglo-American the definitive victor over his Mexican rival. Crane reveals a sense of equality between Anglo and Mexican combatants that is at odds with the popular Western stories of the time. His evenhanded treatment of the Mexican and Anglo displays ambivalence toward the Anglo-American, specifically in myths about the Western hero. Thus, Crane engages the positive figuration—the positive stereotype—of the Anglo male and subverts it. In the second half of the chapter, I focus on the emergence of the "greaser" stereotype in the films of D. W. Griffith from 1907 to 1910, and argue that the greaser constitutes not the reproduction of dime-novel stereotypes but an ambivalent form of racial discourse. Griffith's inconsistent appraisal of the Mexican suggests that Anglo-America's relation to ethnic minorities in general and Mexicans in particular encompasses contradictory feelings of derision and desire.

Because film relied heavily upon popular literature for its narrative and stereotypical tropes at the turn of the century, an assessment of the early cinema requires a comparison with its literary precursors. Juxtaposing Griffith with Crane in particular is appropriate because these men were nearly contemporaries: Crane wrote his Mexican stories at the end of the nineteenth century, at a moment when writers were beginning to question the heroic themes of the Western adventure story; Griffith began his career at the beginning of the twentieth century, and among his earliest movies are precursors to film Westerns. Each man, therefore, engages with the Western adventure story at a pivotal moment in its development. Furthermore, Crane and Griffith take up the representation of the Mexican in an idiosyncratic fashion, breaking with the expectations of the Western genre: Crane departs from an established tradition, while Griffith confounds an emerging genre before its conventions are established. Although they maintain canonical status within their respective art forms, each has been criticized for his depiction of ethnic identities. In Crane's case, such critiques not only lack nuance but also misread his evaluation of the heroic codes of conduct practiced by Anglos and Mexicans alike. In Griffith's instance, critiques of his racist cinematic practices are well founded, but do not account for the contradictory moments when Griffith admits the Mexican's humanity. Placing Crane's stories and Griffith's films in comparative tension demonstrates that "negative" stereotypes of Mexican identity are never strictly negative. The ambivalent re-articulation of the Mexican in Griffith and the Anglo in Crane reveal that these subjects are constructed using similar stereotypical operations, that the derogation of one subject requires the exaltation of the other.

Stephen Crane was not the first American writer to represent Mexican identity in his fiction. The representation of Mexicans in American literary and historical texts goes back to the early 1800s, when Anglos encountered these strange folk on their migrations West. Because these two groups were of different national and cultural origins, competition for land and resources often took deeply antagonistic proportions, and the subsequent representation of Anglos and Mexicans fell along respective lines of good and evil. In the creation of the archetypal white hero of the frontier, "Mexican villainy was an essential ingredient" (Robinson, 18). The process of the hero's creation required the denigration of the Mexican Other, giving rise to terms such as "greaser" in the early part of the century (De Leon, 16). At a broader social level, the Mexican's denigration went so far that even the word "Mexican" came to acquire a pejorative value, and one had to avoid using it if one did not wish to be insulting. In the literary sphere, scholars have well documented the instances of antipathy for the Mexican, as in Zebulon Pike's chronicles of his travels in the Southwest, wherein his racialist views deem the Mexican "a biological catastrophe" due to his miscegenated racial make-up (R. Paredes, 86). The Mexican "greaser" emerges out of the need for the Anglo-American to define himself as the morally and physically dominant inhabitant of the Texas territory and the West. In conquest fiction, "the concept of Anglo-Saxon superiority and Mexican inferiority . . . is sustained by constant repetition of tried and tested positive American projections of themselves juxtaposed to negative projections of the Mexican as opposition" (Pettit, xx).[2]

The cultural antagonism between Anglos and Mexicans determines the criteria for establishing the "'Tex-Mex' formula scoundrel" in the Western adventure novel, which include: "the fictional need for villains who offer maximum contrast to the heroes; the actual presence of some difference in skin color between the two ethnic groups; the unabashed racial bigotry that characterized the United States between the first years of manifest destiny and the outbreak of the Civil War" (23). The characters contained in this type of story include lazy peons, cruel dons, and beautiful señoritas, but the most prevalent are the greaser *bandidos*, who are "burdened with a formidable set of easily identified, ethnic, stereotyped features," including "long, greasy hair coiled under huge sombreros, scraggly *mustachios* . . . tobacco-stained fingers and teeth, and grotesque dialect and curses. Above all, the Beadle [publishing house] bandidos are characterized by complexions shading from pitch black through dark brown to orange, yellow, olive, and gray" (Pettit, 39–40). By 1859, these negative characterizations are fully established and incorporated by the writers of the Beadle and Adams publishing house, widely recognized for introducing the dime novel (Robinson, 27).

The most often used descriptive words for the Mexican in popular Westerns are "coward" and "greaser." In *Bernard Lile, an Historical Romance* (1856), Jeremiah Clemens repeatedly employs the word "greaser" to describe Mexicans: "The people are greasy, their clothes are greasy, their dogs are greasy, their houses are greasy—everywhere grease and filth hold divided dominion" (214). Raymund Paredes has argued that the Mexican is so reviled by the 1880s that "the Mexican—and not the Indian—is the most contemptible figure in western popular fiction" (171). The Mexican "functioned as the ultimate villain, leering out from behind his grimy *serape* and invariably clutching his deadly *cuchillo*" (180). Provocatively, Stephen Crane would take up the image of the serape and transform it into something other than the expected negative stereotype.

Stephen Crane and the Mexican

The doleful picture of the Anglo's estimate of the Mexican in nineteenth-century Western fiction, critics aver, continues into the twentieth century (Pettit, 111). More recently, in a discussion about the representation of Mexican sexuality in Western fiction, José Limón observes that if "the Mexican woman in her full eroticization has critical meanings and possibilities beyond the stereotype," the Mexican male has "none of the exotic sexuality, the freer play of the erotic given the figure of the Mexican woman"; thus "he is a rhetorical construction that exemplifies the term 'stereotype' in its most negative sense" (136). Limón concludes that in the case of the "rhetorical construction of Mexican men, there is no ambivalence, no rhetorical quarter given; nor . . . has this unambivalence attenuated in our own time" (137).

There is, of course, a great deal of truth behind Limón's assessment. *Bernard Lile*, written during the nineteenth century, refers to the greaser as a "born thief" who "would murder his brother for a *peso*" (215). Still, some degree of affinity does exist between Anglo and Mexican combatants. Limón writes that "in the context of the Anglo male's symbolic desire for the Mexican woman, we can now see between these two men a psychological relationship of difference but also of identity, aggression, and mutual narcissism" (136). Significantly, however, identity occurs not only in his desire for the Mexican woman, but also in the Anglo's recognition and grudging admiration—narcissistic or otherwise—of something of himself in the Mexican. We see the vacillation between recognition and negation even in the most dyspeptic representations of the Mexican—even in *Bernard Lile*, in which the narrator accepts that in the battle of Palo Alto, the Mexicans "are said to have fought bravely as well" (213).

At the turn of the century, Stephen Crane's short stories about the West and Mexico recognize the Mexican's equality with his Anglo-American rival. Yet if we are to accept the views of some critics, Crane's Western stories enact a Darwinian struggle between Anglo and Mexican and express a familiar contempt for the Mexican, whose fate it is to lose.[3] Crane, however, is actually less concerned with deriding the Mexican than with deflating the myth of the Western hero, which he achieves partly through an unprejudiced depiction of Mexican characters. I see a notable degree of play, discrepancy, and respect for the Mexican in Crane's stories, particularly in "One Dash-Horses" and "The Three White Mice," in which Crane questions the popular Western novel's vision of the cowardly and villainous Mexican in contrast to the heroic Anglo.

"One Dash-Horses" recounts the near-death experience of Richardson and his servant, José, during their travels in Mexico. The two men encounter trouble one night at a lodging house, when Mexican bandits enter Richardson's sleeping quarters and threaten to steal his gun and saddle. Richardson faces the Mexicans in a seemingly stoic manner while José cowers in the background. A closer examination of this story, however, reveals that Richardson does not act with quiet heroism; rather, he is catatonic with terror. Additionally, it is not Richardson's cool response to danger but José's efficiency and watchfulness that saves Richardson from certain death. In the initial encounter between Richardson and the Mexican bandits, Richardson is woken by a guitar and hears a Mexican gruffly telling his companions that if the American does not hand over his pistol, saddle, and money, "I will kill him! . . . if he will not give them, you will see!" (15) Unlike the hero of *Bernard Lile*, Tom Simpson, who unflinchingly confronts numerous greasers, Richardson "felt the skin draw tight around his mouth, and his knee-joints turned to bread. He slowly came to a sitting posture. . . . This stiff and mechanical movement . . . must have looked like the rising of a corpse in the wan moonlight" (15). As he responds to the threat, the "tumultuous emotions of Richardson's terror" render him incapable of understanding Spanish and demonstrate the extent of his fear (16).

Crane's first visual depiction of the Mexican seems to follow the stereotypical tropes of the dime novel, and its visceral impact gives the reader pause: "the red light of a torch flared into the room. It was held by a fat, round-faced Mexican, whose little snake-like mustache was as black as his eyes, and whose eyes were black as jet. He was insane with the wild rage of a man whose liquor is dully burning at his brain. Five or six of his fellows crowded after him" (16). This description of the Mexican, undoubtedly stereotypical, helps us understand why critics of racial representation have responded so strongly to Crane. We have before us the Mexican bandido in all his un-ambivalence. But for all the negativity that we may read in the Mexican's portrayal, we should not lose sight of Crane's representation of the Anglo "hero" as well.

As the Mexican enters, Richardson sits "very straight and still, his right hand lost in the folds of his blanket" (16). The reader knows that within the folds of the blanket lies the pistol to which he clings. The bandit does not see the pistol, but he suspects it is nearby, since this is the object he covets. Although the Mexican threatens and curses, Richardson remains still, "staring at the fat Mexican with a strange fixedness of gaze, not fearful, not dauntless, not anything that could be interpreted. He simply stared" (16). Richardson is, in other words, frozen beyond fear by the situation. Crane infuses the narrative with humor in showing the Mexicans confused by Richardson's response. "Ah, well, sirs, here was a mystery. At the approach of their menacing company, why did not this American cry out and turn pale, or run, or pray them mercy? The animal merely sat still, and stared, and waited for them to begin. Well, evidently he was a great fighter; or perhaps he was an idiot. Indeed, this was an embarrassing situation, for who was going forward to discover whether he was a great fighter or an idiot?" (16). A reading that assumes derogation may see the Mexicans' indecisiveness as a sign of their fear before the brave American. Cecil Robinson, for instance, claims that the Mexicans back down as Richardson holds the revolver in front of them: "for all their drunken rage, as the American held a gun on them and stared coldly in their direction, they kept back. Not one of them was quite drunk enough to want to be the sacrificial victim that would be required if the American was to be overpowered" (192). To state that Richardson "stared coldly" is to seriously misread the nuances of the story. The American is actually immobilized by sheer terror. As the lead Mexican delays pouncing on him, "this pause was a long horror [for Richardson]; and for these men who could so frighten him there began to swell in him a fierce hatred." Though he feels hatred, he does not act but only longs "to be capable of fighting all of them" (17). The Mexicans' hesitation is due to their calculating stance; they are waiting for an excuse to pounce. The Mexicans, furthermore, are not deterred by the gun pointed at them since they cannot see it pointed at them—it lies under the folds of a blanket. Since it is the gun they have come to steal, the reader must assume they know it is at hand.

A classic interpretation of the Mexicans' depiction following the positive/negative binary would see their actions as simply negative. A reading of the stereotype's ambivalence, on the other hand, examines the specific deployments of the Mexicans' characterization in relation to the supposedly superior Anglo-American. In the agonizingly long moment when Richardson awaits the Mexicans' attack, José stirs, and the bandits begin beating and berating him. As they bully Richardson's servant, they "continually turned their eyes to see if they were to succeed in causing an initial demonstration from the American." Clearly, they are testing Richardson to determine if he is brave enough to come to José's defense. Though he holds the gun under his blanket, Richardson merely looks on "impassively" (17). Thus, Crane's Mexicans are not simply bullies, but experts in the arts of provocation and intimidation. The Anglo is not stoic, but incapable of mastering his fear. This reversal is clearly at odds with critical expectations and assumptions.

The stereotypical inversion extends still further. While the Mexicans return to their drinking and carousing, the Anglo experiences the unlikely emotion of longing "to run" (18). At dawn, Richardson and José finally manage their escape. Both men exhibit nervousness and fear, but it is José who keeps his wits. We learn, for instance, that while Richardson makes all kinds of loud noises with his clanging spurs, José capably "had his own saddle girth and both bridles buckled in a moment. He curled the picket ropes with a few sweeps of his arm." Richardson, on the other hand, is still too shaken for quick and effective action. His fingers "were shaking so that he could hardly buckle the girth. His hands were in invisible mittens" (20). Unexpectedly, this scene suggests the Mexican's efficacy and grace, not the Anglo's.

In his treatment of Richardson's false courage and lack of judgment, Crane again uses humor and irony to destabilize the Anglo hero's image. For instance, as Richardson and José escape their would-be attackers, the Anglo looks upon the Mexican and sees a weaker man: "Riding with José was like riding with a corpse. His face resembled a cast in lead. Sometimes he swung forward and almost pitched from his seat. Richardson was too frightened himself to do anything but hate this man for his fear. Finally, he issued a mandate which nearly caused José's eyes to slide out of his head and fall to the ground like two coins. "Ride behind me—about fifty paces" (21). Richardson's want of judgment lies in his presumption that he rides with an inferior. Although José seems the bigger coward, Crane uses his forced position in the rear guard to show Richardson's feigned bravery and his need of the Mexican's protection. "Richardson had resolved in his rage that at any rate he was going to use the eyes and ears of extreme fear to detect the approach of danger; and so he established his servant as a sort of an outpost" (22). Yet Richardson could have served as outpost just as well, since he has embodied "extreme fear" from the beginning. Crane, therefore, refuses to idealize the Anglo at the expense of the Mexican in his depiction of the relationship between the two cultures. Jamie Robertson has more generally observed that in the myth of Western heroism, "Crane was attracted to the West, but he never succumbed to the dream world of the dime novelist. . . . His heroes participate in the convention of popular Western fiction that individual courage gives meaning to life, but that convention is always ironic" (243). Applied to this story, Crane's deflation of the Western myth means that the Anglo is not so easily the Mexican's superior. At story's end, José once again proves to be the more capable of the two men when Richardson loses the trail and is "recalled to it by the loud sobs of his servant" (22). As the Mexican bandits catch up and give final chase, it is José, "terror-stricken, who at last discovered safety" when he spots the Mexican rural police force just over a ridge, rides to them, and saves his and Richardson's life (23–24).

Although an initial reading of "One Dash-Horses" may lead a reader to believe that Crane's characterization of the Anglo-American is, compared to the Mexican, more positive, careful analysis reveals that Crane felt empathy and respect for the Mexican. Although narrative space concentrates on the figure of the Anglo, we see small instances of admiration for the Mexican, as when José prepares for a night of rest. "José threw two gigantic wings of shadow as he flapped his blanket about him—first across his chest under his arms, and then around his neck and across his chest again—this time over his arms, with the end tossed on his right shoulder. A Mexican thus snugly enveloped can nevertheless free his fighting arm in a beautifully brisk way, merely shrugging his shoulder as he grabs for the weapon at his belt" (14). The narrative viewpoint is objective here. We do not see José from Richardson's perspective but from the perspective of the narrative voice. The movement of the Mexican in this description connotes a speed and finesse, an efficiency and grace that recalls nothing of the lazy greaser.

Stephen Crane's travels in the West and Mexico during the period in which he wrote his Western stories allowed him a glimpse of the way Mexican people of all classes lived on a daily basis. Crane could have come away with an impression of Mexico like that found in *Bernard Lile*, where an American "whose ill fortune has made him for any number of days, a sojourner in the city of Metamoros [sic], can have no difficulty in tracing the origin of the term 'greaser'" (214). Crane, however, sees this intercultural assessment of a different people as part of the ill-informed "arrogance of the man who has not solved himself and discovered his own futility" ("The Mexican Lower Classes," 435). Forewarning the future readers of his Western fiction—and readers of dime novels and adventure fiction—Crane determines in his Western sketches (written as dispatches for American newspapers) that it "perhaps might be said—if any one dared—that the most worthless literature of the world has been that which has been written by the men of one nation concerning the men of another" (436). Thus, Crane exhibits an awareness of the myopic perspective of Anglo-American cultural imperialism.

Crane's precautionary statement guides our reading of "The Five White Mice," which treats the encounter of the New York Kid, the San Francisco Kid, and their friend, Benson, with three Mexican men on a dark Mexico City street. The crucial moment in the story picks up the three Anglo men on their way home. Benson and the San Francisco Kid are inebriated, and the sober New York Kid acts as their escort. As they make their way along the street, they come upon three Mexican men, and Benson bumps one. The Mexican is offended by the American's carelessness and tempers rise, but the encounter ends when the New York Kid brandishes a pistol and the Mexicans are sent on their way. Because the story ends with the Mexicans' defeat, critics have read "The Five White Mice" as yet another instance of the Mexican's denigration.[4] The story, however, demonstrates Crane's attraction to the codes of honor and ritualistic behavior that he sees in masculinity, be it Anglo or Mexican. In one of his dispatches from Mexico City, for example, Crane comments upon the city's bullfighters, who are "a most impressive type to be seen upon the streets. . . . They are always clean-shaven and the set of the lips wherein lies the revelation of character, can easily be studied. They move confidently, proudly, with magnificent self-possession" ("The City of Mexico," 431). In this dispatch, Crane joins Ernest Hemingway in his fascination for the figure of a heroic Mexican masculinity, which also appears in the Mexicans of "The Five White Mice."

The story's tension lies in the disturbance of masculine codes of honor when the Mexican's grievances are not acknowledged by Benson, the drunk American. "The Mexican wheeled upon the instant. His hand flashed to his hip. There was a moment of silence during which Benson's voice was not heard raised in apology. Then an indescribable comment, one burning word, came from between the Mexican's teeth" (46–47). Benson's failure to provide an apology upsets the Mexican's masculine code of honor. With his hand on the pummel of his knife, the Mexican asks if "the señor want fight?" (47) The New York Kid immediately tries to move his friends away, but the San Francisco Kid, himself very drunk, affirmatively answers the

Mexican's challenge. Subverting the stereotypical conventions of the drunk Mexican, Crane presents the Americans' drunkenness as leading them to recklessness. The New York Kid reluctantly joins the fray, and he too stands with his hand at his hip, but his coat conceals a revolver. Crane freezes this moment in the narrative to provide an intimate glimpse of the New York Kid's admiration for and fear of the Mexican. "This opponent of the New York Kid was a tall man and quite stout. His sombrero was drawn low over his eyes. His serape was flung on his left shoulder. His back was bended and in the supposed manner of a Spanish grandee. This concave gentleman cut a fine and terrible figure. The lad, moved by the spirits of his modest and perpendicular ancestors, had time to feel his blood roar at the sight of the pose" (48). Despite knowing he is better armed than the men he faces, the "Eastern lad suddenly decided that he was going to be killed" (48).

The reader would expect the Anglo to act bravely and without hesitation at such a decisive moment, in accordance with Western hero conventions, but instead the New York Kid's hand is only "tremoring on the trigger" (50). Realizing that they are outmatched, the knife-carrying Mexicans finally show their own fear. "The fulsome grandee sprang backward with a low cry. The man who had been facing the 'Frisco Kid took a quick step away. The beautiful array of Mexicans was suddenly disorganized" (50). Crane presents the scene with a sense for its choreography, and he shows the Anglo and Mexican standing as equals in their capacities to experience fear and in their attempts to hide it with false courage: "The cry and the backward steps revealed something of great importance to the New York Kid. He had never dreamed that he did not have a complete monopoly of all possible trepidations. The cry of the grandee was that of a man who suddenly sees a poisonous snake. Thus the Kid was able to understand swiftly that *they* were *all* human beings. *They* were unanimous in not wishing for too bloody combat. There was a sudden expression of *equality*" (50, emphasis mine). The use of "they" and "all" applies to both groups, who share in the "equality" of fear and loathing as they sense their own mortality.

Finally seeing his position of advantage, the New York Kid "pounced forward and began to swear. . . . He was bursting with rage because these men had not previously confided to him that they were vulnerable. . . . And after all there had been an equality of emotion, an equality: he was furious" (51). Crane's framing of the New York Kid's thoughts suggests that one man's bravery increases in direct proportion to the other's fear. Crane shows that Anglos and Mexicans alike struggle with controlling these impulses. In the story's ending, there is little to suggest the Mexicans' lack of bravery and nothing that implies the Anglos' contempt. The New York Kid is furious, but he is furious because the Mexicans "had not previously confided to him that they were vulnerable"—that is, they had not previously evinced that they were as emotionally vulnerable as the New York Kid. Thus, the New York Kid feels angry that he lacked an understanding of the "equality of emotion" all the men feel.

In a dime novel, when the Mexican greaser sees the Anglo pull out his weapon, he runs. In "The Five White Mice," the Mexicans and Anglos act according to the masculine rituals of a duel. Realizing that they are literally outgunned, the Mexicans step backward, but they do not turn their backs on the Americans. Their leader acknowledges defeat, but he does not lose his dignity. He speaks to the New York Kid "in a tone of cynical bravado" and asks, "Well, señor, it is finished?" To this, the New York Kid responds, "I am willing" (51). And most significant of all, the two groups of men bid each other goodnight as each group disappears into the Mexico City streets. This final exchange implies, once again, that Crane undermines the strict conventions of heroic Anglos and cowardly Mexicans in favor of a view in which these combatants stand shoulder to shoulder, each drawing from the same masculine codes of conduct.

Crane's Mexican fiction enables a different reading of the Mexican and Anglo than does the typical dime novel. His critique of the inflated myth of the Western hero, along with his treatment of the Mexican as the Anglo's equal, permits a questioning of the stereotypes that sustained the relation of dominance between Anglo and Mexican during the nineteenth century. Significantly, Crane's ironic reversal of these stereotypes provides us the critical lens with which to examine the American cinema, which was just emerging as Crane's stories were being published. If Crane's stories demonstrate a manifest subversion of Mexican stereotypes in critical opposition to the norms of popular literature, then D. W. Griffith's early Western movies stand somewhere between subversion and affirmation, evidencing a latent desire for the Mexican even as they deride the Mexican "greaser."

From Western Novels to Western Movies: The Greaser in D. W. Griffith's Films, 1907–1910

Thus far, I have argued that Stephen Crane presents a Mexican subject who stands his ground against the Anglo-American hero, contrary to ethno-critical interpretations of the seventies and eighties. In American film, D. W. Griffith is regarded as one of the utmost practitioners of racist cinematic representation, and this identification is well deserved. Notwithstanding this incontrovertible assessment—especially with respect to Griffith's treatment of African Americans—Griffith may nevertheless be positioned beyond the either/or binary of the conventional critique of the stereotype. Mexicans appear in several of Griffith's early films set in the West, and in the title of one film, Mexican identity is explicitly and derogatorily foregrounded. In spite of the liberal use of the word "greaser" to identify Mexican characters, the presence of *Mexicanidad* in Griffith's early Westerns encompasses contradictory points of attraction and repulsion.

Griffith started making Westerns for the Biograph Company in 1907; only a year later, Mexican characters began to appear regularly in his films. Because copies of Griffith's early movies are extremely rare—sixteen-millimeter copies of the paper prints are currently housed at the Library of Congress[5]—critics have only a tenuous understanding of these films' racial politics. Most critics, especially those writing in the seventies and eighties, base their analyses on secondary accounts, and they assume that early films reflexively follow the models set by their literary predecessors.[6] In general, these assessments are correct, for popular literature greatly influenced—and it continues to influence—the kinds of films being made at the inception of narrative film. Yet there is a way in which these critiques fall into a binaristic trap: representations are either completely positive or, more usually, they are wholly negative. The approach required, however, is a critical analysis that takes into account the complexity of ethnic representation, a way to see the moments in which literary and cinematic texts express a conflicted attraction for the ethnic subject.

Derision and desire coexist in the emergence of the "greaser" stereotype in Griffith's work from 1907 to 1910. During this period, Griffith directed at least seven films whose Mexican content runs the spectrum between sympathetic and hostile representations, depending on a particular film's narrative imperatives. Such films include *The Fight for Freedom*, *The Tavern Keeper's Daughter*, *The Greaser's Gauntlet*, *The Red Girl*, and *The Vaquero's Vow*, all from 1908, as well as *The Thread of Destiny* and *Ramona*, both from 1910. It is instructive to note that, with the exception of *The Thread of Destiny*, the ultimate fate of Mexican characters in these Griffith films is deleterious; characters either die or vacate the narrative space to make way for the Anglo-American hero. Still, the greaser stereotype constitutes not merely the reproduction of dime novel stereotypes; it is an ambivalent racial discourse. Griffith's films place the Mexican subject in multiple representational postures and allow us to see the stereotype's "*effectivity*," its "repertoire of positions of power and resistance, domination and dependence" (Bhabha, 67). A reading of Mexican identity representation in terms of the analytic of ambivalence allows us to see the limits of stereotypical discourse and the complex relation of attraction and repulsion between the Anglo subject and the Mexican who is the object of stereotypical fixation. This relation reveals the impossibility of simplifying any culture to the imperatives of the stereotype and demonstrates the limitations of the positive/negative critique that has traditionally responded to stereotypical production.

It is difficult to imagine that the director who created *The Birth of a Nation* (1915) may be read "ambivalently." One of *Birth*'s commentators, Clyde Taylor, notes that this film constitutes "an incomparable racial assault," one of those "national allegories in which the definition of national character simultaneously involves a co-defining anti-type" (15). We could assume that the Mexican fares no better in Griffith's representational universe, and if we were to read the July 24, 1908, issue of the *Biograph Bulletin*—a promotional playbill—these critics' assertions would seem to be borne out. The *Bulletin* introduces the main character in *The Tavern Keeper's Daughter* (1908) as "the fairest flower that e'er blossomed in the land of the golden sun." Then, it ominously introduces her antagonist as "one of those proletarian half breed Mexicans, whose acidulate countenance was most odious, particularly to the girl" (qtd. in Usai, *Griffith Project*, vol. 1, 71). Yet despite all indications to the contrary, the Mexican does not constitute a "co-defining anti-type"—he is not wholly odious, but a very complicated and ambivalent figure. Several of Griffith's early Westerns suggest a strong fascination with Mexican character that goes beyond the race hatred that critics ascribe to Griffith in the case of African American characterization.

The Fight for Freedom treats the story of Pedro and Juanita, a Mexican couple who must escape a lynch mob when Pedro kills a man who cheated him at poker. When the sheriff gives chase, Pedro kills him and Juanita is jailed in Pedro's stead. During the course of their escape, Juanita is killed and Pedro captured; Pedro is "bound and carried back to prison to meet his inevitable [demise]," according to the July 17, 1908, issue of the *Biograph Bulletin* (qtd. in Usai, *The Griffith Project*, vol. 1, 63). In a brief critical commentary, Patrick Loughney observes, "though the title suggests sympathy for the wrongly accused Juanita, little of that sentiment is actually apparent on the screen. The story is set in a Texas border town and the villains are Mexicans" (*Griffith Project*, 64). While *The Fight for Freedom* presents little regard for Juanita, we should not mistake the representation of her constant suffering as a lack of sympathy. In the film, Juanita's goodness is signaled by her stalwart defense of her husband and her willingness to risk her life for his safety. Griffith's narrative typifies the first silent features because it is "spare and fast moving, with no effort of time . . . spent on character development" (64). This means that we can only deduce the film's attitude toward its characters by their actions, not through characterization. If this is the case, then the film ultimately sympathizes with Pedro and Juanita, for every action they take is in defense of their lives.

The statement that "the villains are Mexican" also calls for closer examination. Pedro seemingly embodies the dime novel greaser: he angers quickly and takes murderous action when he discovers the cheater. He also kills a sheriff. In the context of the Western setting of the film, however, Pedro is no different from his Anglo-American counterparts. In the opening scene of the movie, for example, Pedro and two other men sit at a card table, and their demeanor indicates equality. Interestingly, all the men are dressed similarly, so there is little "ethnic" differentiation between Pedro and his counterparts. (Juanita, on the other hand, is clearly marked "Spanish" or "Mexican" by her style of dress.) When Pedro discovers that another man has cheated in the card game, events transpire quickly, and the viewer is hard pressed to assess guilt. When all three men begin to shoot—with three bystanders joining the fray—the action takes place within the context of an early Western action film (before the full emergence of the genre). The narrative does not attempt to single out any of the men, thus naturalizing the violence as part of its setting. Pedro, therefore, is no more a villain than the other men at the saloon. By distinction, the posse that hunts down Pedro and Juanita does not convey an empathetic or heroic image, for members of the posse kill an innocent woman, an action seen as taboo even in the most sensationalistic popular fiction.

The Fight for Freedom leaves the viewer with a query that it refuses to answer, namely, whose "fight for freedom" is this? The *Biograph Bulletin* states that it "almost makes us question the justice of fate that the innocent should suffer for the crimes of the guilty" (63), but it never tells us who is innocent—Juanita or the sheriff—nor who is guilty—Pedro or the lynch mob. Although we can deduce that the Biograph Company masks the film's sheer spectacle and sensationalism with a title that connotes respectable entertainment and moral instruction, we must nevertheless allow for the possibility that audiences may have "question[ed] the justice of fate" in a way favorable to Pedro and Juanita.

The Tavern Keeper's Daughter and *The Greaser's Gauntlet* inaugurate the thematic of the bad Mexican redeemed. In these types of films, "the lustful greaser is sometimes allowed to reform, usually by saving the Anglo heroine from defloration . . . we meet for the first time the Mexican male of low blood but good heart. His is an unenviable lot, as he is doomed to wander between the longed-for world of the Anglo and the stigmatized world of the Mexican, held forever in a middle position between Saxon heroes and greaser villains" (Pettit, 134–35). *The Tavern Keeper's Daughter* is an example of the surprising change of heart in a greaser caught in the "middle position" between Anglo and Mexican worlds, although he only desires the Anglo woman. The sensationalistic fashion in which the *Biograph Bulletin* describes the story's conflict bears repeating twice here: "Among those who frequented this rustic hostelry was one of those proletarian half breed Mexicans, whose acidulate countenance was most odious to all, particularly the girl" (qtd. in Usai, *Griffith Project*, vol. 1, 71). In this typical fear-of-miscegenation plot, the Mexican makes unwanted advances, is rejected, and subsequently returns with rapacious intentions. The Mexican reveals his "cruel, black nature" and his behavior is that of an "infuriated beast." But at the moment when this "brute" is poised to commit the awful act, he sees a baby in the room, his "heart is softened by the pure, innocent chatter of the child, and he drops on his knees before the crib and prays to God to help him resist his brutal inclinations" (71). I quote from the *Biograph Bulletin* extensively because in the silent era before the introduction of inter-titles, such a promotional publication strongly shaped an audience's understanding and interpretation of a film's narrative and ideological structure. For instance, without the aid of this publication, the audience might not have interpreted that the villain is a "half breed Mexican," since his costume is more "western" than "ethnic"—although we should note that the kerchief on his head is a marker of his Mexicanness.

The language of the *Biograph Bulletin* synopsis naturalizes the Mexican's psychology. An insatiable desire for the white woman is part of his "cruel, dark nature," and he must beg God to deliver him from his "brutal inclinations." Although the titillating language of the bulletin is reprehensible, the film nevertheless stops short of having the greaser commit an act that would be unacceptable to its emerging middle-class audience. *The Tavern Keeper's Daughter*, then, reveals several ambivalent aspects of early film. First, the film displaces a prurient, pornographic desire to witness the spectacle of rape. This displacement occurs through the convenient location of this desire in an ethnic Other, as well as in the final and safe prevention of the actual act. Second, the film reveals Anglo-America's ambivalent relation to those ethnic subjects it came to dominate. The film is most probably set in post-1848 California; thus although the Mexican is dangerous, he has already been defeated, his lands taken. What remains is for Anglo-American values to take hold, and the film's paternalistic, almost revival-tent denouement produces the salvation the Mexican requires. Third, it is crucial that the Mexican contain within himself the possibility of Christian salvation. This means that, even as we consider the Protestant aversion to Catholicism, the film implicitly recognizes the commonality of the Anglo's and Mexican's Christian faith.

The plot structure of *The Greaser's Gauntlet* follows a pattern similar to that of *The Tavern Keeper's Daughter*, but with significant additions. Initially, the title character of *The Greaser's Gauntlet* is not a despicable personage; according to the *Biograph Bulletin*, Jose is a "handsome young Mexican" who "leaves his home in the Sierra Medra [sic] Mountains to seek his fortune in the States" (qtd. in Usai, *Griffith Project*, vol. 1, 75).[7] He travels to a border town where a new railroad line is being built. In the convoluted story, Jose is accused of stealing money from another man and is subsequently saved from hanging by Mildred, who discovers that a Chinese servant has in fact taken the money. Mildred saves Jose a moment before he is to be hanged, and Jose expresses his gratitude by presenting her with the embroidered wrist of a gauntlet. The embroidery is of a cross sewn onto the gauntlet by Jose's mother, who gave it to him as a reminder of his Catholic values and heritage. Jose "swears that if she ever needs his help he will come to her," with the gauntlet symbolizing "a token of his pledge" (76).

Working against the interdiction of romance between an ethnic male and a white female, *The Greaser's Gauntlet* requires the attraction between Mildred and Jose for its narrative coherence. From their earliest encounter, when Mildred walks into a saloon with her fiancée, Mildred and Jose are fascinated by one another. With many people in the room, the two stand facing each other, and Jose removes his hat in salutation. Mildred simply keeps her eyes level with his and smiles. As she leaves, she turns to look at Jose one last time. It is through this short encounter that Mildred intuits Jose's "goodness" and innocence, even before she discovers the Chinese servant's guilt. Thus, although the couple exchanges neither romantic words nor overt gestures, the *Biograph Bulletin* describes Mildred as "pleading" his innocence because she "really believes him" (76). The *Bulletin* makes her conviction sound innocent, but from their first encounter onscreen, we see an intense attraction. Later in the narrative, when she has just saved Jose from hanging, Mildred and Jose stand alone, facing one another as Jose offers her the glove. The moment is charged with their unspoken fascination for each another. Jose gives Mildred the glove, and "as she takes it her eyes sink deep into his heart, enkindling a hopeless passion for her," while she "promises to always keep his token with her" (76). That *The Greaser's Gauntlet* should use the attraction between a white woman and a "greaser" to maintain narrative tension goes against the conventions that the film Western would establish only a few years later. In *Broncho Billy and the Greaser* (1914) and *An*

Arizona Wooing (1915), for instance, the greaser makes unwanted advances upon the white female, only to be repulsed by her hero and suitor.

Although Mildred and Jose demonstrate mutual attraction, Mildred is engaged to another man—the head engineer, Tom Berkeley. The main villain of this story, as it turns out, is not Jose, but Bill Gates, the assistant engineer who also has an intense desire for Mildred. When Mildred and Tom marry, Jose "takes to drinking and goes to the depths of degradation" because he "cannot obliterate the sweet face of the girl" (76). One day, Bill encounters Mildred and becomes "insultingly persistent," but Tom arrives in time to thwart him. Gates becomes infuriated, "swears vengeance and going to a low tavern for help comes upon Jose, drunk of course, and with him and another greaser, they waylay Tom's carriage" (76). The men kidnap Mildred and take her back to the tavern. Jose, who is now Bill's lackey, initially does not recognize Mildred because he is too drunk. It is at this point in the story that the gauntlet reappears and makes possible Jose's redemption.

> There upon the floor is the cross embroidered wrist of the gauntlet, which Mildred has dropped. . . . Jose seizes it and the truth at once dawns upon him. 'Oh, God! What have I done? Yet it is not too late to undo it.' So with the ferociousness of a wolf he leaps at the throat of Gates and after a terrific battle, drops him lifeless to the floor, as the husband and friend burst into the room. The tables are now turned and Mildred has a chance to thank him for his deliverance. Jose at the sight of the cross, makes a solemn resolution which he immediately fulfills—to return to his dear old mother in the mountains in whose arms we leave him. (76)

In the film, Jose does not send Gates "lifeless to the floor," but spares the man's life at Mildred's behest. Thus, Jose is twice redeemed, first by his mother's cross, then by Mildred's intervention.

Jose undergoes a spectacular redemption in *The Greaser's Gauntlet*, one that reveals the conflicted relationship between Anglo-Americans and Mexicans in particular, and between Anglo-Americans and other ethnic subjects in general. On the surface, Griffith's vision of the Mexican in this film seems paternalistic: the Mexican is presented as essentially good but in need of moral guidance. He cannot act from his own volition; instead, he is led astray by the evil Bill Gates and later redeemed by the saintly Mildred. A more nuanced reading, however, uncovers the latent meaning of the Mexican's redemption. Jose is clearly Catholic, and the gauntlet signifies his adherence to his faith. We can read Jose's redemption, then, as evidence of the strength of his religious values. He does not require a paternalistic guidance, but can draw upon his own Catholic resources. Whether or not Griffith intended this, there is an embedded recognition of the Mexican's Christian faith, as well as a recognition, on perhaps a deeper level, of common values shared between the Anglo-American and the Mexican.

Consistent with the film's paternalism is its refusal to accept the Mexican on American land. By making Jose an "immigrant," *The Greaser's Gauntlet* elides the history of Spanish and Mexican settlement in the southwestern United States before the Anglo-American's arrival. Jose is thus made alien in a land that fellow Mexicans had long inhabited. At the end of the film, he must return to Mexico to his mother, for there is ultimately no room for his cultural values in the American West. The film positions Jose's chivalry and faith above the amoral drunkenness that pervades the lower sectors of this western town, but it is ultimately the moral strength of people like Mildred's husband, Tom Berkeley—a strength symbolized by his role as an engineer and builder of the railroad—that will claim the West for the Anglo-American nation.

The film is more problematic with respect to other ethnicities, specifically Chinese Americans. If we recall, Mildred saves Jose from lynching when she discovers that a Chinese waiter is responsible for the theft. Thus, it is only by replacing one despised ethnic subject with another that the film is able to deliver the greaser from harm. In this way, *The Greaser's Gauntlet* reenacts the historical machinations of Anglo-American railroad companies during the construction of railroad lines in the Southwest. With the availability of cheap Mexican labor along border towns, the preferred labor pool consisted of Mexicans rather than Chinese, and the film expresses this change by placing the Chinese waiter below the greaser in its racial hierarchy. Notwithstanding the film's seeming stereotypic complicity with U.S. dominance, ultimately the film's ambivalence still subverts this complicity.

One source of the film's more ambivalent representation is the way *The Greaser's Gauntlet* merges technical achievement with ethnic representation: it is the first American film to employ the "cut-in" within a narrative framework, and it does so in the lynching scene in which Mildred saves Jose. As a camera technique, a cut-in produces "an instantaneous shift from a distant framing to a closer view of some portion of the same space" (Bordwell and Thompson, 478). Not to be confused with a "close-up," a cut-in has the effect of enlarging—in either an intermediate or a close-up shot—an important detail within the frame. Tom Gunning provides a detailed analysis of this significant moment in the film in his study, *D. W. Griffith and the Origins of American Narrative Film*. Gunning describes and comments upon the sequence of shots immediately after Mildred saves Jose from the lynching and they stand facing one another.

After this dramatic climax, the filmic discourse takes an unusual turn. We cut in to a shot which frames Jose and Mildred beneath the tree, but from a much closer camera position. . . . The full figures of the actors appear in this shot, from head to toe. . . . This cut-in creates a spatial relation between shots that had not appeared in any of Griffith's films to this point. Rather than presenting an entirely new space, the closer shot enlarges a part of a space already established. In contrast to the earlier monolithic and neutral presentation of the bar scene, the camera seems to respond to the action within the frame, moving closer to emphasize it. (78)

Gunning notes that although the cut-in is "not a Griffith invention," this film marks the first use of a cut-in to present "a detail essential to the story" (78).

I call attention to Griffith's use of the cut-in in *The Greaser's Gauntlet* because, as with his use of the close-up in *Ramona* (1910), this is an instance in which "technical 'innovations' are a means of ideological encoding that have been used in highly precise ways," as Chon Noriega has argued about that film ("Birth of the Southwest," 217–18). Furthermore, the cut-in in the case of *The Greaser's Gauntlet* produces a racial encoding of startling dimensions. Griffith's use of the cut-in confounds critical expectations because one would infer, based on *The Birth of a Nation*, that Griffith would employ this narrative technique to highlight the purported deviousness of the Mexican or to focus on the negatively valenced racial difference between these two figures. This is what I expected coming to the film after having read a short description of the cut-in.[8] Instead, the "exchange between Mildred and Jose . . . carries emotional overtones of gratitude, unspoken love, and devotion which affect later narrative development. The cut-in brings us closer to the human figures at an emotional moment. . . it transforms the actors from distant figures to recognizable characters with visible faces and expressions" (Gunning, 80). Surprisingly, Griffith's use of the cut-in brings the viewer closer to the racial difference between Jose and Mildred, but not in a denigrating manner. The fullness of character the cut-in produces means that in this particular moment, Jose the greaser escapes one-dimensionality (figs. 2 and 3). Despite Griffith's conflicted relationship with American ethnicity, the movie gives the Mexican a human complexity. Additionally, the detail shot of Jose bestowing the gauntlet upon Mildred adds a historical dimension to his character, since the presentation of the gauntlet forms a "narrative armature" linking Jose, his mother, and Mildred (80). In terms of ethnic analysis, this linkage gives Jose a history and a connection to an ethical universe that the typical film greaser does not enjoy, further humanizing the Mexican.

FIGURE 2. Jose and Mildred in *The Greaser's Gauntlet* (Biograph, 1908), after Mildred saves Jose (frame enlargement courtesy of the Library of Congress, Motion Picture, Broadcasting, and Recorded Sound Division).

FIGURE 3. The cut-in used to emphasize the relationship between Jose and Mildred (frame enlargement courtesy of the Library of Congress, Motion Picture, Broadcasting, and Recorded Sound Division).

Griffith's ambivalent and contradictory relationship with ethnic representation adhered to other groups as well. In *The Red Girl* (1908), Griffith again expresses paternalistic sympathy for an ethnic subject, the Native American "Red Girl" in the film's title. Not unlike what we see in *The Greaser's Gauntlet*, however, *The Red Girl's* sympathy toward the Native American heroine requires that another ethnic subject be placed in the role of the villain. This time, Griffith chooses a Mexican woman as the scoundrel, and she is particularly evil. The unnamed Mexican sets the story in motion when she sneaks into Kate's hotel room and steals her gold. In her escape, the Mexican woman convinces the Red Girl and her "half-breed" husband to hide her, but she then betrays the Red Girl by seducing her husband. The "Mexican Jezebel" convinces the half-breed to kill the Red Girl. "To this end they plan a torture. Binding her hands and feet, they take her to a large trunk of a dead tree, which overhangs the river and there they hang her" (*Biograph Bulletin*, qtd. in Usai, *Griffith Project*, vol. 1, 94). Eventually, the Red Girl frees herself and helps Kate find the thief, and the Mexican woman is arrested. Like *The Greaser's Gauntlet*, in which the Chinese servant serves as a scapegoat for the tacit acceptance of the Mexican, *The Red Girl* places the Mexican woman in the role of scapegoat, and she makes possible a symbolic reconciliation between whites and Native Americans. In its depiction of the Mexican woman, the film veers toward titillation that is only explainable as an attempt to shock audiences into returning to theaters. In the film's most sensational scene, the Mexican woman ambushes a sheriff's deputy, then shoots, slaps, and kicks him, all the while laughing at her victim's fate.

In its antipathy and misogyny toward the Mexican woman, *The Red Girl* shows the uneven characterization of Mexican identity in Griffith's films. A short time later, in his production of *The Thread of Destiny* (1910), Griffith would return to a favorable presentation of Mexican identity. *The Thread of Destiny* is the most sympathetic of the early Griffith films that treat Mexican characters. The film treats a young couple, Frances Deland and Pedro Juan Moreno y Calderon, who meet and immediately fall in love. The inter-titles describe Frances, played by Mary Pickford, as "a delightful bit of American girlhood." Curiously, the film shows an awareness of the constructed nature of stereotypes, for it notes that Pedro is "a Spanish aristocrat to his countrymen—only 'another impudent greaser' to the white settlers." Between their affections stands Buck Larkin, who insults Frances and is easily defeated by Pedro. Buck turns the townsmen against Pedro by accusing him of cheating at cards—a familiar trick—but in the end, Pedro and Frances escape and get married. When the townsmen see them again, Buck attempts to stir up another posse, but miraculously the sight of a married couple "awakens the boys to their better selves," and they leave Frances and Pedro alone as the narrative concludes (21).

The Thread of Destiny is worthy of note for several reasons. First, the narrative explicitly treats an intercultural, if not interracial, relationship. Second, Pedro is clearly the male protagonist of this movie, and he is shown as physically and ethically superior to Buck and the townsmen, who are depicted as rabble-rousing gamblers. Third, the film's antagonist is a white American. Finally, the Mexican survives through the last reel without meeting a violent end. Although *The Thread of Destiny* sympathetically portrays the Mexican, it remains ill at ease with racial representation in its attempt to distinguish Pedro as a Spanish aristocrat. The film's inter-titles emphasize his class position, and his costume is highly ornate. The film, then, is pulled in several directions at once: it elevates the Mexican greaser to the status of upper-class Spaniard in order to make the bond between the Mexican and a white woman acceptable to its audience.

As we watch these movies, one question we may ask is why Griffith chooses to populate his films with so many ethnic subjects, be they Native, Chinese, African, or Mexican American. Part of the reason is that these figures represent Other-ness, thus providing the visual spectacle required to attract early filmgoers. Additionally, these ethnic subjects offer a titillating yet containable threat. Scott Simon comments that the "number of Mexicans populating Griffith's early work suggests they were more than an excuse for eye-catching set design and exotic costuming. Mexicans could be assumed to be hot-blooded and violent, never terribly far from crimes of passion" (Usai, *Griffith Project*, vol. 1, 114). These viewer assumptions notwithstanding, we cannot ignore the instances in which, for some Mexican subjects, Griffith gives ethnic representation a degree of complexity and stirs the viewer to identify with ethnic characters. These early films exemplify the ambivalent qualities of stereotypical representation, demonstrating that we need to expand our vision beyond the positive/negative binary to understand that amidst and through even the worst stereotypes, the American imagination expresses simultaneous derision and desire for the Mexican.

Yet questions remain with regard to the marked differences between Griffith's representations of Mexicans and Native Americans and his representations of African Americans. One possible reason for this difference is the racist political agenda Griffith pursues in *The Birth of a Nation*, which necessitates the completely dehumanized figures he produces. *Birth* instantiates white fear of an empowered African America, which was very palpable to conservative whites in the post–Reconstruction era. Recall, for instance, the scene in the statehouse, in which blacks are shown taking charge of state politics. On the other hand, within the Western genre at this moment, ethnicity is less threatening and—at this time at least—the American West is the only setting in which a Mexican or Native American may be viewed. As Gregory Jay has noted, a "pervading myth about the final days of the Indian spread throughout U.S. culture" at the turn of the century (8). Perhaps the sense of guilt for an accomplished conquest also applied in relation to the Mexican, who had lost his lands in the U.S.–Mexico War of 1848, although it appears that the eruption of the Mexican Revolution and the emergence of the Western hero reinstated the image of the Mexican as a threat, as I argue in the following chapter.

A second and more plausible reason for Griffith's variety of representation with respect to Mexicans and Native Americans may have to do with the youth of the Western genre in the years 1907–10. Gunning observes, for instance, that the "hallmarks of Griffith's early Westerns . . . contrast a great deal with the genre as it developed later." One major difference, Gunning points out, is that "the emphasis on a masculine and ethical Western hero remains absent" in Griffith (Usai, *Griffith Project*, vol. 1, 94). As the Western genre established itself in the second decade of the twentieth century, actors such as Broncho Billy Anderson, William S. Hart, and Tom Mix came to symbolize the white, masculine, and ethical hero to which Gunning refers. These heroes defined themselves—and by extension, the American character—against an anti-type that came to be played by the Mexican villain.

Griffith and Crane stand at seemingly opposite ends of the trajectories of their respective art forms, yet they produce similar results. Griffith's inconsistent appraisal of the Mexican suggests a film genre in its early stages, still to establish its conventions of greaser villains and Anglo heroes. Crane's ironic and critical stance vis-à-vis the Western hero places him outside the conventions of the Western adventure story. Griffith's Mexican is alternately untrustworthy, rapacious, and cowardly, but also brave and noble. The Mexican's contradictory representation in Griffith enables us to see the limitations of stereotypical discourse. Crane, on the other hand, consciously avoids depicting the Mexican as a stereotypical greaser or bandit, and he evinces deep unease for the transcendent Anglo hero. Critics who have concentrated exclusively on José's servility or the grandee's treachery have overlooked Crane's admiration for José's competence and his respect for the grandee's code of honor. The appearance of Mexican identity in both Griffith and Crane, finally, confirms the strong fascination that the American imagination has held for Mexican culture and suggests that the unequal relation between the two cultures has provided the ground upon which the United States has defined itself, particularly in relation to American masculinity.

My alternative and ambivalent reading of turn-of-the-twentieth-century literature and film stereotypes suggests, more broadly, that ethnicity generally and Mexicanidad specifically have always been fundamental constituents of American identity. The Mexican presence in American culture has appeared not only in the oppositional and binary relationship between the Anglo and the Other but also in the more complicated relation of attraction and repulsion between these two figures. Provocatively, because Anglo-America has dominated the production of the discourse on identity, various ethnic subjects have often been relegated to the "negative" position—the Chinese in *The Greaser's Gauntlet*, the Mexican woman in *The Red Girl*—depending on the ideological imperatives of a particular discourse. In chapter two, for instance, I propose that the figure of the greaser or bandit, in its conflation with that of the Mexican revolutionary, occupies the negative position during the 1910s. Yet despite this stereotypical hardening, a reading of the stereotype based on the notion of ambivalence allows us to see the continuing fluidity of the stereotype, the lack of fixity that permits the ethnic subject to subvert its negative determinations and uncover its constructed character. The stereotype's fluidity suggests that ethnic subjects must affirm their undeniable presence in the American imaginary in a far greater range of texts than was previously understood.

Greasers, Bandits, and Revolutionaries

The Conflation of Mexican Identity Representation, 1910–1920

The Mexican Revolution changed everything. This pronouncement constitutes an oversimplification, but in some ways it is also an understatement. Without discussing the revolution's deep societal impact, without delving into its influence upon future generations of Mexican immigration into the United States, and without describing its effects for the next eighty years on Mexico's political corruption and economic underdevelopment, we can say with certainty that it entirely altered the character of Mexican identity representation in American film. The revolution inspired the most recognizable villain in the American film Western canon, the Mexican bandit, or *bandido*. With bandoleers as armor, blazing guns as weapons, and a sneering, sweaty brow as threat, the Mexican bandit indelibly locked himself into the American imaginary, with appearances in a wide-ranging list of films as characters including Holbrook Blinn's Pancho Lopez in *The Bad Man* (1923), Wallace Beery's swaggering Villa in *Viva Villa!* (1934), Alfonso Bedoya's "Gold Hat" in *The Treasure of the Sierra Madre* (1948), and Emilio Fernandez's General Mapache in *The Wild Bunch* (1969). By the time the Mexican Revolution was coming to a close in 1920, the *New York Times* evidenced the prevalent view of the Mexican: "to the average American the Mexican today is an insurgent or bandit or, at any rate, a conspirator against his own government" (qtd. in Delpar, *The Enormous Vogue*, 5). Because the movies—Westerns in particular—reinforced such an assessment, the *Times* statement highlights the ideological conflation occurring during this period: the Mexican was an insurgent *and* a bandit, or, worse yet, a bandit revolutionary. While D. W. Griffith's pre-1910 Westerns demonstrate a degree of play in their representations of the Mexican male, between 1910 and 1920, the Mexican image in American films attained a seeming fixity as the Mexican loomed ever larger as a threat to American society.

But unlike the almost wholly negative cinematic portrayal of the Mexican, the literary assessment of this subject during the revolution was often wholly affirming. Guided by left-leaning intellectuals and progressive writers, the literary vanguard championed the potentially liberating social movement in Mexico, along with its agents. Jack London was among the writers who examined the Mexican Revolution in his fiction, principally in "The Mexican," a story about a young revolutionary working in the United States to raise monies for the cause. The story, whose main action takes place in the boxing ring, is brutally violent, and in it London produces a one-dimensional characterization of the single-mindedness required to carry out a revolution. Nevertheless, "The Mexican" stands out for its critique of the stereotypically negative view of the Mexican revolutionary subject as it would be portrayed in American film.

The U.S. Print Media, Hollywood, and the Revolution

By the second decade of the twentieth century, the motion picture industry had moved most of its production facilities to California, and it was beginning to make extensive ties, through newsreels, with newspaper conglomerates such as the Hearst media empire. Hearst was also by this time investing in film production and distribution, so its interests were converging with those of the film industry's. Perhaps the beginning of the Mexican Revolution, with its spectacle of carnage, came at a perfect time for these media groups, for in this cataclysm of violence, newsreels found a ready-made product for the public to consume, and motion picture companies stumbled upon an easy villain for their Anglo heroes to defeat. By the beginning of the Mexican Revolution in 1910, moreover, Mexico had become the main backdrop for U.S. films about Latin America. During the silent film era, in fact, more than five hundred films covered Mexico and its citizens as subjects for representation. Alfred Charles Richard speculates that "the convenience of an enemy so easily found just across the border aided the rapid growth and development of the film industry" (xiv). Mexico's upheaval threatened U.S. interests and strengthened the perception of Mexicans as lawless bandits. Furthermore, the assassination of Francisco Madero in 1911 "began more than four and one half years of almost continuous confrontation between the two nations. Before the inevitable interventions, it was a war of words and images in which the press and motion pictures played a significant and active role" (xxiv).

American opposition to the revolution's different fighting groups was frequently expressed in newspapers, and newsreels and documentaries often amplified the sentiments expressed in print.[1] *Juarez After the Siege* (1911), *A Trip Through Barbarous Mexico* (1913), *The Tampico Incident* (1914), and *Villa—Dead or Alive* (1916) satisfied the movie-going public's hunger for news about the revolution. That filmmakers were swayed by newspaper headlines and newsreels is evident in the films they produced. A brief survey of film titles made during the revolutionary period indicates the kind of interest the revolution generated: *Across the Mexican Line* (1911), *The Mexican Spy* (1913), *A Mexican Defeat* (1913), *At Mexico's Mercy* (1914), *Captured by Mexicans* (1914), *A Mexican Spy in America* (1914), and *Under Fire in Mexico* (1914) are among the most suggestive, and many more were made.[2]

William Randolph Hearst was among the most adamant opponents of revolution in Mexico. It is well known that Hearst owned a newspaper empire that included the *San Francisco Examiner*, but he also owned vast land and natural resources in Mexico. Hearst's properties incurred attacks from Francisco Villa's forces, so his economic interests were directly threatened. With his newspapers at his disposal, Hearst criticized events in Mexico, and he helped propagate the idea that the United States was under direct threat by events in that country. Hearst newspaper editorials also supported U.S. intervention (Brownlow, 90). A typical *Examiner* analysis of the revolution's leaders appeared on December 14, 1913, attacking Venustiano Carranza and Villa: "Carranza and his general [Villa] are all tarred with the same stick. They are simply organized brigands" (qtd. in Anderson, 91). The Hearst-Selig News Pictorial was among the first to present documentary images of the revolution, but with the addition of Hearst's slanted views: "the way to impress the Mexicans is to REPRESS the Mexicans" (qtd. in Brownlow, 91–92). Hearst's news conglomerate, furthermore, was not the only news and media outlet critical of the revolutionary movement. The *Los Angeles Times* and the *Chicago Tribune* also opposed the revolution, and printed regular editorials condemning the various factions involved in the fighting (Anderson, 55). American newspapers concentrated on three perceived aspects of the Mexican character in their depictions: backwardness, racial limitations, and moral decrepitude (123). These themes are consistent with the views of the "greaser" expressed by popular Western adventure novels during the nineteenth century, but they focus on the Mexican's stereotyped propensity for violence, and thus express the unease the revolution occasioned.

The correlation between the press's characterization of the revolution and the film industry's depiction of the revolutionary becomes readily apparent when we consider that some news syndicates, principally Hearst, also owned film-making operations. Additionally, many of the best-known early studios—Kalem, Pathe, Selig, and Mutual among them—produced newsreels that fanned the public's interest in events in Mexico. The earliest newsreels covered the revolution in a straightforward manner. In *Juarez After the Siege* (Kalem 1911), filmgoers watched the aftermath of a battle between revolutionary and federalist forces, with apparently little editorial comment from inter-titles (Richard, 42). Pathe Newsreel #22, *Del Rio, Texas* (1911), showed Mexican cattle drovers taking their livestock across the U.S. border, purportedly trying to escape both federal and revolutionary forces (73). Although the picture makes no overt condemnation of the revolutionary upheaval, it differs from *Juarez After the Siege* in its implication that the revolution would disrupt life along the border for Americans.

As interest in the revolution grew, so did the length and sensationalism of the films covering it. In 1913, the trade publication *The Moving Picture World* advertised the documentary *A Trip Through Barbarous Mexico*, promoting it as a "five thousand foot masterpiece that will appeal to the masses" (March 13, 1913, 1142). Indicative of the ambivalence that pervades the U.S. relation to Mexico, the advertisement promised viewers "Mexico as she really is today, mingling its beauties and its terrors." The main antagonists of the conflict are featured in bold type, in the style of a boxing match advertisement, "Madero versus Diaz" (1142).[3]

Two events in particular affected the U.S. perception of the Mexican character. The first incident was the 1914 confrontation at Veracruz between Mexican army troops and U.S. Marines sent to occupy Veracruz in opposition to the Huerta dictatorship (Bazant, 143). In response, Pathe filmed *The Tampico Incident* (1914), a newsreel in three parts that, according to an uncredited source, depicted Veracruz "under the firm kindly rule of the American occupation" (qtd. in Richard, 133). The second event, Villa's raid on Columbus, New Mexico, in 1916, had the greatest effect on the U.S. stance toward the revolution. Villa's incursion into the United States was a provocative response to the U.S. backing of Venustiano Carranza in Mexico. The United States in turn responded by sending troops into Mexico in pursuit of Villa. The immediate cinematic outcome can be seen in Pathe's Newsreel #30, *Somewhere in Mexico* (1916), in which the ad notes U.S. flyers braving "the treacherous air currents of the Mexican desert looking for Villa's bandits" (qtd. in Richard, 183). Among the most damning of the newsreels is *Villa—Dead or Alive* (1916), which exhorted American preparedness in the face of Villa's attacks upon the United States (Richard, 199).

Evidence of newspaper and newsreel impact on Hollywood may be found in the dramatic increase of negatively valenced film titles during the revolutionary period, especially the years 1914 through 1916, when relations between the United States and Mexico were at their worst. During this period, American filmic depictions of the Mexican began to coalesce and take on an antinomial quality, with the victorious Anglo in a struggle against a duplicitous, violent Mexican. In *A Mexican Defeat* (1913), a Mexican army captain tries to frame an American couple, and he displays lecherous intentions toward the woman. The two Americans outwit him and narrowly escape across the border. A year after that film was released, with tensions between the United States and Mexico growing and with the perceived threat to American business interests heightened, films such as *At Mexico's Mercy* (1914) and *Captured by Mexicans* (1914) introduced audiences to the trope of the bandit revolutionary. In *At Mexico's Mercy*, a revolutionary general extorts an American mining operator in exchange for allowing the American to continue running the mine. The general is depicted not as a revolutionary, but as an outlaw, and he is defeated in the end (Richard, 97, 112). Similarly, *Captured by Mexicans* blurs the distinction between bandit and revolutionary as Mexican rebels steal a horse and kidnap an American before they are themselves captured by the *federales* (*The Moving Picture World*, April 4, 1914, 98). Films that continue the conflation of bandit and revolutionary include *Under Fire in Mexico* (1914), which *The Moving Picture World* called "a powerful story of guerilla cruelty and American heroism," and *The Americano* (1915), in which, according to the same trade magazine, "bandit soldiers" attack an American oil company (qtd. in Richard, 136, 139). *The Insurrection* (1915) defended the U.S. occupation of Veracruz by claiming that Mexico was about to attack American ships (Brownlow, 101). The *San Francisco Examiner*, the *Los Angeles Times*, and the *Chicago Tribune* had already carried these news stories, and their often slanted interpretations spilled over into newsreels and influenced Hollywood's depiction of the Mexican as villain.

To be sure, there are instances in which Hollywood took a somewhat less hostile, but still opportunistic, approach to the revolution, as when the Mutual Film Corporation signed a $25,000 contract with Pancho Villa for exclusive filming rights to his battles, resulting in *The Life of General Villa* (1914). This film was more concerned with providing sensational footage of Villa in battle than in depicting the life of Mexico's most (in)famous revolutionary. Desperate for the cash necessary for munitions and food, Villa accepted the money, and he took extraordinary measures to help the filmmakers get the footage they wanted, including allowing filming to take place in full daylight and restaging battles to obtain better footage. The monetary exchange between Villa and Mutual only reinforced the idea that the revolutionary figure was a disposable commodity of the U.S. entertainment industry. In their willingness to pay for real carnage, the filmmakers signaled the importance of the Mexican male in the life of the movies. In all his realness, the Mexican revolutionary paradoxically attains an unreality, for his value is not measured in terms of his life and death, but in terms of his ability to entertain audiences. In both life and image, the revolutionary became both malleable and expendable.

The year of Villa's raids on New Mexico, 1916, marks a nadir in the U.S. response to the Mexican male subject. *Liberty*, which *The Moving Picture World* called a "startlingly realistic drama of warfare along the Mexican border," envisions Mexico as a tyrannical country and the United States as the defender of the cause for liberty (qtd. in Richard, 179). *Patria*, a multi-part serial funded by Hearst, imagines Mexico and Japan plotting to undermine the United States. Finally, in *Taint of Fear*, a young man proves his bravery by participating in the capture of Lopez, a Mexican bandit modeled after Pancho Villa (184, 189). If we take *Patria* as a barometer of the ratcheting of hysteria, then the Mexican Revolution was rapidly morphing into the sinister root of America's worst fears.

Was 1910, the beginning of the Mexican Revolution, a watershed year for the representation of the Mexican male in film? Is it possible to argue that pre-1910 Westerns exhibit a degree of ambivalence that post-1910 Westerns do not? Movies such as *The Patriot*, compared with the Griffith films of a previous generation, certainly lead us to this conclusion. Still, these questions are difficult to answer, especially because prints of many of the films under consideration are very rare, in a state of deterioration, or simply not extant. And while we have access to their advertisements and brief plot reviews as evidence of their content, we do not have the benefit of seeing the movies themselves from a longer historical vantage point. Although other factors influenced the representation of the Mexican after 1910—for instance, the solidification of the Western as a genre, as I discuss below—between 1910 and 1920, the revolution heavily tilted the balance of Mexican representation in a negative direction, and the tremendous number of titles produced during this period provides a damning insight on the period.[4] In the years 1914 through 1916 alone, 176 films were produced in which Mexican characterization was a significant element, and Pancho Villa appeared in 36 of these. Villa and other revolutionaries were often depicted as both rebels and bandits, and these representations were mutually reinforced by the movies and newspapers (Richard, xxvi; Pettit, 135).

Dress as Marker of Villainy and Sign of Bandit/Revolutionary Conflation

The Mexican Revolution produced other significant changes in the representation of the Mexican male. Iconographically, it altered the screen Mexican's style of dress, for the Mexican's costume reflects the ideological transformation from greaser bandit to bandit revolutionary, and we can see this change in the modes of dress used before and after the revolution. *The Greaser's Gauntlet* (1908), discussed in the previous chapter, serves as an early example of the style of dress used to depict the Mexican before the revolution. Jose, the greaser of the title, is attired in the costume of a Mexican *charro* or *vaquero*. In addition to the actor's brown-face, the Mexican character can be differentiated from his Anglo-American counterpart because instead of a Stetson, he wears a round, charro-style sombrero, and rather than denim pants, he wears epaulet-trimmed leather pants. As in other films of this early period, the Mexican generally wears embroidered jackets and pants in the Spanish style, with a bandana, sash, or poncho to match. The Anglo's costume is simpler—plain denim pants and cotton shirt—as befits the Anglo Protestant belief in utility over style. A sharper differentiation between villain and hero appears several years after *The Greaser's Gauntlet* in *An Arizona Wooing* (1915), in which "Mexican Joe," who lusts after an Anglo woman and pays dearly for it, wears an even larger sombrero. Unlike Jose, Mexican Joe wears heavy, greasy brown-face that further distinguishes him from the hero. The film's ideology seems to state that the larger the sombrero and the darker the skin, the greater the Mexicanness and negativity of the character.

Although the charro style predominates in early silent Westerns, films such as *Broncho Billy and the Greaser* (1914) show a second mode of dress. Here, the greaser—listed in the credits as "the half-breed"—wears a Stetson, denim pants, and a western shirt, much like his Anglo counterpart. The similarity in costume makes the differences between the Anglo hero and the greaser villain harder to discern, though the ethnic difference is transferred to class difference, apparent in the character's dress. Broncho Billy wears a distinctly shaped, light-colored hat and a form-fitting shirt. The half-breed, by way of contrast, wears a ragged, somewhat deformed black hat and a loosely fitting patterned shirt. The differences in dress between Broncho Billy and the half-breed are subtle—we should keep in mind that as a cowboy, Broncho Billy is a working-class hero—but their effect is to give the half-breed his lowly caste. Additionally, it is clear by the Mexican's actions and the inter-title descriptions that he occupies the role of "badman." Whether they are dressed as charros or cowboys, the Mexicans in *An Arizona Wooing* and *Broncho Billy and the Greaser*—movies made after 1910—are irredeemable villains. Unlike Jose in *The Greaser's Gauntlet*—a movie made before 1910—Mexican Joe and "the half-breed" express neither guilt nor a change of heart as a result of their actions.

The Mexican Revolution introduced the third and most strongly differentiated mode of dress: the revolutionary iconography produces a stronger differentiation between the Mexican and the Anglo-American hero. As Charles Ramírez Berg writes in *Latino Images on Film*, the *bandido* stereotype in Hollywood films is iconographically recognizable by the "dark, sweaty, unshaven face . . . the *bandoleras* . . . the wide-brimmed sombrero" (1). The bandido Ramírez Berg describes is the one with whom contemporary filmgoers are most familiar, but he is differently attired than the bandit of the earlier greaser films. The updated Mexican bandit wears a larger, charro-style hat; his most significant accouterments are the bandoleers across his chest, making him not only far more threatening than his predecessors, but also more easily discernable. We should remember that men who wore these bandoleers and hats were primarily revolutionaries, not bandits, yet what has occurred in American Westerns is the collapse of two distinct stereotypical figures—the bandit and the revolutionary—into a single iconographically recognizable character. For contemporary filmgoers, all Mexican revolutionaries are also bandits, and there is no distinction between these originally separate characters.

Because many early Westerns do not survive, we cannot exactly determine when the iconographic conflation of bandit and revolutionary began, but we can guess that newsreels about the revolution and the (semi-)documentaries about Pancho Villa played a crucial role in the creation of the bandit revolutionary. As the most famous of all the Mexican revolutionary leaders, Villa was actually known for banditry on both sides of the border, and the United States' ideological need to vilify him made this label stick. As a bandit and rebel, Villa captured the imagination of the American film industry and the news media—for good and ill. Henceforward, his image was so dominant that nearly all representations of Mexican characters in Westerns would reference him, even if at the most sublimated levels.

The Bad Man, a movie I discuss in depth in the next chapter, is perhaps the first film to fully consolidate the visual elements of the bandit revolutionary, though this film did not appear until 1923. The Villa-derived representation of the bandit revolutionary in *The Bad Man* became the dominant depiction of the Mexican in the Western genre. The conflation of bandit and revolutionary has meant that we cannot think "bandit" without associating the descriptors "treacherous" and "cowardly," and without picturing the sneering look, the dirtiness, the large sombrero, and—the most important link with the revolution—the bandoleer belts across the chest.[5] Because the stereotypical image of the Mexican greaser or bandit long precedes the image of the revolutionary, nearly every American film about Mexican revolutionaries also carries associations with banditry. Even when the Mexican revolutionary acts heroically, he is usually indiscriminately violent.

Establishment of the Western Hero, Emergence of the Mexican Villain

As early as 1911, *The Moving Picture World* complained that the Western had become predictable and stagnant: "always the same plot, the same scenery, the same impossible Indians, the wicked half-breeds, the beautiful red maidens" (qtd. in *Treasures from the American Film Archives*, vol. 1). Pronouncements about the Western's extinction were prevalent during the teens, but in truth, the Western genre would not truly establish itself until the appearance of what Richard Slotkin has called the "myth-hero" during the 1910s, the same period in which the Mexican Revolution took place. It was in this era also that William S. Hart established himself as the preeminent star of Western films, thus having a foundational influence on the development of the genre (243). The "myth-hero" is the center of the Western, for he is the highest representative of Anglo-American values and he is the embodiment of the "Myth of the Frontier." That American film founded the Western hero at this historical moment is significant for Mexican representation, for this is also the moment when the film industry conflated the Mexican revolutionary with the bandit. If the early Western positions the Mexican as the nemesis the hero must overcome, then this binary placement is further emphasized by the threat that the Mexican Revolution instantiated in Hollywood filmmakers' imagination.

The "Myth of the Frontier" has proven foundational in its power to influence "the life, thought, and politics of the nation." As a "mythic expression of ideology," the Myth of the Frontier functions as "a set of symbols that is apparently simple yet capable of varied and complex uses; that serves with equal facility the requirements of progressives and conservatives . . . that is rooted in history but capable of transcending the limitations of a specific temporality" (Slotkin, 4–5). The Myth of the Frontier, in other words, serves as a flexible, explanatory narrative for the ideological assessment of a historically diverse set of national circumstances, especially American identity during times of crisis or change. And the Western's ability to concretely express national concerns enables a reading of American identity in relation to its most persistent Other, Mexican identity. William S. Hart's founding vision for the Western most strongly positions itself vis-à-vis Mexican male identity, for he constructs the paradigmatic Western hero in opposition to this particular ethnic subject.[6] In the teens, Hart set a pattern that would continue throughout the Western's history. While Hollywood's relationship with the Native American would continue to be deeply troubling, Hart's main opponents were not Indians, but "greasers," "half-breeds," bandits, and bandit revolutionaries. As the following discussion suggests, Mexican identity came to signify the negative Other to Hart's Anglo-American heroism.

Three films directed by and starring Hart exemplify the necessity of creating a Mexican villain in order to establish the Anglo-American male as the Western's preeminent hero. *Hell's Hinges* (1916) aptly instantiates the wholesale transference of villainy to the Mexican—or Mexicanness, in this case. *Hell's Hinges* has attained the status of classic among silent Westerns, especially in consequence of its release as part of the *Treasures From the American Film Archives* series of historically significant films.[7] *Hell's Hinges* is an unusually bleak Western about a badman, played by Hart, who is redeemed by helping to annihilate a town stained by sin. Interestingly, the film does not directly treat Mexican identity, since no half-breed, greaser, or bandit shows up to antagonize the hero. The absence of a greaser notwithstanding, the film establishes a covert racial dichotomy in its differentiation of the story's hero, "Blaze" Tracy, from its villain, "Silk" Miller. In the narrative, an early inter-title describes "Blaze" Tracy as the "embodiment of the best and worst of the early West. A man-killer whose philosophy of life is best summed up in the creed, 'shoot first and do your disputin' afterward.'" As the inter-title makes clear, initially Tracy is no hero. His redemption, however, may be possible only if his adversary is established as wholly despicable. To this end, the film characterizes "Silk" Miller as mingling "the oily craftiness of a Mexican with the deadly treachery of a rattler, no man's open enemy and no man's friend" (fig. 4). Miller's appearance, while not apparently raced, is definitely more sinister than Tracy's. He wears a mustache, which in the Western is a facial feature reserved for gamblers, badmen, and Mexicans.

Hell's Hinges establishes a narrative structure based on the covert opposition between the Anglo and the Mexican early on, and thus suggests two

FIGURE 4. Alfred Hollingsworth as "Silk" Miller in *Hell's Hinges* (Kay-Bee, 1916) (DVD frame enlargement courtesy of the National Film Preservation Foundation).

points. First, the plot makes clear that in 1916, the mere association of a character with Mexicanness was enough to confirm his ultimate villainy. Second, and more importantly, the plot sets up the necessary antinomy from which the hero emerges, and this antinomy is built on an implicit racial difference. The film champions "Blaze" Tracy as the center of its moral universe—and he embodies an unassailable Whiteness alloyed by the armor of a Protestant moral compass. Furthermore—and this is the most important point—Whiteness needs a relational Other; it does not exist in and for itself in a moral vacuum. In *Hell's Hinges* and other Westerns, Whiteness elevates itself in relation to what it rejects, which in this case is the moral corruption and evil represented by the subsumed Mexican character of "Silk" Miller.[8]

In *The Aryan* (1916), Hart plays Steve Denton, a former miner turned outlaw who leads a band of Mexican renegades on attacks against westward-moving settlers. Hart's character finds redemption through the graces of a white woman, who convinces him to change his lawless ways and protect the whites who are under attack from the Mexican renegades. The woman senses his goodness, but she also confides "implicitly in the fact that Denton is an 'Aryan' and as such [is] instinctively bound to protect all women of his race" (Slotkin, 250). Not only does he protect white womanhood, Denton also makes possible the accomplishment of the United States' "manifest destiny" by clearing its path of the Mexican threat. *The Patriot* (1916) follows a similar thematic structure. In this film, Hart's character, Bob Wiley, joins the revolutionary Mexican forces of "Pancho Zapilla" after unscrupulous politicians steal his mine claim, betraying his loyalty to America. Familiarly, the film's plot is based on Pancho Villa's attacks on Columbus, New Mexico. When the band prepares a raid on the United States, Wiley has a last-second change of heart that restores his patriotism. His transformation is made possible by the purity of a child, paralleling the moral redemption in *The Tavern Keeper's Daughter*. This time, however, Wiley is the one redeemed, not the Mexican. In these Westerns, the Anglo-American hero defines his moral worth, his goodness, and his patriotism against the Mexican's villainy. Furthermore, these mid-decade films established Hart as the cowboy hero of his generation. Finally, *Hell's Hinges*, *The Aryan*, and *The Patriot* address key themes within Anglo-American identity—heroic redemption, White-ness, and nationalism—and they take up these themes by tacitly or overtly positioning Mexicanness as the evil the Western hero must defeat.

In other Westerns, the Mexican displaces conflicts within Anglo-American communities by taking on the main role of villain. This is the case in *An Arizona Wooing* (1915). The plot for this movie is based on the struggles between cattle ranchers and sheepherders on the western range. Tom Mix plays Tom Warner, a sheepherder threatened with severe harm if he does not take his flock far away from a cattle ranching community. Unfortunately, he is in love with an elder cattleman's daughter. Conveniently, "Mexican Joe" also loves the girl, and he kidnaps her, intending to force her into marrying him. Tom, who had been tied up by several Anglo cattle ranchers and then cruelly jeered by "Mexican Joe," informs the girl's father of the situation. The man releases Tom, who then rescues the girl. "Mexican Joe" is captured and taken off-screen to meet a certain end. The Mexican thus acts as an odd scapegoat—no pun intended—for the historical conflict between cattle ranchers and sheepherders in the West. The film ends with peace between the two groups as it introduces fans of the Western to another of the genre's early stars, Tom Mix.

The vilification of the Mexican takes other forms still. Some early American films with Mexican characters follow a disturbing racist logic similar to that seen in films with African American characters. It is not an accident, as Richard Flores has pointed out in *Remembering the Alamo: Memory, Modernity, and the Master Symbol*, that the film *Martyrs of the Alamo* (1915) closely parallels *The Birth of a Nation* (1915) in its racist paradigms. In fact, Christy

Cabanne, the director of *Martyrs*, assisted D. W. Griffith in the production of *Birth*. Both *The Birth of a Nation* and *Martyrs of the Alamo* depict blacks and Mexicans as menacing and violent. Additionally, both films place special emphasis on African American and Mexican rapacity, and thus rely upon the familiar Anglo-American fear of miscegenation. The "abhorrence of miscegenation has been called the one enduring American taboo and while the feeling against it is most strong in terms of alliances between Whites and Negroes, it carries over to include the mating of Whites with dark peoples other than Negro" (Robinson, 75). *Martyrs of the Alamo* justifies the taking of the Texas territory from Mexico by representing the sexual-racial threat that the Mexican posed. Through the film's racial logic, the Mexican is presented as a danger to the emblem of Anglo Texas civilization, the Anglo-Texan woman. White womanhood must be protected at all costs, and the white woman inspires the heroes of Texas liberty to a fervent commitment that runs as deep as the famous battle cry itself.

The Mexican male occupies a cluster of interrelated positions during the years 1910 to 1920. He is the ultimate villain for the white hero to defeat, he is a fall guy for other conflicts in the West, and he is the rapacious sexual threat to white womanhood. Above all, though, the Mexican is a bandit revolutionary whose ideological conflation continues well past the end of the Mexican Revolution, and even into the present day—see *And Starring Pancho Villa as Himself* (2003), for instance. Examined from a broad perspective, the Mexican male has performed a complicated psycho-social function: he has been the Other—the double in the mirror—against whom the U.S. imaginary has crafted a vision of American masculine identity. The U.S. relation to Mexican identity is characterized by open disavowal in order to produce difference, but the relation, as I argue further in the next chapter, is also characterized by sublimated identification, which is a feature of ambivalence.

Jack London and the Mexican Revolutionary

As I have argued, the period of the Mexican Revolution coincides with an increasingly denigrating portrayal of the Mexican subject in popular media. During this same era, however, literary production took a different turn, as American writers began a serious reconsideration of the Mexican subject (Delpar, R. Paredes). Essayists such as Charles Macomb Flandrau in *Viva Mexico!* (1908) and John Kenneth Turner in *Barbarous Mexico* (1910) criticized the Díaz regime and accused the United States of participating in the peon's enslavement. In fiction, Willa Cather's *Song of the Lark* (1915) depicts the

Mexican in a more hopeful manner. These are but a few examples, but what is important to register is that American literature would present an oppositional voice and alternative history to the mass cultural perceptions as defined by newspapers and the movie industry. Placed against contemporaneous developments in motion pictures, literature added a complexity to the public discourse on Mexican identity. If the cinematic output during the era dogmatically held out the Mexican male as threat, the literature was more varied, expressing hope and admiration, but also condescension and fear. The literary record, then, expressed contradiction and ambivalence in its depiction of the Mexican. Jack London's "The Mexican" (1911) exemplifies the level of contradiction, for London's main character is by turns idealized and villified. "The Mexican" was first published in the *Saturday Evening Post* in 1911, near the inception of the Mexican Revolution, and it preemptively responds to the idea that newsreels and the motion picture industry would disseminate, namely, that the Mexican was a bandit revolutionary.

Jack London, whose radical politics veered between intense loyalty to socialist causes and disaffection for those causes, stands as an incongruous spokesperson for the Mexican rebel. In "The Mexican," he champions and even idealizes the revolutionary movement and the main character of the story, Felipe Rivera. Yet by 1914, he would vilify the revolution and the "half-breed" Mexicans fighting on its behalf. Writing for *Colliers*, London called the revolutionary a member of the "half-breed class that foments all the trouble, plays childishly with the tools of giants, and makes a shambles and a chaos out of the land" (qtd. in Anderson, 138). This statement forms part of London's bigoted legacy, for even in his best writing, "his fiction was warped by misguided ideology, often of the most embarrassing racist kind" (Crow, 46). London's racial politics, as the previous chapter's discussion of Griffith demonstrates, are not unusual in their conflicting positionalities. Although London admired the working classes, his racial views tended toward Darwinism, and he considered Indians, Chinese, blacks, and other races inferior to the Anglo. Nevertheless, as Andrew J. Furer has argued, London's "admiration for the spiritual and physical power to be found among those whom popular opinion . . . held to be inferior . . . persists through all the contradictions of his racial views" (171). In stories such as "The Mexican," London exalts the ethnic subject as one whose will and tenacity should be neither underestimated nor regarded at the level of base stereotype.

"The Mexican" is the story of Felipe Rivera, a Mexican boy of eighteen working in the United States on behalf of the revolution. Rivera is a member of a socialist organization in the United States that is raising funds to help arm the Mexican rebels. Rivera is idealistic and angry, having witnessed the murder of his family by the *federales*. Although he possesses modest intellectual and economic resources, he is physically strong and determined. Demonstrating a zeal unequaled in his fellow revolutionaries in the United States, Rivera decides to enter a boxing match against a seasoned fighter, with the hope of winning the prize money that he will then donate to the revolutionary cause. He endures a tremendous beating, as well as the taunting of a biased ringside crowd, but in the end he overcomes great odds and wins the fight.

The narrative opens with a statement about its protagonist, the young Rivera, that could well apply to the popular American attitude toward the Mexican revolutionary: "Nobody knew his history" (70). As the story unfolds, London simultaneously rejects the emerging stereotype of the bandit revolutionary and creates an idealization of the primal, almost animalistic power of the Mexican. London writes, for instance, that to his comrades, Felipe Rivera is "something forbidding, terrible, inscrutable. There was something venomous and snakelike in the boy's black eyes" (70). Another revolutionary sees him as a "power—he is the primitive, the wild wolf, the striking rattlesnake, the stinging centipede" (73). While these visions parallel a different stereotype about Mexicans—that they are primitive and close to the earth—it is a far cry from the view of the Mexican as simply a violent bandit revolutionary.[9] And although Rivera is compared to a snake, there is nothing "sneaky" about his representation. The story, in fact, admires the main character's revolutionary dedication, albeit in overblown language: "He is the revolution incarnate. . . . He is the flame and the spirit of it, the insatiable cry for vengeance. . . . He is a destroying angel moving through the still watches of the night" (73).

Although London gives way to idealism in his depiction of the Mexican character, he also demonstrates an acute knowledge of the thwarting of the revolutionary movement by the U.S. government and media. The reader learns, for example, that the U.S.-based junta Rivera joins is busily involved raising funds and writing letters, "appeals for assistance, for sanctions from the organized labor groups, requests for square news deals from the editors of newspapers, protests against the highhanded treatment of revolutionists by the United States courts" (71). London is one of the few American writers—along with Ambrose Bierce and, later, Katherine Anne Porter—to critique the U.S. government's and media's responses to the Mexican Revolution, and he does so from a position of critical awareness.

London's critical appraisal of U.S. institutions, we should recognize, comes not as a consequence of an attraction for the ethnic subject but because he championed workers, underdogs, and anarchists. A longtime proponent of socialism, London demonstrates his allegiance to the lower classes when he exuberantly imagines their toppling of the Díaz dictatorship.

> The border was ready to rise. One Yankee, with a hundred I.W.W. men, waited [for] the word to cross the border and begin the conquest of Lower California . . . the Junta in touch with them all and all of them needing guns, mere adventurers, soldiers of fortune, bandits, disgruntled American union men, socialists, roughnecks, Mexican exiles, peons escaped from bondage, whipped miners from the bullpens of Coeur d'Alene and Colorado who desired only the more vindictively to fight—all the flotsam and jetsam of wild spirits from the madly complicated modern world. (74)

London's defense of the peon, then, results from his support of the subaltern classes, who are in this example led by a single Yankee. While we should keep in mind the framing of this Yankee's implicit racial superiority, it does not diminish London's positive re-articulation of the Mexican revolutionary.[10]

London's most significant contribution to the depiction of the revolutionary is in his reversal of four distinct statements implied by the cinematic stereotype then under way: that the revolutionary was a bandit, that he was without revolutionary commitment, that he was inferior to the Anglo ethically and physically, and that he was underhanded and sneaky. As "The Mexican" opens, the revolutionary junta seeks monetary support from various workers' unions. The story characterizes the junta's activities as legitimate and above board. For his part, Rivera also raises funds for the revolution, contributing what little money he earns to the cause. While his compatriots view the source of his contributions with a great deal of suspicion—after all, he is only a kid, dressed in tatters and half-starved—we later learn that he has acquired his money honestly, by winning small-time prize fights. Furthermore, through prize fighting—this time against Danny Ward, the champion—Rivera plans to contribute the much-needed five thousand dollars the junta requires to continue the struggle.

London portrays Rivera's commitment to the revolution by contrasting it with his opponent's selfish desire for money and leisure. "Danny Ward fought for money and for the easy ways of life that money would bring. But the things Rivera fought for burned in his brain" (81). While Ward thinks only of his own material gain, Rivera cannot but mentally relive the death of his parents and other Mexican people who died at the hands of the federales. In the moments before the fight begins, as he awaits Ward's arrival at the ring, Rivera recalls the "death-spitting rifles that seemed never to cease spitting, while the workers were washed and washed in their own blood" (81). While

Ward represents materialism and greed, Rivera symbolizes unselfishness and the idealism of fighting for a cause larger than oneself.

Most films about the Mexican Revolution made during the 1910s—whether for or against the struggle—imagine the Mexican as the Anglo's ethical and physical inferior, and even movies supporting the revolution show the Mexican in need of the Anglo hero's aid. London, by contrast, renders Rivera as self-possessed and determined. As the bout is to begin, we get a picture of Rivera as "more delicately coordinated, more finely nerved and strung than any" of the mostly white spectators at the fight with Ward. "The atmosphere of foredoomed defeat had no effect on him. His handlers were gringos and strangers" (80). London shows Rivera as capable of understanding the Anglo prejudice against the Mexican, and able to stand above it. When Ward finally arrives for the fight, the physical differences between the champion and the man whom Ward has labeled a "little Mexican rat" are palpable (82). The reader also gets a sense of the fight audience's perceptions of the differences between the two boxers when Rivera disrobes for the fight. "A groan went up as Spider Hagerty peeled Rivera's sweater over his head. His body seemed leaner because of the swarthiness of his skin. He had muscles, but they made no display like his opponent's. What the audience neglected to see was the deep chest. Nor could it guess the toughness of the fiber of the flesh, the instantaneousness of the cell explosions of the muscles, the fineness of the nerves that wired every part of him into a splendid fighting mechanism. All the audience saw was a brown-skinned boy of eighteen" (83). London shows that the physical differences between the two men are racially overdetermined, and that the Mexican's ethical and physical strength cannot be established by his swarthy skin. In fact, Rivera's dark skin prevents the audience from seeing his inner strength.

Finally, London refuses the stereotype of the sneaky Mexican by depicting Danny Ward, and not Rivera, as the unfair fighter. As the fight begins to turn in Rivera's favor, Ward "stalled, blocked, fought parsimoniously, and strove to gather strength. Also he fought as foully as a successful fighter knows how. Every trick and device he employed" (86). Rivera, for his part, fights cleanly, and must endure not only Ward's tactics, but also the unfairness of the Anglo referee. London's reversal of the Mexican and Anglo's efficacy in this case has its antecedents in London's sports reporting, as Andrew Furer has noted. In an article London wrote relating the bout between James Jeffries, who was white, and Jack Johnson, who was black, London recognized the superiority of Johnson, regardless of the color of his skin. Furer writes that London "inverts the era's stereotypical oppositions of civilized white man and savage black man—he declared that Johnson's abilities were those of a scientific boxer while Jeffries' were those of a primitive fighter: 'Jeff is a fighter, Johnson is a boxer'" (qtd. in Furer, 169). In "The Mexican," London similarly reverses stereotypes of the Mexican's underhanded tactics. He declares that Rivera boxes honorably and according to the rules—like a scientific Jack Johnson—while Ward cheats throughout the fight—like a primitive James Jeffries.[11]

In the end, Rivera outlasts Ward and attains his goal of supplying guns for the revolution. Rivera stands alone; there are "no congratulations" for him (89). He faces the unbelieving crowd of gringos in anger and defiance; there is no cowering and no hiding from the enemy, as the movies would depict the "bandit revolutionary" doing a short time later. Rivera looks before him as "the hated faces swayed back and forth in the giddiness of nausea," and he recalls his purpose. "The guns were his. The revolution could go on" (89). The Mexican protagonist closes the story dignified and victorious, in a completely different posture than the lowly "greaser" of the D. W. Griffith films and popular adventure novels of the nineteenth century (and even of José in Crane's "One Dash-Horses"). In the years that followed the 1911 publication of "The Mexican," American newspapers, newsreel documentaries, and Hollywood films would take the Mexican and transform him into a "bandit revolutionary," a violent and immoral figure devoid of true revolutionary ideals. The concurrent emergence of the film Western as the repository of Anglo-American values only amplified the Mexican male's seemingly villainous nature.

Provocatively, much like Crane and Griffith, London also muddies the waters of representation, creating in "The Mexican" a character constituted by the forces of ambivalence. Although London's Mexican is presented with great admiration—the revolutionary figure inflamed London's own social and political commitments—his depiction is troublingly one-dimensional and, ultimately, animalistic, indicating a deeply seated hatred or fear of the Other. We cannot deny, then, that the Mexican London championed appears to us in two contrasting facets—one, on the surface, is attractive and heroic, while the other, at sublimated levels, is marked by derision. As for the movies treating the Mexican revolutionary, these too contain the contradictory pulls of derision and desire, but only as the revolution draws to a close and the perceived Mexican threat diminishes. As I argue in chapter three, the Mexican who was denigrated in American movies of the 1910s is linked to American identity through unconscious identification as we move beyond the Mexican Revolution. This identification gives way to an unacknowledged admiration, and it is an admiration for Mexican masculinity that will suffuse the Western with ambivalence and give way to a reversal of the bandit revolutionary's fortunes by way of the "good badman."

The Western's Ambivalence and the Mexican Badman

The Western, it would seem, is the genre *par excellence* for the unhesitating declaration of American values and identity—yet, arguably, the Western is founded on ambivalence, for while its dominant motifs and iconography are avowedly 'American,' they are not exclusively native to the Anglo-Protestant worldview. In actuality, many of the constituent features of the Western film cowboy are produced through an interplay with the modes of masculinity as expressed in the values of the Spanish and Mexican *vaqueros* who preceded the American cowboy in the West. Because the 1910s are also the moment when the Western as a genre comes into being, the Western itself is constituted through deep ideological contradictions. It is not a genre of monolithic vocality, as its creators and admirers would like to think. The Western's wavering quality, in fact, is evidenced by its very overt attempt to declare the moral preeminence of its hero, the white Anglo male. The greater effort to declare the unassailability of this subject position is a measure of its anxiety. The Western, then, must grapple with an anxiety over its origins or influences. The genre's logic ultimately depends upon a set of values and iconography that are isomorphous with one of its principle Others, the Mexican male, who is often depicted as a "greaser" or "badman."

Few films demonstrate the Unites States' deep psychic dependence on Mexico for its vision of itself more than *The Bad Man*, a movie adapted for the screen from Porter Emerson Browne's play of the same title. *The Bad Man* first appeared in 1923 and saw two more major productions, in 1930 and 1941, and it signals a transition in the representation of Mexican identity. No longer merely the heavy of the Mexican Revolution, the Mexican badman was glamorized for his rough yet gallant demeanor and id-driven approach to life. He was feared, but he was also admired. In the films' narratives, he must eventually meet his end, but not before he can serve as mirror for the examination of American values and self-conception. Although the figure of the bandit revolutionary in its most despised form would live on in future film productions in various guises—from gangster to gang member to corrupt general—the 1920s witnessed a shift in the way the Mexican villain was portrayed. No longer simply a villain, the Mexican badman acquired likeable three-dimensional qualities, and he was usually on the side of good rather than evil. The fact that this "good badman" appeared at the same time that the Western genre was constituting the enduring image of the heroic cowboy marks a coincidence that cannot easily be reconciled.

The Western's Ambivalence

Between 1910 and 1920, as I have contended, the representation of the Mexican was characterized by an increasing fixity. Nonetheless, an examination of a broad array of films indicates varying degrees of ambivalence. We cannot ignore, for instance, the number of films that indicate an attraction toward the Mexican subject. *An American Insurrecto* (1911) and *A Prisoner of Mexico* (1912) express support for the incipient revolutionary movement—although they have no faith in the Mexican's efficacy, since they feature American heroes winning battles on behalf of the Mexican rebels (Richard, 33, 48). In *The Mexican Revolutionist* (1912), the main character, a Maderista rebel, is favorably presented (70). *The Mexican* (1914), directed by and starring Tom Mix, treats the story of a Mexican who, after being persecuted and fired from his job, saves the life of a child and then regains his job for his heroics. The movie "suggests the innate prejudice of some whites toward all Mexicans and may be considered an early example of a social problem film" (Langman, 288). *The Mexican* is notable because in it, an early icon of the film Western plays an ethnic subject, albeit before the height of his popularity. Finally, *Rio Grande* (1920) depicts a Mexican heroine who works on behalf of cultural understanding between Mexicans and Americans along the border (376).[1] While these sample films demonstrate a positive appraisal of the Mexican, he appears most consistently as a villain in numerous Westerns of the period.

Paradoxically, the derision of Mexican identity occurs within a genre, the Western, whose constitutive quality is ambivalence, as Jim Kitses has argued. In his foundational study, *Horizons West*, Kitses describes the ideological oppositions embedded within the idea of the West, and he conceptualizes a binary model of meanings that structure the "dialectical play of forces" in the constructions of American identity. "Was the West a Garden threatened by a corrupt and emasculating East? Or was it a Desert, a savage land needful of civilising and uplift?" (13) The answer is neither and both, for an ideological uncertainty, an undecidable, double-valenced opposition cuts through the genre: "this ideological scheme positions the Western hero between the nomadic and the settled, the savage and the cultured, the masculine and the feminine" (13). The major opposition within the Western is that between the Wilderness and Civilization, and this opposition is subsumed by several others, including that of Individual/Community, Nature/Culture, and West/East. Yet Kitses cautions that this schematic "must be seen not as a prescriptive taxonomy but rather as an exploration of the frontier mythology that defines the world of the genre" (14). In other words, the mythic structures of the West constitute oppositions that stand simultaneously, that blur and contradict each other, that are marked not so much by ambiguity as by ambivalence.

The contradictory groupings of meaning described by Kitses fit the genre's hero appropriately, for he often figures as the bulwark between civilization and the wilderness. Therefore, he necessarily straddles two worlds: he must know the ways of the wilderness in order to successfully fend off its threats against the establishment of civilization. In fact, it is often the case that the hero desires to escape from the strictures of civilization. Thus, it is not surprising that an early Western film hero such as Broncho Billy Anderson on numerous occasions played the "good badman," a character who stood within and outside social norms. The image of Anderson as a good badman is especially significant in light of the fact that during the genre's early years, Anderson "was by far the most coherent and attractive character on the Western screen" (Buscombe, *BFI Companion*, 25). William S. Hart followed a similar route, playing a badman who was "still essentially a cowboy figure," but "one who has strayed outside the law" (29). As his career developed, Hart made a virtue of holding the good-bad opposition in tension.

Provocatively, the theme of the badman who becomes good brings the Western hero in strikingly close proximity to the Mexican villain and exposes an ambivalence expressed as mimicry. Specifically, the theme recalls Griffith's Biograph Westerns such as *The Tavern Keeper's Daughter* and *The Greaser's Gauntlet*, in which the Mexican begins as the badman and is later redeemed. Anderson and Hart also followed this formula, and in the process they displaced the Mexican from the position of possible redemption. The plot structures of Hart's films in particular prove to be highly telling, for he often "played a 'bad man' of one kind or another—an outlaw, gambler, or just a hard customer—who finds redemption through the love of a good woman (or a pure young girl). The formula was used over and over, with minor variations. Sometimes the hero would be unjustly accused of crime;

sometimes he would be a genuine criminal who redeems himself through some charitable act" (Slotkin, 244). As discussed earlier, in *The Tavern Keeper's Daughter*, the greaser finds redemption when he gazes upon the face of an innocent child; in *The Greaser's Gauntlet*, the drunk and violent Jose sees the face of the woman who saved his life and in return he saves hers. The plot structures of Hart's Westerns adhere to a similar pattern, but they transfer the possibility of redemption from the Mexican subject to the Anglo-American hero. Hart's Mexican antagonists have no option but to play the villain through the final reel. The transference of redemptive action from Mexican to Anglo marks not only the increasing rigidity of the Mexican stereotype, but also the representational closeness between Anglo and Mexican definitions of masculinity, and it is a sign of the deeply ambivalent character of Mexican identity representation in particular.

In a sense, then, the Mexican is the original "good badman" whom the Anglo-American hero comes to mimic. Homi Bhabha discusses colonial mimicry as the third-world subject's imitation of European cultural forms. Although mimesis and transformation of the colonial subject remains incomplete—and thereby maintains a subversive possibility—Bhabha nevertheless concludes that mimicry "emerges as one of the most elusive and effective strategies of colonial power and knowledge" (85). The kind of mimicry that adheres in the Western also functions as a strategy of power, but it is reversed: rather than the Mexican mimicking the Anglo-American, it is the Anglo who makes use of the theme of redemptive heroism from the Mexican, producing a form of power that operates through the displacement of the Mexican's redemptive position.

The level of mimicry as power extends yet further. The Mexican is, in a very real sense, the original cowboy—the *vaquero*—of the West. If the Native American is the first inhabitant of the West, it is not the Anglo who comes afterward, but the Spaniard or Mexican. When the Anglo cowboy arrives on the scene, he imitates the vaquero's ways. While both the Anglo and the Mexican appropriate the survival skills of the Native American, ultimately the Anglo comes to adapt many of the customs of the Mexican. The Anglo imitates the vaquero's utilitarianism, and he adopts the names that the Mexican has given to the objects of the West. When we consider the number of Western cultural artifacts with Spanish names, it is as if the Spaniard/Mexican and not the Anglo is the West's "American Adam," to borrow from R.W.B. Lewis's use of the term in a different context.

We begin to see, then, the degree of ambivalence the Mexican's presence produces. We also recognize the anxiety vis-à-vis Anglo-American identity formation that the Mexican induces, because the Western is so deeply preoccupied with American identity: "[T]his shifting ideological play illuminates the genre's basic function, its inquiry into the roots and circumstances of American character" (Kitses, 13). In the world of the Western, therefore, it is not the Indian with whom the Anglo is predominantly concerned, but the Mexican. Native Americans were mostly displaced once the Mexicans and Anglos began encroaching upon their land. The final antagonist, then, is the Mexican, with whom the Anglo shared similar aspirations, as Américo Paredes has noted: the "colony of Nuevo Santander [in South Texas] was settled much like the lands occupied by westward-pushing American pioneers, by men and their families who came overland, with their household goods and their herds" (*With His Pistol*, 8). As the first conqueror of the native land, the Mexican must necessarily be demonized and differentiated as much as possible if the Anglo is to position himself as the true "myth-hero" of the West. By the 1870s, "the Indian danger was past, [so] it was possible to idealize the Plains savage. But the 'Mexican problem' remained" (Paredes, *With His Pistol*, 21). The result has been the creation of stereotypes about the Mexican, such as the "Anglo-Texan legend," which holds that the Mexican is, by his miscegenated nature, prone to cruelty, thievery, and cowardliness (15–16).[2] These are qualities over which no single race holds a monopoly, but which have been attributed to the Mexican in order to justify the Anglo's presence in the West and to make the Anglo hero unassailable.

As a symbol of American identity, the Western hero is white. Yet the real cowboy of the Western range upon whom the hero is based came from different backgrounds: "at least one-tenth of 'American' cowboys were Hispanics, generally mestizos. Blacks and mulattoes comprised about a fifth. Already at the turn of the century, though, many Americans had conveniently forgotten this racial mixture lest it tarnish an increasingly mythologized being" (Pike, 1, 37). If survival on the range depended on confraternity, regardless of race, endurance in the Western novel and on the Western screen depends on racial differentiation and the exclusion of all but the conquering Anglo-American hero.

Enter the Badman

True difference, however, is never fully achieved, and, from a diachronic standpoint, the wide variance of Mexican identity representation during and after the Mexican Revolution only highlights the contradictory relation between the Anglo-American and the Mexican male. *The Bad Man* (1923) cogently exemplifies this vexed relationship. The film's very title speaks to the representational closeness between these two figures. "Badman" recalls the kind of character made famous by Broncho Billy Anderson and William S. Hart. In the case of *The Bad Man*, however, the badman is Pancho Lopez, a Mexican bandit modeled after Pancho Villa. And like those Anderson and Hart characters, this badman is not fully bad, for although he is a wanted revolutionary and cattle rustler, he acts from a sense of duty and justice on behalf of an American rancher who previously saved his life. When Lopez recognizes the rancher, he helps the man recover his losses and saves his love interest. This badman never stops being bad—he is a thief and a killer—but his good and simple heart and his zest for life inspire admiration even from the people he threatens.[3] The film's premise was so compelling, if not popular, that studios remade it twice—in 1930, with Walter Huston as Pancho Lopez, and again in 1941, with Wallace Beery (not coincidentally, of *Viva Villa!* fame) playing the lead.[4] In *The Bad Man*, we observe a second order of mimicry: Pancho Lopez mimics Hart's badman mimicking the Mexican badman of *The Greaser's Gauntlet* and other early Westerns. Racial representation would make a complete circle, further highlighting the often indeterminate and always multivalent nature of stereotypical representation.

The Bad Man, in fact, has a history that precedes its cinematic iteration. All three of its major filmed versions are based on Porter Emerson Browne's play, *The Bad Man*, which debuted in New York's Comedy Theatre on August 30, 1920, and which received highly favorable responses from audiences and reviewers alike (Mantle, 269). Writing for the *New York Times* about the play's opening night, critic Alexander Woollcott noted "such ostentatious salvos of applause and sharp Continental [sic] cries of 'Bravo! Bravo!' as are usually reserved for really great occasions in the theatre" (August 31, 1920). During its year-long run at the Comedy Theatre, *The Bad Man* was performed no less than 342 times, making it the fourth most frequently performed play of the 1920–21 season (Mantle, 351). The number of times the play was performed suggests that Mexicanness as a concept—in its multifaceted and often misguided readings—held great fascination for American audiences.

Yet for all the attraction for the Mexican subject that Browne's *The Bad Man* may suggest, the play was primarily a satire concerned less with Mexican identity per se than with commenting upon American culture and society. To critique American social mores, the play uses the reckless behavior of the carefree and amoral Mexican bandit as a foil for its examination of American customs and rules of propriety. Furthermore, the play's context should also be kept in mind: *The Bad Man* opened at the end of two major wars—World War I, which affected every American in a direct way, and the Mexican Revolution, which also affected Americans, but in a more diffuse although no less significant fashion.

In the play's opening, Gilbert Jones has just returned from serving his country in France, and he comes back to find his Texas ranch on the verge of bankruptcy and foreclosure, for his cattle have been stolen and the mortgage is due. Circling him like vultures are Jasper Hardy, the sheriff and lien holder of Jones's land, and Morgan Pell, a New York investment banker who suspects that Jones's land holds oil riches. Hardy and Pell are guests at Jones's ranch. Lucia Pell accompanies her husband Morgan, but she was also, in her former life, Gilbert Jones's great love, the woman he left to make his fortune. The badman of the play's title, Pancho Lopez, does not appear until the end of Act I. His late and sudden appearance, however, functions as a crucial plot device, for he arrives just in time to save Lucia Pell from the abuses of her husband. In the course of the first act, Morgan Pell discovers the still-smoldering feelings between Gilbert and Lucia. In a vindictive move, he takes her to their bedroom, where he decides to teach her a lesson. He takes hold of a spur that sits at a table and intones, "Horses don't always know who they belong to. (*Drags spur on table.*) So they are branded. (*Lucia shrinks.*) There is no reason why women equally as ignorant shouldn't be similarly treated" (Browne, 38).

At the same instant, Lopez and his band of horsemen enter the scene, guns blazing, unintentionally preventing Pell's awful deed. Lopez closes the first act with the pronouncement, "*Senors, Si Senoras* [sic]. *You are my prisoners*" (39).[5] These lines and many others are written—and likely were delivered—with a high degree of exaggeration, and they played well with audiences. In his review for *Theatre Arts Magazine*, Kenneth MacGowan noted that the play was "quite extraordinarily acted by Holbrook Blinn as the bandit" (9). Other reviewers agreed with MacGowan's assessment that Blinn's acting carried the play. "Mr. Blinn swaggered through his role with a superb sense of its picturesqueness. . . . Capital performance" ("Highly amusing comedy," 7). Blinn, whose career to this point was deemed "uneven" by a *New York Times* reviewer, was so convincing and entertaining that he was the only cast member to also appear in the 1923 film version of the play.

As the second act begins, it is apparent that Lopez has not arrived at the ranch to rescue anybody. He is there to take away the women, the cattle, and whatever loot there is to be found. His arrival coincides with the presence of Sheriff Hardy, his daughter Angela, and the Pells. Lopez sees in the assembled bodies an opportunity to steal from and perhaps even kidnap a rich American in order to finance his ongoing insurgency against the Mexican government. As he lustily looks Lucia over, he decides to take her to Mexico, too, as his woman.

LOPEZ: What's your name?

LUCIA: Lucia.

LOPEZ: Lucia. Ees putty name. Come 'ere. Come 'ere! (*Goes to her—draws her to him. She winces.*) I would see more of you. (*Lifts her skirt, she slaps his hand.*) Not bad. 'Ow you like to go wiz me to Mexico?

LUCIA: What?

LOPEZ: Well? You 'eard what I said.

LUCIA: But I couldn't do that!

LOPEZ: Why not?

LUCIA: I'm married.

LOPEZ: (*Sits on R. of table*) Well, we will not take ze 'osband. Just you and me. We go to ze bull fight. I rob ze jewelry store for you. We get plenty dronk. I show you 'ell of a good time. Well, 'ow you say? (41)

Lopez's early exchanges with Lucia reveal much of what critics found so appealing about this 'Mexican' character. He is a free spirit, unaffected by American norms of morality and propriety. In this instance, the audience would have laughed at and sided with Lopez's comment about Lucia's husband, for Morgan Pell is clearly the villain of this story.

Pancho Lopez is also openly critical of the double standards and hypocrisy contained within American society, as more than one critic has observed. The play's imputed critique of American social norms, of course, is always presented lightly and in a comedic fashion. For instance, Lopez compares the United States and Mexico on the subject of individual freedom.

LOPEZ: Tell me, Senora [*sic*], 'ave you never been to a free country?

LUCIA: A free country?

LOPEZ: Si, like Mexico, for instance?

LUCIA: Don't you call the United States a free country?

LOPEZ: The United—Bah! Ees the most unfree country what is. Every man, every woman, is slave—slave to law, slave to custom, slave to everysing. You get up such time; eat such time; every day you go to work such time; every night you go to bed such time; every week, Madre de Dios, you take a bath such a time! And yet you call it a free country! Ees only one free country. Ees one in which man does as she dam' please. Like Mexico. (44–45)

Lopez's pronouncements are pure exaggeration and ironic inversion, but perhaps America's puritanical values, industriousness, and war-weariness weighed heavily on theatre-goers of the 1920s, especially in comparison with the perceived openness of Mexico, as Helen Delpar has documented in *The Enormous Vogue of Things Mexican*. Lopez's statements describe an America regimented by clocks and rigid customs—it was a society against which Mexico promised the freedom to do as one pleased.

Audiences could not but assume that the Mexico in question was a real place, and they took Pancho Lopez's realism (or lack thereof) for granted. One of the most interesting issues brought about by the play and subsequent film adaptations, then, is the idea of an uncertain verisimilitude in relation to the representation of Mexicanness on the stage and on the screen. The play was successful for several reasons, and not least because its audience bought into the idea that they were somehow seeing Mexicanness on display, whether or not they had any a priori idea of what Mexicanness entailed. MacGowan, for instance, praised Blinn's performance for what he judged to be its closeness to an idea of authentic Mexicanness. In his review, MacGowan avers that in the play "we have an American player who can achieve physical as well as spiritual impersonation. In aspect, voice and mood, he creates a fresh and living character. The gusto of his performance is delightful" (9). MacGowan does not directly make a claim for verisimilitude, but the notion that Blinn approaches "physical" and "spiritual impersonation" strongly implies the satisfactory attainment of an essential Mexicanness.

When Blinn adapted his role for the screen, film reviewers were no less impressed by his ability to represent the Mexican. When we consider that the first filmed version of the play was a silent movie, it becomes apparent that it was upon Blinn's physical action and appearance that reviewers based their judgments. The *New York Times* noted that Blinn's acting "is a lesson for motion picture players, for he is never at a loss for a smirk, a smile, a look of surprise, threatening gestures, or interest in what is going on around him. Blinn's hands and feet appear to suit the very expression of his darkened countenance" ("Whimsical Bandit," 17). Writing for *Life* magazine, Robert E. Sherwood declared the movie "exceptional," and added that Blinn, "appearing as the engaging Mexican bandit, loses nothing in his transition from the spoken word to the silent drama" (26). These comments take Blinn's ability to inhabit Mexicanness as a given; they do not question its presentation as *re-presentation* and interpretation.

I want to emphasize that neither the playwright nor the main actor nor audiences had but a second-hand knowledge of the attributes of Mexicanness; yet in Blinn's words, in his appearance (aided by brown-face, as advertising photos demonstrate), and in his physical movements, the actor as the Mexican bandit fulfilled the expectations of Mexicanness for Americans.

Both producers and consumers of this Mexican figure had acquired their understanding of Mexicanness from the adventure and conquest stories of the late nineteenth century, from the silent movies made during the first twenty years of American filmmaking, and from newspaper articles about the Mexican Revolution. Yet none of these representational models approached what we can call an authentic or realistic description of Mexicanness; each of these media carried its own agenda, and none of them were concerned with representational accuracy as the highest priority.

The assumed realism in the Mexican's representation is especially noteworthy in light of its departure from previous norms, for *The Bad Man* and its first film adaptation in 1923 ironically marked a transformation in the way the Mexican was depicted. The Mexican figure, in almost one fell swoop, went from being a cunning and murderous adversary of American values to becoming a jovial and good-hearted fellow, someone interested in ensuring justice, respecting property, and extending the blessings of marriage to those who truly deserve it. Further, in *The Bad Man*, Pancho Lopez becomes a gentle critic of American character. He is comical and absurd, yet he is suddenly likeable. Reviews of the play and film regarded Lopez as "picaresque," "picturesque," "uncomplicated," and even "pungent," a character who "knows just what to do" when it is time to mete out justice. He is attractive because of his ability to cut to the chase, unencumbered by the "drawbacks of civilization" (Woollcott, 16). MacGowan and other reviewers were particularly impressed by the scene in which Lopez coolly solves Gilbert Jones's personal problems: Lopez unceremoniously orders the execution of Jones's enemy, Morgan Pell, to make possible Jones's reunion with Lucia.

The secret to the Mexican's precipitous climb to acceptability is explainable by the fact that he remains, through comedy, a figure of thinly veiled derision. As revealed by the phonic renderings of the script, his English is abominable—of course, since he is Mexican—but his Spanish is just as mangled. Although the few Spanish phrases contained in the script can be attributed to Porter Emerson Browne's probable limited Spanish proficiency, the audience surely responded to Lopez's pidgin Spanish with laughter aimed at the Mexican's—not the playwright's—ineptitude. Of far greater importance than the Mexican bandit's language limitations, however, are his crude ideas concerning justice, which are efficient yet barbaric. For instance, when Lucia confronts Lopez on his attitude toward killing other men, his response contains a casually debased logic.

LOPEZ: You sink it wrong to kill?

LUCIA: You talk of killing so matter of factly!

LOPEZ: Why not?

LUCIA: Does life mean as little to you as that?

LOPEZ: Life? To be 'ere is life. Not to be 'ere, is death. Life is a little thing unless it is one's own.

LUCIA: You do kill your prisoners, then, as they say?

LOPEZ: Certamente. You capture ze prisoner. You 'ave no jail to put 'im in. You cannot pack him around wiz you. If you let 'im go, 'e come back to fight you again. So you kill him. Sabe?

LUCIA: But it seems so *cold*-blooded!

LOPEZ: To you, perhaps. It is ze difference between zose who live in safety and zose who live in danger . . .

LUCIA: It's too horrible.

LOPEZ: Ees life. (43)

Lopez's rough but effective beliefs were beyond the pale for middle-class theatre-goers of the 1920s, and it is likely that these comically rendered beliefs were attributed to Mexicans in general. Middle-class American audiences could enjoy the Mexican's violent tendencies while comforting themselves that their values, however restrictive, were superior in their moral uprightness. By placing the Mexican at arm's length, Americans could examine their own beliefs and find them preferable to the Mexican's.

At the same time, the perspective implied by the quoted lines also caused audiences to see in Mexico an alternative and liberated space, one governed by simple, clear-cut rules. MacGowan supports this conclusion in his comments for *Theatre Arts Magazine. The Bad Man*

> startles its audience with keen and double-edged satire on the social habits of America and Mexico. Porter Emerson Browne . . . has brought forth a colorful picturesque and exciting play in which a border bandit discusses the shortcomings of American life, and by his own mental attitude not only clarifies our own view of ourselves, but lets us see the oddities of life below the Rio Grande. Again and again come sharp and pungent pictures of our hide-bound society set off against the happy land of the south where all is happiness and freedom—"if you don't get shot" (8).

McGowan's last statement richly puts *The Bad Man* in the American context. At this point in the twentieth century, Mexico represented a contrastive space of freedom and possibility—although not a space Americans would ultimately choose—much like the American West would have symbolized a generation earlier.

To put both the play's bold outlook and the audience's attraction toward it into perspective, we have to also consider that the viewers who were thrilled by the badman's lines were the same New York audiences who saw 350 performances of *Enter Madame*, a comedy play about a "world famous prima donna" on the verge of divorce, and they were the same audiences who witnessed 204 performances of Eugene O'Neill's *The Emperor Jones*, a now-classic one-act drama about an African American who installs himself as the emperor on a Caribbean island (Mantle, 98, 299). These comparative examples suggest that 1920s audiences welcomed exotic fare into their theatre repertoire, and in this sense they were not different from nineteenth-century readers of adventure novels, or the first attendees to the nickelodeon. All these audiences, regardless of class or social standing, were interested in the spectacle of exotic locales, exotic peoples, and exotic points of view. Perhaps as a way of drawing in its female audience, the play further encourages identification with Pancho Lopez and his ideas by having the second female character, Angela Hardy, fawn at the badman's every move or statement. Angela finds his rough techniques alluring and the prospect of being kidnapped and taken to Mexico romantic. The possibility of adventure and romance, along with the Mexican badman's cavalier views on life and mortality, brought audiences back again and again.

And they would continue to come back, this time at the urging of movie studios, to see three versions of *The Bad Man* on the screen. As I have noted, in 1923 Holbrook Blinn reprised his starring role in *The Bad Man*, and it was a critical success on the same order as the play. Reviewers praised the movie for its fidelity to the script and for including more action than its stage predecessor (Sherwood, 26). Although extant prints of the 1923 movie are unavailable, the film was by all accounts very faithful to the original script, for as the *New York Times* noted, there "is hardly a better example of filming a play" than *The Bad Man*, and the director, Edwin Carewe, "deserves great praise for the clever and restrained manner" in which he adapted it ("Whimsical Bandit," 17).

One of the questions that impresses itself upon the discussion of the abrupt change in fortune for the Mexican badman is: What altered so quickly to make him a palatable character for American audiences? The answer, as my analysis of such films as *The Greaser's Gauntlet* and *The Thread of Destiny* implies, is that the Mexican does not so suddenly go from being hated to being loved. In actuality, the Mexican figure has always walked the line between derision and desire. Yet certain political factors and societal views did change during the 1920s. For one, as the descriptions of the New York theatre scene make clear, the post–World War I era saw a relaxing of

American guardedness towards new ideas and different peoples. Furthermore, with specific regard to the Mexican badman, by 1920 neither the Mexican Revolution nor Mexico's possible involvement with German agents plotting to disrupt the U.S. government (a highly suspect idea to begin with) posed a threat to America's well-being.

The final factor in the transformation of the badman's fortunes had to do with the economics of the film industry. Even as early as the 1920s, Hollywood was exporting its films to Mexico and Latin America, but its products were often deemed offensive or propagandistic by Latin American governments. By 1922, Mexico had grown tired of Hollywood casting its citizens as bandits, villains, and badmen, and in February of that year the Mexican government took formal steps to ban American movies from entering its country if those movies were deemed derogatory or politically damaging to the nation. As reported by the *New York Times*, the ban was "so sweeping that it places restrictions on any company seeking to do business in Mexico, [and] comes on the eve of an attempt by motion picture companies in this country to expand their business there." The Mexican government's move was received, at least initially, as a serious and far-reaching admonition. The *New York Times* article quotes a consulate official stating that the warning "applies to all pictures made by companies which produce films featuring the Mexican bad man, no matter where they are sold. . . . 'The usual portrayal of the Mexican in moving pictures is as a bandit or a sneak, and naturally the Mexican government wishes this stopped'" ("Mexico's Ban," 15). American production companies' response, ostensibly, was to make their Mexican characters less offensive. Perhaps it is no coincidence, then, that Porter Emerson Browne's "positive" rendition of Mexican character was seen as a viable story to be mined by filmmakers.

Looking upon available photos of the first filmed version of the play, we can see at least partly why Blinn's badman was so likeable (fig. 5). His costume is clean and tidy, a far cry from the greaser's of an earlier decade. He wears a classic *charro* outfit, composed of pants and a matching short jacket made of suede or another soft fabric, as well as a sash and a tall white hat that looks new—not malformed, crushed, and battle-worn like the bandit's hat. Across his waist sits a single gun belt; absent are the menacing bandoleers of the Mexican Revolution era. He sports a simple mustache and well-groomed hair; he is devoid of the scruff or unkemptness of the bandit revolutionary. On top of all of this, Blinn's demeanor as Pancho Lopez is dignified as he stands in the slightly exaggerated formal manner suiting the acting conventions of the silent period. Of course, my interpretation of these traits is speculative, since it is based on production stills, so I cannot

FIGURE 5. Holbrook Blinn, far right, played Pancho Lopez in *The Bad Man* (Edwin Carewe Productions, 1923) (magazine cut-out, origin unknown).

incontrovertibly confirm that this was a self-respecting bandit. By comparison, Lopez's second-in-command, Pedro, is given a scruffy appearance, has a heavier mustache, and does wear bandoleers across his chest.

In any case, it is not difficult to imagine that, coming closely on the heels of the Mexican consulate's broad warning, the 1923 *The Bad Man* crafted its interpretation of Mexicanness so that it would please the Mexican government. Further, the representation by Blinn of a clean-cut Mexican also pleased the American audiences who viewed it. The photograph in question is interesting for one other reason: it shows the scene in which Lopez arrives in the nick of time to save Lucia Pell from her jealous husband. In the photograph, the American male is the villain, as he is about to sadistically inflict physical harm upon his own wife.

Comparing production stills of the film with photographs from the original play contained in the Samuel French edition of the script, it is apparent that the major difference between the two productions is in the use of make-up: Blinn wore brown-face for the theatre production only. Otherwise, the costuming is very similar for the play and film, as are Blinn's formal gestures and calm demeanor. In photos, Blinn looks more like the stereotype of the regal Spanish Don than like that of the Mexican bandit. In the Samuel French photograph, he stands calmly next to the character of the uncle, one hand in his pocket and the other gesturing. We see no violence or extreme action in these gestures.

By 1930, when *The Bad Man* was made yet again, any pretense of respectability seems to have gone out the door. The 1930 version stars Walter Huston, who a year earlier had played the evil Trampas in the adaptation of Owen Wister's *The Virginian*, a film starring Gary Cooper in the title role (Huston went on to win the Best Supporting Actor award for *The Treasure of the Sierra Madre* in 1948).[6] A 35-millimeter copy of the 1930 film is available for viewing at the UCLA Film and Television Center, complete with sound. Huston's badman leers behind heavily made-up eyelids and dark makeup; his curled mustache and broad smile give him a mischievous countenance. This Pancho Lopez moves quickly and assertively, he speaks loudly, and his mood veers between extreme joviality and anger. A production still of Huston dressed as the badman shows him posing with a six-shooter at his shoulder, cigarette hanging from his lips (fig. 6). Huston smirks sideways at the camera. His costume, far more elaborate than Blinn's, calls attention to his bandit's aggressive personality. A tall man, Huston could be dashing and athletic, handsome and charming despite his cunning look. In the transition between Blinn and Huston, the badman becomes less smooth and far more threatening. Simultaneously, he loses some of his dignity. In an attempt to heighten the comedy, this badman is over the top; he is becoming a buffoon, a transformation that is complete by 1941 in the person of Wallace Beery.

Reviewers of the 1930 *The Bad Man* drew comparisons between Blinn and Huston, giving the nod to Blinn for originating a cool, philosophical bandit capable of critiquing American society's weaknesses without alienating audiences. The *New York Herald Tribune* noted in Holbrook Blinn "the suavest, subtlest and most facile of our actors . . . never more deft or more shrewdly satirical than as the straightforward Mexican brigand, whose simple, frank barbarity pierced the tortuousness of effete American civilization" (Watts, Jr.). While reviewers generally commended Huston's acting, all agreed that Blinn's original could not be surpassed. The *Chicago Daily Tribune* noted that Huston was "magnificent in the role rendered forever memorable by Mr. Blinn, proving a picturesque, virile, lovable, and terrible Robin Hood of the west. His teeth flash under cocky black mustachios. Beneath beetling brows his eyes fairly stab you with their brilliancy" ("The Bad Man," 31). These words describe an energetic performance, but they also make clear that Blinn's bandit contained an openness that Huston's steely eyes seemed to obliterate.

FIGURE 6. Walter Huston as Pancho Lopez in *The Bad Man* (First National Pictures, 1930) (production still courtesy of the Margaret Herrick Library, Academy of Motion Picture Arts and Sciences).

The 1930 edition of *The Bad Man* follows the original dramatic script closely, but it also contains some notable exceptions that help us understand the continuing ambivalent rendering of the Mexican. After a brief introduction of Gilbert Jones and the main conflict, the 1930 film includes a scene with Pancho Lopez that is indicative of the farcical direction the film will take. In the scene, Lopez and his men have captured an American whom they believe to be a spy. The American, however, claims to be a reporter seeking to write a story about Pancho Lopez, the infamous Mexican revolutionary. Nonchalantly, Lopez orders the American's execution, but he has a change of heart when he notices the American's stoic manner. Lopez studies the reporter, has a laugh, and decides to spare the man's life. The reporter asks Lopez what he is doing in the United States, and Lopez responds that Mexico is too dangerous. "Is much better United States." The reporter then asks Lopez how he became a revolutionary. Lopez retorts, in deadpan, "Because of women. Chasing, running from, looking for. . . . I have no women, I am lonely." This comedic introduction to the bandit is not in the script of the original play, and it has no relation to the play's satiric intent. Thus Lopez's first appearance in the 1930 version signals the film's greater willingness to ridicule Mexican character traits, in this case the stereotype of the Mexican's insatiable sexual hunger.

The second and more telling difference between the 1930 film and its predecessors may be found in its ending: in its final reel, *The Bad Man* reverts to the plot device of early greaser films in which the Mexican is disposed of to create the possibility of Anglo-American heterosexual union and to ensure America's safety. While the play and its first film version produce closure by having Pancho Lopez bid his adieu to a reunited Gilbert and Lucia, the 1930 film kills off the bandit. In the play, the ending is happy and light, with Lopez wishing that his "frands . . . may . . . always be so happy like what I have make you" (93). The 1930 film, following its trajectory of farce, takes the good-bye to an absurdist extreme. Lopez jokingly tells the reunited couple that they must name their first boy after him, Pancho. But "if he's a girl . . . " He does not finish this sentence, for at the same moment the Texas Rangers—whose pursuit he has always cleverly evaded by employing the moving-picture trick of a stunt double—catch him by surprise. He takes flight, but he is ultimately shot and captured just outside Gilbert's ranch. Gilbert and Lucia run out to help, but it is too late and the bandit utters his final words, which reinforce the notion that this Mexican is to be mocked, even in death: "If he's a girl, Panchita!" With these words, he expires, having died at the hands of the Texas Rangers.

By 1941, *The Bad Man* as a film franchise had run its course (though a British television movie crediting Browne for its screenplay was made in 1947). Wallace Beery, an Academy Award winner (Best Actor for *The Champ*, 1931) and one of the greatest badman character actors of his generation—also known as Long John Silver in *Treasure Island* (1934) and King Richard the Lion-Hearted in *Robin Hood* (1922)—starred as Pancho Lopez. Beery had previously played Pancho Villa in *Viva Villa!* (1934), a film I discuss in the next chapter, so Pancho Lopez was not a stretch for him. Even more than its immediate predecessor, the 1941 *The Bad Man* was a complete farce, and it was negatively received by critics. "Episodes in the script calling for comedy hit the burlesque side too frequently," complained *Variety* ("The Bad Man"). Other reviews were far harsher, all but dismissing Beery as the Mexican badman: "Ever since 'Viva Villa,' Wallace Beery has periodically shaded his squinting eyes under a broad sombrero and assumed an even broader Mexican accent for the benefit of a South-of-the-border adventure." The comedy, furthermore, was seen as dated and past relevance. *The Bad Man* "is so old he's decrepit. His bones creak and it's painful to watch him act young" ("Wallace Beery Plays . . . "). This final comment was meant to apply to the movie as well as Beery, who was fifty-four years old when the movie was made.

Production stills of the movie show Beery, corpulent and greasy, stuffed into a charro outfit with a gun holster at each hip (fig. 7). He sneers at the camera in every photo. While his outfit is not dirty or sloppy, it is gaudy, with a shiny belt and buttons festooning him from head to foot. With one eye closed and pointing his pistol, Beery looks brutishly menacing. But still more telling than Beery's appearance is that of Chrispin Martin, the actor who plays Pedro. Consistent with his role as "Gordito" ("Fatty") in the Cisco Kid series of movies, Martin's Pedro is rotund, and the wide-eyed and vacant expression on his face is supposed to be evidence of his dim-wittedness (fig. 8). Martin appeared in more than fifty Westerns, often playing to the stereotype of the mentally slow sidekick who is the butt of all the jokes. The production stills of Pedro unmistakably confirm that he stands for the Mexican bandit as buffoon. As I argue in the next chapter, Beery's rendition of Pancho Villa in *Viva Villa!* would inaugurate the Mexican's slide into a clownish figure.

Despite its ignominious final version, *The Bad Man* was not simply a minor film franchise. The three major film productions of *The Bad Man* starred some of the most popular if not talented actors of their time—Holbrook Blinn, Walter Huston, and Wallace Beery. The 1941 version of the film also

FIGURE 7. Wallace Beery as Pancho Lopez in MGM's 1941 version of
The Bad Man (production still courtesy of the Margaret Herrick Library,
Academy of Motion Picture Arts and Sciences).

FIGURE 8. Chrispin Martin (right) as Pedro in the 1941 version of *The Bad Man* (production still courtesy of the Margaret Herrick Library, Academy of Motion Picture Arts and Sciences).

featured Lionel Barrymore and Ronald Reagan. All this is to say that these films were not small productions with limited runs projected for them. The production companies saw in these films the potential for high economic return, and the actors saw them as viable career vehicles. These were ambitious films, and they reached broad audiences. Thus, for some twenty years after the Mexican Revolution, the Mexican badman lived on in the American imagination, standing as a figure to be simultaneously feared and admired— and ultimately ridiculed.

The four dramatic versions of the Mexican badman launched between 1920 and 1941 demonstrate a schizophrenic quality in the American production of Mexican masculine identity. The original play and the 1923 movie depict the badman as a romantic and admirable figure, while the 1930 film starring Walter Huston shows him as aggressive and cunning. By 1941, in the Wallace Beery edition, the movie shows the badman as an aging and overweight buffoon. The earliest renditions of an admirable Mexican badman seem almost like aberrations, for they owe their provenance to an individual sensibility, that of Porter Emerson Browne. Still, though created by a single writer, the play and 1923 filmed version were admired and enjoyed by many. The striking transformation from admiration of the play to gradual levels of denigration of the subsequent movies is the product of a complex set of social factors, beginning with the more receptive American attitudes in the years immediately after World War I, and progressing to the narrowing of viewpoints at the onset of the Great Depression and then World War II. Although it was also during this period that Hollywood tried to appease Mexico's concerns about the importation of negative views about the Mexican, in a few short years, the possibility of a cultural trade embargo had dissipated. The Mexican male, in his subsequent cinematic iterations, would become less a character to be feared, and more a personage to be laughed at and scorned. A speculative reading of the diminishment of the Mexican as threat might link this change to the waning of revolutionary potential in the United States and abroad. Especially as the United States entered World War II and as the Mexican Revolution and its attendant concerns faded into memory, the Mexican badman was simply no longer the same menacing figure. If his subsequent cinematic appearances are any indication—from his semi-comic renderings in *The Treasure of the Sierra Madre* (1948) to his screwball antics in *The Three Amigos* (1986)—then eventually the Mexican badman became a figure of neither derision nor desire, but of insignificance and bemusement.

Stereotype, Idealism, and Contingency in the Revolutionary's Depiction

The films *Viva Villa!* (1934) and *Viva Zapata!* (1952) tell the highly fictional-ized stories of Mexico's best-known revolutionary leaders, Francisco Villa and Emiliano Zapata. These movies, however, sharply contrast one another in their ideological positions vis-à-vis the representation of their Mexican male subjects. The films' disparities are immediately apparent when we consider the actors contracted to play Villa and Zapata—Wallace Beery and Marlon Brando, respectively. Beery's Villa, like many of the badmen he played, is rough, violent, and often buffoonish; Brando's Zapata, on the other hand, is reasoning, idealistic, and focused. The two characters stand at extremes, exemplifying the multivalent qualities in the depiction of the Mexican revolutionary at mid-century.

In this chapter, I apply the thesis of the Mexican's ambivalence to the films *Viva Villa!* and *Viva Zapata!* and Américo Paredes's novella *The Shadow* (1955). In the two films—both Anglo-American productions—the bandit revolutionary is a figure of attraction and repulsion: *Viva Villa!* articulates its central character following the classic norms of stereotypical representation, even as the film presents him as the hero; *Viva Zapata!* operates in a more complex manner as its Mexican protagonist paradoxically takes on the role of an "Americanized" hero. Finally, Paredes's *The Shadow* also functions at a complex ambivalent level, but from a distinctly critical Mexican/Mexican American perspective. The novel seemingly responds to the previous films' facile categorizations of Mexican identity by displaying deep distrust for the Mexican hero of the revolution, proposing instead that we cannot rely on the myth of a transcendent, heroic subject of history, since the revolution's failures make this subject untenable. Paredes's novel, which examines the revolutionary subject's ideological displacement in capitalist modernity, creates a questioning and haunted "mimic man" who destabilizes the fixed and unexamined stereotypical assumptions in *Viva Villa!* and the idealistic reproduction of a mimetic Americanized Mexican in *Viva Zapata! The Shadow* reveals that Mexican identity is ultimately contingent, thereby presenting an early literary instance of Mexican American anti-essentialist identity construction. For Paredes, the Mexican stands neither as an object of the stereotype nor as a subject of an unrealistic transcendence; rather, the Mexican must possess the knowledge that self-identity and agency are only possible when the subject understands the histories and discourses of power through which identity is constituted.

Pancho Villa: Peon, Bandit, Soldier

Jack Conway's *Viva Villa!* (1934), starring Wallace Beery, dramatizes the life of Francisco Villa, the Mexican revolutionary who used guerilla tactics to fight the governments of Díaz, Carranza, and Obregón during Mexico's years of upheaval. Based on Edgcumb Pinchon's *Viva Villa! A Recovery of the Real Pancho Villa, Peon . . . Bandit . . . Soldier . . . Patriot* (1933), the film makes Villa the hero of Mexico's emergence as a democratic society. *Viva Villa!* is important in the history of Mexican identity representation because it was, up to this moment, the most publicly viewed instance of the United States' ambivalent fascination for the stereotyped Mexican subject. Additionally, the film established a model for future representations of Mexican identity, for it succinctly encapsulates the conflation of revolutionary and bandit.

According to Sander Gilman, the stereotypical construction of the Other originates from an early psychological impulse to create categories of difference between the self and the object world (18). In his study of the production of stereotypical discourse in nineteenth- and twentieth-century European texts, Gilman makes two important points that help us understand the ambivalent nature of stereotype production. Gilman writes that in our relation to the Other, we "can move from fearing to glorifying. . . . We can move from loving to hating. The most negative stereotype always has an overtly positive counterweight. As any image is shifted, all stereotypes shift. Thus stereotypes are inherently protean rather than rigid" (18). Second, in his discussion of the European vilification of blackness, Gilman observes that we cannot "deny that the black was [also] perceived as an attractive sexual object in fin-de-siècle Vienna" (110). The presence of these often contradictory and changeable feelings of love and hate for the Other produce the necessity for the stereotype's mutability. Because the stereotype springs out of contradiction and uncertainty, its dominant characteristic is ambivalence.

In his analysis of the European fascination with and construction of stereotypes about the Other, Gilman identifies three "basic categories of difference [that] reflect our preoccupation with the self and the control that the self must have over the world," and he adds that because "the Other is the antithesis of the self, the definition of the Other must incorporate the basic categories by which the self is defined." Our "sense of mutability, the central role of sexuality in our nature, and our necessary relationship to some greater group" constitute the categories by which the self/Other are defined (23). Gilman uses the terms "illness," "sexuality," and "race" to concisely describe the operation of these three categories in the definition of the Other. Although Gilman limits his analysis to European literature and culture's representation of Jews and blacks, his examination of stereotypes through the fundamental categories of illness, sexuality, and race remain very consistent when applied to the American cinema's representation of Mexican masculine identity, particularly in the case of a film such as *Viva Villa!*

From its beginning, *Viva Villa!* constructs its main character by employing the same stereotyped categories of illness, sexuality, and race, even as it champions the cause for which he fights. The movie, in fact, opens with a primal scene that is to scar Villa psychologically and shape his personality and revolutionary posture toward the *hacendado* ruling class. In the scene, Pancho as a boy witnesses his father's brutal lashing and death at the orders of an hacienda owner. The event pushes Pancho to madness and revenge as he kills the hacendado and flees to the mountains to lead the life of a rebel and bandit. Thus, from its opening scene, the film links the Mexican Revolution with Villa's psychic damage. As Gilman notes, illness is a phenomenon perceived to exist outside the self and is structured as outside or Other to the self. "We have the 'healthy' and the 'pathological' self. Likewise, concepts of mental illness . . . recapitulate the 'realist' definition of illness as dichotomously opposed to 'health'" (24). For Villa, to be mentally unstable is to be alien or Other in relation to the American audiences watching him.

The next scene further establishes Villa as a pathological figure. Many years have passed and we see Villa's forces attacking the town of La Concepción. Villa and his army storm the town and overwhelm the *federales*. Villa rides up on his horse, powerful and angry, sporting bandoleers and a large

FIGURE 9. Wallace Beery as Pancho Villa in *Viva Villa!* (MGM, 1934)
(production still courtesy of the Margaret Herrick Library, Academy of
Motion Picture Arts and Sciences).

sombrero, his visage sweaty and unkempt (fig. 9). This is the viewer's first
glimpse of Villa as an adult. In contradistinction to the previous sequence, in
which Villa was only a frightened boy, this is the revolutionary at his most
menacing. And although Villa is supposed to be the hero of this story, this first
image of him could not but reinscribe the idea of the bandit revolutionary.

The first order of business at La Concepción is to mete out the Villa style
of justice. In the moments just preceding Villa's arrival, several *campesinos* had
been accused of stealing and were then unfairly tried and executed. Villa enters
the courtroom in the aftermath of the trial and holds the judge and other
government authorities at gunpoint. He then proceeds to try his own case
against the government's men. Propping the dead peons on chairs, Villa uses
them as jury and asks for their verdict. His form of justice is quicker and more
severe than that of the judge before him, as he orders the judge and the rest

of his enemies shot where they stand. The several acts of violence that initiate the narrative serve to construct Villa—as well as the Mexican oligarchy, the revolution, and the Mexican nation itself—following a model of pathology.[1]

At different moments, the film affirmatively presents Villa as a well-meaning man who loves his country and his people, a man whose acts of violence are carried out because of his revolutionary commitment. This favorable framing notwithstanding, Villa's violent acts often occur unexplainably and randomly, not so much emerging from revolutionary zeal as from instinctive and irrational urges. Villa angers quickly and resolves conflict with the use of overwhelming force. He does not respect the rule of law and steals when the need arises. In one particularly disturbing instance, Villa murders a bank clerk for no particular reason other than that Villa is unfamiliar with modern banking practices. His constant and inexplicable use of violence is a primary marker of Villa as pathological and Other in relation to the American audience watching the film.

Villa possesses other uncontrollable tendencies and desires. He behaves in a loud and uncouth manner and exhibits a voracious appetite for food and drink. But his most unrepressed desires are for women and sex, which the film codes as Villa's penchant for getting "married." *Viva Villa!* therefore introduces an uncontrollable sexual appetite as the second category of difference between its hero and its audience. As Gilman writes, one "major category which pathology is often associated with is human sexuality," and the "sexual dimension of human sexual experience is one of those most commonly divided into 'normal' and 'deviant'" (24). In the definition of the self, "sexuality and the loss of control associated with it must be projected onto the Other. Fantasies of impotency are projected onto the Other as frigidity, fantasies of potency as hypersexuality. . . . Sexual norms become modes of control. . . . The analogy between the 'ill' and the 'perverse' is ubiquitous" (24–25). *Viva Villa!* posits that the nature of Villa's sexual pathology is due, in part, to his uncontrollable hypersexuality, which leads him to acts of seduction and rape.

The film's representation of Villa's excess sexuality places him outside the norms of American values, yet it is a representation ambivalently expressed as a simultaneous anxiety about and desire for sexual plenitude. In the film, Villa's rampant libido appears as the most striking marker of difference between him and his Anglo-American heroic counterparts. Wherever Villa goes, he meets a woman with whom he seeks sexual union, and the film makes humorous light of this insatiable thirst. In his first contact with the opposite sex in the film, for example, he gathers as many women as he can find at a cantina so that he can choose whom he'd like to "marry." When Johnny Sykes, a reporter, learns that Villa is to marry Rosita, Sykes responds with naïve excitement. Second-in-command Sierra, however, knows better and remains unimpressed. Sierra tells Sykes in a deadpan manner, "that's what he likes, he likes to get married. He gets married all the time." To this, Villa responds with child-like innocence, "That's the way I was brought up, religious." The film invites its audience to laugh at Villa's ingenuousness, lack of moral understanding, and want for sexual inhibition.

Richard Slotkin has argued that the "most significant difference between the Mexican and the American versions of the social bandit is expressed through the metaphor of sexuality" (414). The distinction between the two lies in that the American hero, no matter how violent he may be, no matter how far outside the norms of society he may exist, remains monogamously devoted, or at least potentially so, and this loyalty marks his "redemptive link to middle-class and domestic values" (414). The Mexican revolutionary bandit's sexuality, on the other hand, "is rampantly *macho*, the erotic expression of the willful violence that makes him an effective revolutionary fighter" (414). This distinction, based on a lack of sexual morality, is an important one because it links with the earliest marker of difference attributed to the greaser in silent films. As early as *The Tavern Keeper's Daughter* (1908), for instance, the narrative involves the rapacious desires of a greaser for the Anglo-American woman. Both in this early film and in *Viva Villa!* the Mexican's sexual excess is threatening, especially to the realm of domesticity, represented by the white female.

Villa's hypersexuality threatens the domestic values the film attempts to finally champion—and his rapaciousness is his final undoing, for he is murdered by the man whose sister, Teresa, he earlier attempted to rape. In terms of screen time, Teresa's role, played by Fay Wray, is relatively minor, but it contains major symbolic implications. Having just starred in the original *King Kong* (1933), Wray was once again cast as the object of a brute's desires. This time, the "gorilla" is an unbridled Pancho Villa, who attempts to seduce her but then accidentally kills her during their struggle. One of the movie posters produced for the release of *Viva Villa!* shows the beautiful Wray with the menacing Beery looming above her, six-shooters in his hands. In scale, he is much larger than she is, giving the viewer a monstrous sense of his pathologies. On the screen, Wray's skin is lighter than any of the other actors', and her costume is a light and bright dress. These contrasting features strongly convey the idea of white femininity put in peril by the Mexican male.

Part of this stereotype's ambivalence lies in its being simultaneously scandalizing and tantalizing for American audiences. Slotkin alludes to this contradiction when he recognizes that audiences "could excuse, even enjoy, the radical violence of 'Villa's' methods, because they were identified with the alien mythic space called 'Mexico'" (415). Mexico, in other words, acts as the space within which American ideologies are tested, while American fantasies and desires are given free play. Anglo-American audiences are able to vicariously enjoy Villa's violence and sexual exuberance while seemingly adhering to their own middle-class American values. Furthermore, the oblique enjoyment derived from this representation is not dissimilar from the pleasure derived by readers of popular Western novels, who consumed the sexual licentiousness of, for example, the Anglo male's amorous advances toward the Mexican woman while remaining morally outraged and racially removed from the action.

The multivalenced elements of attraction and repulsion contained in Villa's sexuality produce another contradictory layer of meaning, one involving the simultaneous preproduction and blurring of the socially inscribed boundaries between the masculine and the feminine. While I concur that Villa represents an excessively macho sexuality, I would also maintain that Villa's sexuality carries an obverse element that is homologous to the erotic attractions of the "sexy señoritas" with whom adventurous cowboys were wont to have amorous congress in nineteenth-century Western fiction. Surprisingly, Villa's behavior oscillates between the domineering and the acquiescent, and thus exhibits behaviors coded as either masculine or feminine.

The reproduction and blurring of the differences between traditionally defined masculine/feminine boundaries potentially threaten definitions of American and Mexican masculinity and, at the same time, potentially throw definitions of masculinity into productive play. The first site at which we may find a challenge to traditionally defined masculinity is Villa's body itself, made corpulently evident in Wallace Beery's performance. In Rabelaisian fashion, Beery's Villa constantly threatens to overspill his corporeal borders, and in doing so, he pushes against the very borders of a self-contained masculinity as defined by Anglo-American values. Recall Hart's brooding "good bad-man," Gary Cooper's Virginian, and later, Clint Eastwood's man-with-no-name—heroes who maintain consummate control of their minds and their bodies—are always prepared for the unexpected. Beery's Villa, by contrast, may appear powerful and manly, but his inability to control his passion for destruction, food, and women implies an unmanly Otherness.

We see, furthermore, an uncertain masculinity in Villa's relationships with the two other principle characters in the film, Francisco Madero and Johnny Sykes. Villa's relationships with these two men are predicated upon emotional dependence and bodily contact that replicate parent-child and traditionally defined masculine-feminine relations. The narrative logic of

Viva Villa! requires that Villa as an uncontrollable and implicitly feminized force somehow be contained. The film deploys Francisco Madero and Johnny Sykes to perform the task of controlling him. Madero and Sykes represent the masculine or fatherly side of the relationship because they possess "reason," a characteristic that has traditionally been coded as male.

When Villa meets Madero, he is smitten by Madero's bold idealism, although Madero is not too impressed by Villa's bandit ways. When Madero castigates him for making war as a bandit and not a soldier, Villa delineates their differences: "I don't think you know much about war. You know about loving people. But you can't win a revolution with love, you've got to have hate. You are the good side, I am the bad side." When Madero insists on proper conduct, Villa storms out like a sullen child. Then he returns, more subdued, and tells Madero, "All right. You tell me once again, what was the orders?" There is laughter between them, the men embrace, and Villa asks, "You like me?" with the voice of a child seeking his parent's approval. Villa's innocence "is a further mark of difference. . . . The Other is like the child, different from the mature sensible adult" (Gilman, 113). Although it is true that Villa's tremendous violence affirms his masculinity, his child-like responses to Madero soften him and make him appear more child-like and more Other.

Villa's relationship with Johnny Sykes, a reporter for the *New York World*, is even more complex. As a journalist, Sykes becomes Villa's mouthpiece, and the illiterate Villa comes to depend on Sykes for everything from writing letters to describing Villa's heroism in battle to performing civil ceremonies whenever Villa has a whim to "marry." Sykes becomes similarly dependent on Villa to win battles in order to be the first to scoop the sensational news. At one point in the movie, Sykes even becomes demanding, expecting Villa to take the town of Santa Rosalia—despite terrible odds—because he incorrectly reported that Villa had already attacked and taken it. This scene is particularly provocative because we see Villa in an un-revolutionary, un-masculine framing. The scene, conceived as a comic moment, shows Villa emerging from a bathtub wearing a long blanket wrapped around him like a dress. With Sykes standing next to him, lecturing him on the necessity of taking Santa Rosalia, the coding of the two men follows the pattern of a heterosexual couple in which the male is dominant. While we cannot go so far as to argue that the moment is homoerotically charged, Villa certainly is presented as less of a "man" than Sykes.

In a similar scene, Villa and Sykes stand together after Villa's first liberation of Mexico. Madero has ordered Villa to disband his army and go home. Faced with the prospect of losing Sykes, upon whom he depends for "fixing up" the narrative of his battles, Villa despondently begs the reporter not to leave him.

Sykes comforts him: "I'd rather be with you than anybody I know. You know how I feel about you." Villa tells Sykes that he needs him, and Sykes responds, "How do you suppose I feel running out on ya?" As Sykes leaves, Villa grabs his arm and Sykes has to break free. Again, the moment is not necessarily homoerotically overdetermined, but it is homosocially ambivalent, with the two men playing lovers about to be parted. Hence if, as Gilman argues, the distinction between a perceived "normal" and a "deviant" sexuality is an instrument that makes possible the defining and controlling of the Other, then the "aberrant" characterization of Villa's sexuality—still deeply embedded within his revolutionary manliness—defines him as radically Other in relation to the Anglo-American hero and the American audience consuming his image.

The third category of Otherness that *Viva Villa!* instantiates, not surprisingly, is that of race. In the production of Villa's racial Otherness, the film completes the conflation of the bandit and revolutionary. We may once again draw upon Gilman's theorizations on the production of stereotypical categories for an understanding of Villa's racial alterity. One mechanism of creating in-group/out-group distinctions is through the category of race: "[W]e search for anatomical signs of difference such as physiognomy and skin color. The Other's physical features, from skin color to sexual structures as the shape of the genitalia, are always the antithesis of the idealized self's." Here, Gilman makes a compelling connection between the categories of race, sexuality, and illness: "sexual anatomy is so important a part of self-image that 'sexually different' is tantamount to 'pathological'—the Other is 'impaired,' 'sick,' 'diseased.' Similarly, physiognomy or skin color that is perceived as different is immediately associated with 'pathology' and 'sexuality'" (25). Villa's excessive corporeality bespeaks the associations of race, sexuality, and illness. Because a Hollywood film could not overtly point to the Mexican's genitalia as a sign of racial/sexual/pathological Otherness, Villa's girth comes to stand in for this ultimate sign of difference. Villa is a large man with a bulging stomach. In addition, his facial expressions are extreme, displaying either a menacing grimace or jovial smile. In close-up, the glisten of sweat or grease is never absent. His hair is uncombed, his mustache is long. Finally, Villa wears a large sombrero and a single bandoleer across his chest. The physically exaggerated differences, along with the accoutrements of his dress, may be seen as metonymies for his deviant sexual, and ultimately racial, Otherness.

The physical and psychological representations of difference help us understand the importance of *Viva Villa!* in framing larger cultural distinctions between Anglo and Mexican males. Because *Viva Villa!* "was an extremely successful film whose images and narrative formula shaped all future treatments of Mexico and the Revolution" (Slotkin, 414), the powerful stereotypical structures of racial/sexual/pathological difference were also more deeply felt. Furthermore, the veiled construction of Villa's racial, sexual, and pathological Otherness calls attention to the American attraction to and need for a certain kind of Mexican masculine identity in order to imagine an Anglo counterpart that was whole, normal, healthy, and—above all—manly.

The creation of a pathological Mexican identity in *Viva Villa!* also meets other needs, including the fulfillment of displaced fantasies for the forbidden, as I have alluded to. Gilman recognizes, in the context of nineteenth-century European literature, that one strain of modernism "condemned the exploitations of the black as sexual object and used this condemnation to veil the authors' fascination with the sexual difference of the black" (120). Similarly, although *Viva Villa!* endorses the Mexican revolutionary Other, the film reproduces categories that reinscribe a pathological Otherness, and the film also suggests an intense fascination with the very categories of Mexican Otherness that it produces. The depiction of a pathological revolutionary in *Viva Villa!* may therefore be read in terms of the underlying Anglo-American desires (and anxieties) it puts on display.

Finally, *Viva Villa!* also constitutes the most significant example of the conflation of the revolutionary and the bandit. The film demonstrates that Anglo-American films that treat Mexican identity do so only insofar as the Mexican functions as a heuristic for America's concerns about itself, whether they are ideological or about identity. When necessary, then, the Mexican male appears as a degenerate bandit revolutionary. The film's logic requires that Villa, while at times heroic, must fail in order that the narrative may preserve notions about American democratic exceptionalism, as is the case with *Viva Zapata!*

Emiliano Zapata: Peon, Revolutionary, "American"

While *Viva Villa!* is the most prominent conflation of bandit and revolutionary, *Viva Zapata!* (1952) transforms the representation of Mexican identity by deemphasizing violence and lawlessness while stressing revolutionary idealism. This transformation, however, depends on the continued need to center Anglo-American values within the representation of the Mexican, for Zapata is made the mimic man of American values. Directed by Elia Kazan and written by John Steinbeck, *Viva Zapata!* differs from *Viva Villa!* in that it attempts to take a strong political stance on the importance of democracy and the role of universally shared revolutionary ideals in making future democratic rule possible. At the same time, *Viva Zapata!* resembles *Viva Villa!* in that, at varying levels, both films use the Mexican Revolution and its most iconic male figures as "thought experiments" for the working-out of American ideology and identity (Slotkin, 418). Thus, *Viva Zapata!* is also a film about Anglo-America and its values.

Viva Zapata! appeared immediately after the U.S. triumph in World War II, its defeat of the Nazi dictatorship, and its victory against Stalin in the Berlin Airlift. The film coincided with a historical moment that witnessed "a new and highly sophisticated form of 'American exceptionalism'" (421–22). Significantly, inasmuch as *Viva Zapata!* deals with American exceptionalism, the film must still engage with the Mexican Other in order to claim America's uniqueness. But rather than reproduce *Viva Villa!*'s anxious categories of difference, *Viva Zapata!* attempts a peculiar rapprochement with Mexican identity by representing Emiliano Zapata as an admirer and imitator of American values. Thus, mimicry as an instrument of hegemonic control sees its full articulation in *Viva Zapata!* for we witness in this film the reproduction of a figure that is almost Anglo, but not quite.

The salient analysis of the concept of mimicry appears in Homi Bhabha's "Of Mimicry and Man: the Ambivalence of Colonial Discourse." In this text, Bhabha explains the workings of mimicry in a colonial situation. Although the U.S. relation to Mexico does not adhere to classic colonialism, the relations of power between the two nations have often replicated the conditions and attitudes of imperial domination, as previously noted. Bhabha recognizes mimicry as an apparatus of power that controls the colonial population by employing native colonial administrators who are educated in the values of the Western imperial power. Bhabha calls these subjects "mimic men" who are "the effect of a flawed colonial mimeses, in which to be Anglicized is *emphatically* not to be English" (87). In its representation of Emiliano Zapata, *Viva Zapata!* reaches an aporia between its desire to depict Zapata as embodying American values and the impossibility of identifying with the Mexican Other. As Bhabha notes, "colonial mimicry is the desire for a reformed, recognizable Other, *as a subject of a difference that is almost the same, but not quite.* Which is to say, that the discourse of mimicry is constructed around an *ambivalence*, in order to be effective, mimicry must continually produce its slippage, its excess, its difference. The authority of that mode of colonial discourse that I have called mimicry is therefore stricken by an indeterminacy: mimicry emerges as the representation of a difference that is itself a process of disavowal" (86). In the case of *Viva Zapata!* the Mexican revolutionary is palatable only if he is capable of being "Americanized," but this "Americanized" Mexican always appears slightly different, as "the representation of a difference" that is ultimately rejected. His disavowal is predetermined and necessitated by the discourse of American exceptionalism.

Kazan and Steinbeck's film stars Marlon Brando as Emiliano Zapata, Jean Peters as Zapata's bride, Josefa, Anthony Quinn as Zapata's brother, Eufemio, and Joseph Wiseman as Zapata's advisor and revolutionary ideologue, Fernando Aguirre. In *Steinbeck and Film*, Joseph Millichap identifies the screenplay of *Viva Zapata!* as one of Steinbeck's greatest post-war literary successes, and he notes that despite the film's limited theatrical release, "it has become something of a cult film, popular with television late-show viewers, college film classes, and Chicano groups" (123). While we may dispute the film's popularity among Mexican Americans contemporarily, the film was generally well received among wider audiences upon its release. Kazan credibly directs the movie, Brando received an Oscar nomination for Best Actor and Quinn was awarded an Oscar for Best Supporting Actor. Furthermore, unlike *Viva Villa!* this film takes the historical record into more careful consideration. *Viva Zapata!* concentrates on the ideologically formative events in Zapata's life to give a sense of the revolution's progress, as well as a sense of Zapata himself. Additionally, the film relies far less than *Viva Villa!* on stereotypical representation to convey Mexican character, and Zapata himself is presented as ethically strong, honest, and selfless.

But although the main representative of Mexican identity escapes the denigration of the stereotype, he does so only by becoming Anglo-Americanized. Furthermore, we encounter a continuing enmity toward the Mexican male when we compare the representation of Emiliano Zapata with that of his brother, Eufemio Zapata. The source of the film's uneven representation lies with its prevailing need to work through American ideological and identity positions in relation to revolution and in relation to the Mexican Other. In this context, Zapata becomes a meditation on American values: "Zapata offers an 'exception' to the rule of revolutions—Mexican and otherwise—which sees as inescapable the pendulum swing between upheaval and dictatorship. Although he is identified as 'Mexican,' many of the values that make Zapata exceptional are drawn from the conventional vocabulary of the American Western" (Slotkin, 422). As the hero of this Western-like movie, Zapata parallels the Western's central character, the Anglo-American male. Zapata, in other words, is not so much "Mexican" as "American" in the tradition of the Anglo-American hero of the Western. He differs from the stereotypical revolutionary bandit because the film requires that he inhabit the space of Anglo-American values. Zapata, therefore, is among the mimic men who are "authorized versions of otherness" (Bhabha, 88).

Eufemio, on the other hand, is a bandit in the tradition perfected by Beery in *Viva Villa!* Notwithstanding the recognition Anthony Quinn received for his performance—an accolade that can only be appreciated with a sense of irony—his character "cynically exploits the revolution for his own gain. . . . [H]e is connected with Pancho Villa, who in turn is presented with some of the Wallace Beery stereotyping that Hollywood grafted onto the historical reality of Mexico's other popular revolutionary hero" (Millichap, 126). In the film, Eufemio is presented as the stereotypical revolutionary bandit even before the revolution begins. Eufemio exhibits loud and boisterous behavior, he refuses to follow any but his own rules, his violence has no equal, and he lusts after women constantly. Eufemio's violent libido is significantly on display throughout the film. When we first see him with a woman, he sits with her in a cantina, leering at her and caressing her chin. When he gets too rough, she pushes him away because he is a threat. A second time, we see Eufemio dancing with a *soldadera*. They dance innocently until he suddenly and forcefully kisses her. The woman, once again, separates herself from him violently and he laughs. Near the film's end, Eufemio takes up residence with a peasant's wife, apparently by force and baldly in the presence of her husband. This is undoubtedly a rape scene, and as with Villa in *Viva Villa!* Eufemio's sexual insatiability and social transgressions eventually cause his death.

The most salient difference between the Americanized Emiliano and the stereotypically Mexican Eufemio remains, in fact, in their respective abilities to control their sexual appetites. Brando's Emiliano—unlike the historical Zapata—stays devoted to one woman, behaving decorously in his courting of Josefa, while Eufemio acquires a harem, loving many women at once and taking them when he pleases. "Zapata's 'freakish' (according to Eufemio) fidelity to one woman thus gives this revolutionary the most important caste-mark of the middle-class American and of the Hollywood romantic hero" (Slotkin, 423–24). In this sense, the coding of the two brothers reverts to classic categories of difference. Emiliano is a "good" Mexican because he is cast within American values, while Eufemio is a "bad" Mexican because he is characterized as oversexed, violent, pathological, Other. In brief, he is a Mexican in the most pejorative sense as defined by Anglo-created stereotypes.

By presenting Emiliano Zapata's monogamy as unusual—for a non-American at least—the film normalizes Eufemio's very "Mexican" sexual appetite. The naturalizing of Mexican libidinousness is expressed in a scene when Eufemio puzzles over Emiliano's love for Josefa. He tells a nodding counterpart about Emiliano's slow courtship of Josefa: "He should have stolen her if he wanted her. . . . I have loved with all my heart one hundred women I never want to see again, and he is still after this one. It escapes me."

The film does not really condemn Eufemio's wantonness. It does, however, respect every man's right to his property—*Viva Zapata!* after all, is ultimately about a man's need for land—and it is for stealing property, partially in the form of a woman, that Eufemio is finally punished when an angry peasant murders him for forcefully taking the peasant's wife as his own. When the revolution is won, Eufemio rewards himself by stealing an hacienda that was to be partitioned. When Emiliano visits Eufemio to force him to give the land back, Emiliano finds his brother drunk, with a terrorized woman at his feet. Eufemio tells Emiliano, "I took what I wanted. . . . I took their wives too." Eufemio then stands, grabs the woman, and takes her into another room. It is at this point that the husband takes action and kills Eufemio. Significantly, Eufemio dies not merely because of his out-of-control sexuality, but also because he has taken another man's property. In *Viva Zapata!* then, woman is as much property as is the land—as one *campesino* comments, "[L]and is like a woman."

Although markedly different from *Viva Villa!* in terms of the representation of its hero, *Viva Zapata!* nevertheless follows some of the same stereotypical conventions as its predecessor. Emiliano Zapata is a strong and just man, unlike the dictators Díaz and Huerta, unlike the weak president Madero, and unlike his own brother. Yet Zapata is different precisely because he is so unlike any other Mexican. He is exceptional in an American sense, and his strength comes from his likeness to Anglo-American heroes. Eufemio, conversely, is placed to stand in for every other Mexican, and it is within this context that his over-sexualized masculinity is acceptable in the film. It is thus not surprising that the Americanized Zapata is played by an iconic American actor, Marlon Brando, while the Mexicanized Eufemio is played by an ethnic actor, Anthony Quinn.

Like *Viva Villa!* before it, *Viva Zapata!* withholds representational freedom from the Mexican, and it is unable to imagine the Mexican as an agent of his or her own history. While in *Viva Villa!* Francisco Villa remains trapped within his pathological violence, hypersexuality, and racial alterity, in *Viva Zapata!* Emiliano Zapata is a genuine hero in the Anglo-American vein, but despite his adherence to American democratic values, Zapata is himself gunned down at the end of the film. Although his death signifies the coming to freedom of the Mexican people, the film shows no real promise that Mexico will be free, for its ending is indeterminate.

The years between the making of *Viva Villa!* and *Viva Zapata!* witnessed a transformation in the representation of Mexican identity, but we see, nevertheless, a continued reliance on a tradition that goes back to nineteenth-century popular Western fiction. Critics praise Steinbeck for thoughtfully giving Zapata a fullness not seen in previous representations of Mexicans, yet we should be wary of this assessment. While Steinbeck gives Zapata a complexity that Wallace Beery's Villa does not achieve, Steinbeck, for one, still carried stereotypical conceptions of Mexico, a country that represented "everything modern America was not; for him Mexico possessed a primitive vitality, a harsh simplicity, and a romantic beauty" (Millichap, 95). We can make a similar assessment about Kazan's directing. While Kazan deserves recognition for the historical faithfulness that he brings to the film, we cannot ignore the instantiation of mimicry that characterizes Zapata's representation. The depiction of a nuanced Mexican identity, of course, constitutes neither Steinbeck nor Kazan's main concern. Partially because *Viva Zapata!* was filmed during the McCarthy political witch hunts, we may read the movie as an attempt by these two artists to defend their allegiance to America's core values by making a film about these values' universal appeal. As a result, *Viva Zapata!* operates by way of a supreme irony: it articulates American identity through a sublimated fascination with the Mexican revolutionary.

Américo Paredes's Critique of Mimicry in The Shadow

Américo Paredes wrote *The Shadow* (1998 [1955])[2] shortly after returning from journalistic service in World War II and during the period of Kazan and Steinbeck's idealistic representation of the Mexican revolutionary. Growing up in South Texas, Paredes was no stranger to cultural conflict and failed revolutions, as his ethnographic work (*"With His Pistol in His Hand,"* 1958) and fiction (*George Washington Gómez*, 1990) richly elaborate. Still, having only recently returned from Japan, where, as José Limón writes, "he covered the post-war trials of Japanese generals accused of atrocities and became . . . suspicious of American racist motives," Paredes was perhaps more acutely aware of "past and present Anglo social domination" than at any other time in his life (*Dancing*, 78–79). Read from this perspective, *The Shadow* evinces deep pessimism with regard to revolutionary idealism in the wake of an "advancing Anglo-American capitalist political economy and culture," both in Greater Mexico and throughout the world (85).

The Shadow takes us from the Anglo-American representation of the Mexican to Mexican self-representation, and from mimicry as an effect of the unconscious assumption of American preeminence to mimicry as an object of cultural critique. *The Shadow* diagnoses the structural and subjective effects of Anglo-American capitalism on the people of Greater Mexico both north and south of the border, and provocatively, it evidences the complicated causal links between an American-centered process of world-economic expansion and the Mexican Revolution, events which figure prominently in the narrative.[3] As the constitutive events of Greater Mexico's emergence into modernity, the global capitalist economy and the revolution powerfully shape the Mexican's subjective and ideological formation. *The Shadow* examines the individual's problematic movement between two poles: on one side, we witness traditional ways of life as they are defined by an indigenous heritage, folk beliefs, and communal values; at the opposite extreme, we see the discourses of capitalist modernity as they are defined by rationality, individualism, and notions of progress. The novel formulates the subject's movement into modernity as mimicry, or, more accurately, as the interpellated acceptance of Western modes of thought. In the novel's main character, Paredes produces a "mimic man" who expresses a "desire to emerge as 'authentic' through mimicry," but only achieves "partial representation" (Bhabha, 88). The form of "authenticity" that is desired is that of Western rationalism as determined by the processes of capitalist modernity.

Set some twenty years after the Mexican Revolution in a northern Mexican communal farm, *The Shadow* narrates its central character's uneasy passage between worlds: Antonio Cuitla is a former rebel leader who disavows his indigenous roots and revolutionary ideals in favor of a perceived rational subjectivity, a subjectivity shaped by capital's uneven entry into Greater Mexico. The novel begins as Cuitla, president of the *ejido* or communal farm of Los Claveles, oversees his men's work from atop his horse. The men are behind schedule due to delays caused by land disputes between the former hacendados and the *ejidatarios*, as well as by disputes between Cuitla and his former friend and comrade-in-arms, Jacinto Del Toro. The former hacendado, Don José María Jiménez, has managed to keep the best of the pre-agrarian reform land, and he plots—and succeeds in the case of Del Toro—to have both revolutionaries killed. On the day Don José María has Del Toro assassinated, Antonio Cuitla is himself on his way to confront and kill Del Toro. But on his way to the other's ranch, Cuitla meets what he initially believes to be a ghost or shadow. Momentarily frightened, Cuitla fires his gun and discovers that he has killed Del Toro's murderer, an outsider from Monterrey named Gerardo Salinas. As the novel progresses, Cuitla is consumed by the guilt of the murder he was to commit, and he is haunted by the shadow of his former friend.

As my synopsis implies, *The Shadow*'s ambiguous title is appropriate, for the spectral figure allegorizes the dying-away of the revolution's communitarian ideals and Greater Mexico's folk traditions; the ghost also represents life under the lengthening shadow of global capitalism as the Mexican economy is transformed from an oligarchic to a communal to an agribusiness system of land management. Most importantly, however, the shadow signals the individual's troubled entry into modernity. In Antonio Cuitla, Paredes creates a protagonist whose intense desire to participate in Mexico's modernization occurs at the expense of his traditional culture. As president of the ejido, Cuitla interacts closely with previous and current power elites, and he emulates what he perceives to be their rationality. As a former revolutionary, Cuitla is one of Bhabha's "appropriate objects of a colonialist chain of command, authorized versions of otherness," which means he is admitted into the structure of governance only insofar as he accepts its rationalist and modernizing discourse (88).

Cuitla expresses his attempted mimicry of modern rationality through a disassociation from his indigenous heritage. Like most Mexicans, Cuitla is a *mestizo* with "that hewn appearance of limb and features sometimes found in mestizos who have much Indian ancestry" (2). Yet Cuitla feels himself above the "Indians" of Los Claveles. For instance, "[e]xcept for the kerchief, Antonio Cuitla's clothes were in the American style: yellow drill trousers, heavy shapeless shoes, and a blue work shirt. . . . His shirttails, gathered outside his belt and tied in a knot over his navel, were another concession to the customs of his native village" (2). Cuitla struggles to subordinate his Indian side in order to mimic what he perceives to be another kind of rational subjectivity represented by the "American style" and by Don José María Jiménez, the fair-skinned, blue-eyed former owner of the ejido land. Don José María convinces Cuitla that being Indian means being barbaric, superstitious, and infantile: "There is something childlike about the primitive mind. . . . It is a mind, in some respects, in the first stage of innocence" (6).

At no time is Cuitla's repudiation of the Indian side of himself more evident than in the moment that catalyzes the narrative, the instant when Cuitla witnesses the ghostly shadow stirring in his path. On his way to the parcel of land worked by Jacinto Del Toro—not only his former comrade, but also his chief political rival in the communal farm—Cuitla intends to kill Del Toro and claim self-defense. As murderous thoughts cross his mind, something on the road interrupts his progress: "He saw it for an instant out of the corner of his eye. He jerked his head toward it, as the horse stopped short. The sorrel shrank back, back and down, as though gathering itself for one tremendous leap" (9). A moment after first glimpsing the shadow, Cuitla regains self-composure. He berates himself for being taken in by the shadow: "Fool! Frightened by nothing, like a superstitious Indian. A man like him, who had read books and seen other countries. It was not for him to go around seeing shadows on the road" (11). Cuitla struggles with his "superstitious Indian" impulses, and believes that a man who has read and who has traveled—a learned, rational man—should not be so easily frightened.

Convinced that the thing he saw was not a ghost, and that he actually startled his own horse by pulling too hard on the reins, Cuitla regains his rational self-assurance: "[a]nother man wouldn't have thought the matter out, and he would have given superstition one more point to stand on. . . . Some day all men would be reasonable, and such things would not be. But, meanwhile, Antonio Cuitla was greatly relieved that he, at least, was a reasoning man and had thought the matter out" (13). Cuitla sees his subjectivity following a rational "Western" trajectory in which the subject comes to a greater consciousness of itself. Cuitla, however, does *and* does not see a ghost, for the shadow acquires an overdetermination of meanings. In reality, the "shadow" stirring in the bushes is Gerardo Salinas, the stranger hired by Don José María to kill Cuitla and Del Toro; on a supernatural level, the shadow is the ghost of Del Toro. Like many of the characters in Paredes's novels and poetry, Cuitla is a subject caught "between two worlds," as the title of this poetry collection implies (1991). On the one hand, Cuitla is a mestizo; he has inherited indigenous and folk traditions which respect the supernatural. On the other hand, Cuitla attempts to emulate a "reasoning man."

In addition to eliding his indigenous identity and folk beliefs, Cuitla attempts to do away with the folk genres that gave voice to the revolutionary spirit and that provide the grounding for the communal life of the ejido. One of these genres is the *corrido* or ballad, which was vital for narrating the revolutionary struggle. To justify his intended murder of Del Toro, Cuitla plans to tell the *peones* that his actions were in self-defense, quoting the words from a song, *"La defensa es permitida* [Self-defense is justified]." In Cuitla's view, his fellow farmers "talked and thought in terms of songs and tales. Like children." Unlike them, he "had put those songs away a long time ago. They were childish, a waste of time" (6). If Paredes's earlier work on the corrido in *"With His Pistol in His Hand"* demonstrates an "antisubjectivist" impulse "because in ballads of border conflict . . . he locates sources of meaning, not in individual subjectivities, but in social relations, communication, and cultural politics," then Cuitla's rejection of traditional folk ballads symbolizes his renunciation of community and his attempt to become a rational, individualistic subject (J. Saldívar, *Border Matters*, 40).[4] By placing Cuitla in the position of radical doubt and by undermining his assumed rationality, Paredes reinscribes the "antisubjectivist" impulse in a way different from the way he presents it in *"With His Pistol in His Hand."* In other words, Paredes questions the Mexican's mimicry of Western individualism.

Cuitla's consistent denial of his inherited beliefs and rituals instantiates itself in his inner conflict with regard to the ghost's authenticity. Cuitla considers that his friend, Del Toro, "would have known" that Cuitla was in danger of being killed by the outsider who also killed Del Toro: "He knew and he was warning me." But then Cuitla reminds himself that this idea is also absurd. Of course there could be no ghost warning him. After all, Cuitla is "an emancipated man, free in body and mind. . . . He did not believe in those dark things that haunted men's minds. He had cast such things away as he had thrown aside the round straw hat and the cotton drawers" (45). Time and again his judgment regarding the ghost's reality and his beliefs' validity falters. He is caught between competing ideologies—in this case, rationalism versus superstition—as he attempts to adopt one while not completely succeeding in disavowing the other.

By placing two belief systems—the bourgeois individualist and the traditional folk communalist—against each other within one person, the novel lays bare the mimicry that is forced upon the Mexican subject. The clashing impulses within Cuitla signify a struggle for dominance between belief systems, one ascendant and the other waning. While Paredes would not deny that forms of belief evolve, he would insist that residual forms of belief are especially useful when they allow a community under attack to cohere (Williams, 122–23). In *The Shadow*, the community of peons is under attack, and in completely rejecting—rather than adapting—his inherited belief system, Antonio Cuitla denies any possibility of communal collaboration against the former hacendado's encroachment. By subverting the tenability of Cuitla's move into a reasoning, nonsuperstitious subjectivity, *The Shadow* questions the validity of the individualistic and mimetic discourses that appear as U.S. capitalist modernity becomes dominant.

Simultaneously, *The Shadow* hints at another idea vis-à-vis the individual and the community in the face of a world in flux: it inquires into the status of traditional modes of belief in a historical moment that threatens traditional patterns of culture. In Antonio Cuitla's case, the particular beliefs he adopts prove destructive to his community's needs (Cuitla parallels Guálinto Gómez, the protagonist of *George Washington Gómez*). Ironically, Cuitla himself understands the power of different ideological formations, such as the communitarian ideals of the revolution. "It had been a relatively easy task to dispossess the old communal owners, to make them turn over the land to men working under a different kind of communal arrangement, one backed by a political philosophy the old one had lacked" (42). In the past, Cuitla acquired a "political philosophy" based on a "communal arrangement"—he became radicalized as a migrant laborer—and he has taught it to his men. While his views have changed, members of the ejido seek coordinated action after the outsider Gerardo Salinas murders Del Toro. Cuitla, however, has acquired a new philosophy, one that more closely mirrors the emerging capitalist order, and he rebuffs the ejidatarios: "Stop talking nonsense" (43). The scene illustrates Cuitla's mimicry of discourses of modernity, beginning with anti-capitalist, anti-oligarchic ideologies, but then acquiring more rational and individualistic belief patterns that he borrows from the *patrón*-turned-capitalist Don José María.

Don José María, as a symbol of an ascendant commercial class, becomes Cuitla's model for his entry into modernity. Don José María, who has retained the best land for himself, befriends Cuitla and the members of the ejido for political reasons: "He became their friend. He visited the colony of Los Claveles frequently and talked about the aims of the Revolution" (26). Cuitla naively accepts Don José María's feigned interest in revolutionary ideals and defers to his superior understanding of agrarian codes. For Cuitla, there are "few men like Don José María, who understood the agrarian law and wanted to see the peon rise and become a man" (43). Cuitla desires to be like Don José María, a "man who understood" his growing sense of alienation. "How often had he wished that life had been different, and that Don José María and he had been born in the same village" (45). Cuitla's aspirations, then, are for the ideals of the patrón and other ruling elites, and this explains his paternalistic attitude toward his men. "They are Indians without shoes, how can they know? They love the land, but they were born too soon. It is up to me to know for them, for their children's sake. It is my burden and my pride" (3). In other words, it is his role as father to take care of his children, the shoeless *indios*. Thus, Cuitla emulates the paternal view of the Indian-as-child from Don José María.

The condescending attitude toward the Indian, of course, goes back centuries, but what is provocative about Cuitla's combination of racial prejudice, insistence on rational thought, and rejection of folk traditions is that it resembles the ideology of what Alan Knight calls "Mexico's 'modernizing elite,'" for whom "racialism justified . . . rational economic exploitation" (167). Interestingly, these "modernizing elites" themselves borrowed from European positivism for their ideology. Cuitla's mimicry, therefore, is enacted as a copy of a copy. Finally, Cuitla's mimicry of Don José María—he tells the former hacendado, "I feel toward you like a brother"—is an acceptance of class hierarchies and takes place at the expense of revolutionary and communal ideals (82). The production of Antonio Cuitla as a "mimic man" occurs not through the subject's desire for modernity but as an effect of capitalist modernity's penetration into Greater Mexico at the beginning of the twentieth century.

Capitalism, therefore, creates the desire for modernity, and the world-systems theory of Immanuel Wallerstein sheds analytic light upon the

production of this desire.[5] In his delineation of the processes of "incorpora-
tion" that the capitalist world economy undertakes, Wallerstein identifies
a "contradiction which the populations of each successively incorporated
zone faced. Should the transformations that were occurring in their zone
be conceived as changes from a local and traditional 'culture' to a worldwide
modern 'culture,' or were these populations rather simply under pressure
to give up their 'culture' and adopt that of the Western imperialist power
or powers? Was it, that is, a case of modernization or Westernization?"
(164). Wallerstein's question seems rhetorical, for undoubtedly cultures
incorporated by the capitalist economy face the continual pressure to
both modernize—this is the case with the communal farm and the former
hacendado—and Westernize—this is the case with Cuitla and the former
hacendado in *The Shadow*.

James Clifford makes a similar observation about the processes of subjectification in his discussion of the "predicament of ethnographic modernity"
in the encounters between Western and non-Western cultures (3). When he
writes about "all of us" (in the West) being "caught in modernity's inescapable
momentum," Clifford recognizes that "[s]omething similar occurs whenever
marginal peoples come into a historical or ethnographic space that has
been defined by the Western imagination. 'Entering the modern world,'
their distinct histories quickly vanish. Swept up in a destiny dominated
by the capitalist West and by various technologically advanced socialisms,
these suddenly 'backward' peoples no longer invent local futures. What is
different about them remains tied to traditional pasts, inherited structures
that either resist or yield to the new but cannot produce it" (5). Cuitla is
one of those people who must confront the transformation between tradition and modernity, and his mimicry of a modern rationality is an instance
of yielding to the new but not inventing it. Paredes's novel represents his
struggle between the old and the new as one of the painful consequences
of the emergence of the world economy in Greater Mexico.

In the novel, the dominant capitalist world economy not only ushers
a transformation in the means of production and exchange, as well as a
revolution in the global division of labor, but it also introduces new ideologies and counter-ideologies that have profound effects on the subject's
self-understanding. As one constitutive process of modernity, capitalism has
rationalized the means of production and at the same time advanced rational,
scientific thought; it has inaugurated the concept of individual wage labor
while it has helped change the concept of the free individual. *The Shadow*,
considered in relation to Clifford's analysis of traditional cultures resisting
or yielding to the West, configures resistance as nearly impossible, and

the novel's representation of the stages in Antonio Cuitla's subject formation allows readers to see the ideological binds of a capitalist modernity in
Greater Mexico.

Initially, the novel demonstrates that one of the strongest counter-
ideological responses to capitalism is revolutionary socialism. We learn, for
example, that Antonio Cuitla's migration to Texas as a farm laborer also
brought him to a radical political consciousness. It was in Texas that he
received a revolutionary education. Having rejected religion, he was "proud
and cynical so that the others called him atheist and were afraid of him. . . .
It was in Texas he first heard men talk of revolution, men of his own sort,
talk about striking off their chains, and of the imprisonment of starvation.
Yes, he had got most of his education in Texas. In the cotton fields and the
coal mines. . . . Texas had a lot to teach the Mexican peon turned migrant
laborer, who looked across the border for a new kind of life" (62). The
evolving world economy creates migrations of labor, which in turn effect a
revolutionary response from those seeking to break the chains of capital's
"imprisonment and starvation." Through strange circumstance, the revolution
sees its birth—partially at least—in the cotton fields, coal mines, and prison
farms of Texas, and many of the revolution's leaders come of age there.

Cuitla's education as a revolutionary is his first step into a modern
subjectivity. This revolutionary subjectivity dialectically links with the
expansion of capital, so it owes its florescence to capitalist modernity. As
he reacts to forms of peonage—whether feudal or capitalist—Cuitla acquires
a political ideology that takes him through the revolutionary period. In this
first movement, Cuitla continues to adhere to the values and folk traditions
of his native village, although he rejects religious doctrine even before his
migration to Texas. Later, Cuitla will reject the communitarian ideals of
the revolution and accept ideologies more closely allied with the emerging
capital order. To repeat Wallerstein, *The Shadow* represents the evolution of
a character "under pressure" to relinquish his culture "and adopt that of the
Western imperialist power" (164).

Another instance of capitalist modernity's shaping of the desire for
mimicry may be found in its reorganization of labor. The narrative suggests
that Antonio Cuitla, Jacinto Del Toro, and even Gerardo Salinas are part of
this reorganization. Salinas, the man hired to murder Del Toro, is an outsider
from the northern industrial city of Monterrey. Cuitla learns this when he
examines the contents of the man's wallet after having killed him. Cuitla
discovers that Salinas was en route to the Texas cotton fields, then under
intense agribusiness development. "Besides a few Mexican bills, there was the
photo of a girl; a guitar string . . . a small pink medallion . . . and a clipping

from a Mexican newspaper. The clipping was about the coming cotton season in Texas and the need for pickers, the high wages being offered" (61). Cuitla recalls that he also "had gone to Texas when he was young, after his father died and he ran away for the first time from the village where he was born" (61). In the movements of these men, the novel charts the migration of labor between Mexico and Texas, illustrating capitalism's organization of its resources. The world economy structures its labor force by producing lack, opportunity, and ultimately the need for survival that is inseparable from a production of the desire for things modern and Western.

To reiterate James Clifford's analysis of the clash between tradition and modernity, the main character of *The Shadow* certainly embodies one of those people "[s]wept in the destiny dominated by the capitalist West" who "no longer invent local futures" (5). The representation of this subject formation points to a very tenuous relation to the traditions of resistance that characterize contemporary interpretations of Chicano/a literature. Yet it is precisely the subject's *relation* to the contradictions of capitalist modernity that *The Shadow* asks us to investigate. I agree with José David Saldívar (1997) when he writes that, in addition to "understanding . . . the dynamics of empire," Paredes's modernist aesthetics instantiate "a desire to produce what Paul Gilroy (1993) calls a counterculture of modernity" (50). For Gilroy, the counterculture of modernity is not merely an aesthetic movement, but "a philosophical discourse which refuses the modern, occidental separation of ethics and aesthetics, culture and politics" (38–39). The counterculture of modernity refuses the very separation between tradition and modernity and reinvents traditions in the face of change. The ghost in *The Shadow* recuperates an elided history and places it in the present, thus making it possible for the subject to stand in critical relation to the processes of modernity.

Finally, the importance of the ghost in relation to the notion of mimicry should not be overlooked. The ghost disrupts Cuitla's assumption of a rational subjectivity by acting as the double and un-incorporable Other of traditional Mexican culture. Because Cuitla cannot rid himself of its presence, his mimicry of the discourses of rationalism and the patrón reveals the *"menace* of mimicry" as a *"double* vision which in disclosing the ambivalence of colonial discourse also disrupts its authority," as Bhabha has argued. *The Shadow's* ghost corresponds to a "double vision that is a result of . . . the partial representation/recognition of the colonial subject" (88); it thus appears as the corrective that constantly ruptures Cuitla's attempt to mimic a Western rational subjectivity and continually reminds him of his crime against the community. The novel inquires upon the individual's difficult entry into modernity, and it asserts that such an entry cannot occur without a continued and uneasy haunting by past traditions. Rather than a negation of traditions, *The Shadow* demands their acknowledgement, and it asks that we come to terms with the presence of our inherited beliefs as we adapt them to new circumstances in our transition between worlds. As it reveals the haunting interplay between rationalism and folk belief, individual subjectivity and community, forgetfulness and historical memory, and, certainly, modernity and tradition, the spectral figure represents a counterculture of modernity, a radical critique and alternative mode of resistance to an ascendant capitalist formation. The novel makes possible an analysis of the structural connections between the development of agribusiness capitalism, the eruption of the revolution, and the displacement of workers, and it places these events in a global context. As *The Shadow* weaves a story of subjective transformation from traditional to modern forms of thought, the work demonstrates, finally, that Greater Mexico's social and subjective emergence into a capitalist-dominated modernity is a troubled and unfinished phenomenon.

In representing the emergence of a mimetic and conflicted Mexican subjectivity as the consequence of the uneven cultural and economic transformations in Greater Mexico, *The Shadow* departs radically from accepted notions of a unified Chicano/a subject in resistance to Anglo-American hegemony. Renato Rosaldo, whose analysis of Chicano/a narratives in *Culture and Truth* charts a historical shift away from such univocal representations, categorizes Paredes as an early instance, a "now . . . dated . . . idealization of a primordial patriarchy" (150). Rosaldo's point of reference, in this instance, is the heroic Mexican American figuration in Paredes's *"With His Pistol in His Hand."* "Once a figure of masculine heroics and resistance to white supremacy, the Chicano warrior hero now has faded away in a manner linked . . . to the demise of self-enclosed, patriarchal, 'authentic' Chicano culture" (149). *The Shadow* anticipates Rosaldo's argument, since it provides no such unified figure of resistance. The novel's "hero," Antonio Cuitla, represents a warrior "faded away" in Greater Mexico's post-revolutionary transformations between tradition and modernity. Thus, this tenuous subject formation demands that critics view Chicano/a identity as contingent and always changing in relation to an evolving modernity. In the next chapter, I examine the popular literary and cinematic adaptations of Paredes's *"With His Pistol in His Hand"* and argue that these mimics of a different order bring further to light ideas about uni- and multivocality, contingency, and the reproduction of Mexican masculinity in literature and film.

Gregorio Cortez in the Chicano/a Imaginary and American Popular Culture

Síganme, rinches cobardes, yo soy Gregorio Cortez. [Follow me, cowardly rangers, I am Gregorio Cortez.]
—from "Gregorio Cortez" (1901 corrido)

Gregorio Cortez, a sus ordenes. [Gregorio Cortez, at your service.]
—from *The Ballad of Gregorio Cortez* (1982)

In all of Greater Mexico, there is no more widely known *corrido*, or narrative ballad, than "Gregorio Cortez." The song, Américo Paredes tells us, "has been reported wherever Mexicans are found in the United States, not only on the border but on the West Coast and in the Great Lakes areas" (*A Texas-Mexican Cancionero*, 31). One reason for the corrido's far-flung influence lies in its concise encapsulation of a single man's heroic action taken in the just defense of his rights as a citizen.

In 1901, Gregorio Cortez was working his small farm in south Texas when Sheriff Brack Morris, accompanied by his interpreter Boone Choate, visited Cortez and his brother Romaldo on the matter of a horse trade gone bad. Through a series of mistranslations on the part of Choate, tensions between the two parties escalated into a gun battle. Morris shot first, hitting Romaldo in the face. Cortez then pulled his gun and shot at Morris as the sheriff shot and missed Cortez. Cortez's shot knocked down Morris, and then Cortez fired on him several more times. Knowing that shooting an Anglo sheriff, even in self-defense, would almost certainly lead to an immediate lynching, Cortez took flight, and thus began one of the greatest manhunts in Texas history. Cortez's actions were celebrated by the Texas Mexican population, and folk songs and legends grew around his deeds. During his flight, Cortez eluded large posses and rode or walked three hundred miles in ten days. When he was finally captured and faced trial, he was exonerated for Sheriff Morris's death but not for a second killing. He spent twelve years in prison and was eventually pardoned. His actions, taken in defense of his rights, live on in songs, legends, and even films.

By 1901, the year of the events recounted in the song, Mexican Americans had long experienced the acts of violence and discrimination visited upon a conquered people, and Cortez's forceful stance, "with his pistol in his hand," united and inspired communities along the border. Furthermore, the ballad and the legend that grew around Cortez's actions received redoubled recognition and inspired a new generation of Mexican Americans when, in 1958, Paredes published *"With His Pistol in His Hand": A Border Ballad and its Hero.* Paredes himself would achieve the status of a culture hero among the young activists of the 1960s–70s Chicano/a Movement, for his study of the corrido and the people who sang it was a breakthrough in several respects: it gave voice to a silenced culture group and its history; it challenged unexamined prejudicial attitudes, often held by leading historians, about Mexican American folklore and culture; and it critically assessed the role of historians, fiction writers, propagandists, and even the Texas Rangers in the dissemination of negative attitudes and images about Mexicans.[1]

The story of Gregorio Cortez, because it has so often been retold, studied, and celebrated, carries special meaning among those concerned with defending the rightful place of Mexican Americans in U.S. society. Paredes was a great admirer of the cultural values Cortez symbolized, so it is not surprising that he would respond critically to interpretations of the story that appeared after the publication of his work.[2] In 1974, Elmer Kelton published *Manhunters*, a novel based on the historical events surrounding Cortez. In 1982, the Public Broadcasting System aired *The Ballad of Gregorio Cortez*, a fiction film adapted by Robert Young. Paredes did not learn about Kelton's retelling until 1982, around the time the movie aired, and in both cases he responded passionately, although privately, to the adaptations of his book. Paredes did not take a public stance on either Kelton's novel or Young's film, but evidence suggests that he saw in both works a betrayal of the ideals represented by the heroic ballad tradition he had so majestically brought to life.

Read together, *"With His Pistol in His Hand," The Ballad of Gregorio Cortez*, and *Manhunters* constitute a continuum in the ideological representation of the Mexican American hero. Each work deals with the efficacy of male action as expressed through violence, but each work emphasizes a different point of view. "*With His Pistol*," as an innovative work of Mexican American historiography, metonymizes the concerns of the ballad's subject, Gregorio Cortez, with those of his Mexican American community in South Texas. *The Ballad of Gregorio Cortez* is deeply indebted to "*With His Pistol*," and its multiple narrative perspectives unambiguously lead the viewer to side with Cortez's plight. *Manhunters*, on the other hand, is one of dozens of popular Westerns by the West Texas writer Elmer Kelton, and it is only loosely based on the Cortez story. While its fast-paced narrative is told from several points of view, its ethical center is with the main protagonist, a Texas Ranger, who ultimately saves Cortez from a lynching posse. Placed one next to the other, these three interpretations of Cortez form an ideological battleground over the proper depiction of Mexican masculinity and identity in the popular culture about Texas and the West.

"With His Pistol in His Hand" *and the Rights of Citizenship*

It is no exaggeration to state that "*With His Pistol in His Hand*" opened a new discursive space in which Mexican Americans were able to contest harmful images of themselves and reframe their social standing within broader discourses of Texas and American history, folklore studies, and civil rights. The character Antonio Cuitla's statement in *The Shadow*, that someday reasonable men would stand as equals, which rang hollow within the dynamics of that novella, rings powerfully true in the body of scholarship Paredes would produce beginning with "*With His Pistol in His Hand*" in 1958, and including such works as *A Texas-Mexican Cancionero* (1976), "The United States, Mexico, and *Machismo*" (1971), and "On Ethnographic Fieldwork Among Minorities" (1977). These are disparate texts, yet they share an abiding sense that, even within the most unequal power relationships—whether those relations be between Anglos and Mexicans, the United States and Mexico, or the ethnographer and the subjects of his or her study—human beings are fundamentally equal in their need to preserve their liberty, dignity, and self-respect.

Without denying the strong communalist inclinations in "*With His Pistol in His Hand*"—Paredes states in the introduction that the book is about "the people who produced the songs, the legends, and the man" (xi)—we should remember that it began as the study of a ballad and the individual man who inspired the ballad. The interplay between the particularity of Cortez's individual experience and its applicability to the broader Mexican community's concerns was important for Paredes in choosing to write about Gregorio Cortez, but first was the man. "I wanted to write on a *corrido* about border conflict. Before the war, I had been writing protest verse, and other things, in Spanish. And then when I looked at what I had written over the years, I saw a pattern emerge from those border stories: of the peaceful Mexican who is goaded into violence by Anglo injustice. . . . 'Gregorio Cortez,' of what I knew at the time, seemed to fit the idea I had formed of the *corrido* hero. So that's why I chose him" (Interview in Saldívar, *Borderlands*, 110–11). Scholars have since focused on the book's central strength—its legitimation of Mexican American cultural values—as they are expressed through Cortez, because he stands in for the whole South Texas Mexican community and its experiences of disenfranchisement.

Thus, Cortez's singular experience is representative of the experiences of the Mexican American people, and the group's ideals are distilled in Cortez. Yet while readers of *"With His Pistol"* celebrate its championing of the community, Paredes was initially attracted to the ballad as a story of a single man defending his individual rights. "Individual acts of violent protest" were initiated by "men without great prominence in the political or social history of the region, but their deeds were engraved in common memory because they were seen as symbols—men who stood up for their dignity as human beings and suffered death or exile for their actions" (*Cancionero*, 34). Ultimately, then, it is most accurate to state that Cortez and the Mexican community exist in a productively dialectical relationship—with the yearnings of the many expressed by the one, and vice versa—especially as they are reflected in the corrido.

We can see the relationship between obligation to the community and the rights of the individual early on in the corrido, in the first moments Cortez speaks.

Decía Gregorio Cortez	Then said Gregorio Cortez
con su pistola en la mano:	with his pistol in his hand:
No siento haberlo matado	I don't regret that I killed him;
lo que siento es a mi hermano.	I regret my brother's death.
(Variant X, 155)	

Here, Cortez's words do not place importance on himself, but on his obligations to a family member, whose loss he feels more strongly than the regret for having killed another man. If the border was, as Paredes describes in *"With His Pistol,"* an organic community in which individuals were linked through extended family bonds, then we can see that Cortez's brother, Romaldo, stands in for the Anglo-persecuted community of Mexicans. The next stanza moves the focus from the community to the individual, as Cortez declares the need to protect his rights.

Decía Gregorio Cortez	Then said Gregorio Cortez,
con su alma muy encendida:	and his soul was all aflame:
No siento haberlo matado,	"I don't regret having killed him,
la defensa es permitida.	a man must defend himself."
(Variant X, 155)	

In the narrative that ensues, we see the exploits of one man in the face of great odds, as when Cortez challenges the posse: "—*No corran, rinches cobardes, / Con un solo mexicano* [Don't run, you cowardly rangers, / From just one Mexican]" (156). The middle section of the corrido thus places emphasis on Cortez's singular bravery and elusiveness as the posse gives chase through South Texas.

Yet by the corrido's end, Cortez does not forget his responsibilities and ties to other Mexicans who have helped him and are now suffering because of him.

Dicen que por culpa mía	It is said that because of me
han matado mucha gente;	many people have been killed;
ya me voy a presentar	I will surrender now
porque eso no es conveniente.	because such things are not right.
(Variant X, 157)	

In its final section, the corrido returns to the broader concerns of the community, and Cortez reconciles his individual struggle for justice with his obligations to the Mexican American people by turning himself in to the Anglo authorities and the hope for a fair trial. The movement of the corrido—from the community to the individual, and back again to the community—demonstrates the dialectical relationship between Cortez and the Mexican people, and the movement is itself symbolic of the story's circulation and production of the feelings of injustice requisite to save Cortez from lynching. Paredes well understood the necessity of this relationship. "It was as if the Border people had dreamed Gregorio Cortez before producing him, and had sung his life and his deeds before he was born" (125).

The ramifications of the emphasis on the relationship between the individual and the community may be found in Paredes's initial compulsion to write about "Gregorio Cortez" and other corridos of cultural conflict. Paredes began "serious work" on these folk forms because they expressed Mexicans' yearnings for "social justice." In interviews, he states, "To use legal terms, perhaps not correctly, I was writing a brief. I was being an advocate for my people" (qtd. in R. Saldívar, *Borderlands*, 121, 70). These legal terms are very apt, for they speak directly to the relationship between the individual and the community: in declaring the rights of the individual Mexican whose rights have been trampled, the corrido—and then Paredes in his study—also advocated for the rights of the Mexican community. Therefore, the language of the ballad, with its references to the right to self-defense and the wrongful suffering of the community, is itself grounded in ethics and the law, and it opens the possibility for the tangible civic redress of the Mexican's standing within U.S. society. In the previous chapter's discussion on *The Shadow*, if such concepts as liberty, justice, and equality seem like grand but empty promises in the agrarian community's evisceration (even as the revolution was *won*), the unity between the individual and the community in "Gregorio Cortez" and *"With His Pistol,"* in contrast, means that the community's ideals are concretized and made possible through the individual's agency and the defense of individual rights.

The actions necessary to right the wrongs inflicted on Cortez involve violence, first in actuality, and then symbolically in the corrido. In 1901, violent action in self-defense of one's rights and resistance to Anglo domination was the only recourse for Mexicans, for as Paredes makes clear, Mexican Americans' uncertain citizenship status—they were officially citizens but in reality treated as outsiders without rights—made peaceful legal recourse untenable. It would not be until after World War II that Mexican Americans would make "greater use of the mechanisms for political and social action offered by existing institutions in the United States." But at the turn of the twentieth century, Gregorio Cortez "epitomized the idea of the man who defends his rights *con su pistola en la mano*" (*Cancionero*, 28, 31). Cortez and others like him represent an ideal of masculine agency for Paredes, one embodied in the "old values of heroic resistance against a new political and social order" (qtd. in R. Saldívar, *Borderlands*, 120). Paredes sees in Cortez a peaceful, law-abiding citizen, a man who respects his elders and authority, but also a man full of dignity and self-respect. That he must resort to violence is an unavoidable consequence of his social condition, as well as an outcome of the need to preserve his dignity and basic human rights. If his violence then comes to be celebrated in song, this is so because it was his only course of effective action.

Scared Little Peon: Performance of Male Agency in The Ballad of Gregorio Cortez

When Paredes wrote *"With His Pistol in His Hand"* in 1958, he strongly sensed that he was giving voice to a previously silenced Mexican American cultural consciousness. Paredes reminds us that the "first part of my study was my attempt to show border Mexican communities from their own point of view, not that of [Texas historian] Walter Webb" (qtd. in R. Saldívar, *Borderlands*, 112). His book constitutes a counter-discursive act in response to biased histories and negative images about Mexicans. One of his stated goals was to demonstrate "the remarkable ways in which their communities held together under great external pressures from discrimination and other social injustices" (70). It stands to reason, therefore, that the adaptation of Paredes's famed study into a film should have garnered positive attention and provided Paredes with much gratification. The 1982 PBS television debut of *The Ballad of Gregorio Cortez*, however, was anything but auspicious. Chicano/a critics rejected the film for what was perceived to be its Anglo-centric perspective. The critics claimed that neither Cortez nor the Mexican community are given a voice as *The Ballad of Gregorio Cortez* explores the legal injustices visited upon Tejanos at the turn of the twentieth century. In the most sustained critique of the film, Rosa Linda Fregoso praises Robert M. Young for his "antiracism politics," but she critiques the film for its "subordination of Cortez within the narrative discourse" (*Bronze Screen*, 70). Still, not all the criticism of the movie has been completely unfavorable. Chon Noriega, for instance, argues that the film effects "an intertextual dialogue with previous Hollywood representation," while it "deconstructs both the classical western and the silent 'greaser' genre of the period depicted" ("Between a Weapon," 153).

While numerous Chicano/a scholars have taken a position on the movie, Paredes's own sentiments over the cinematic adaptation of his most celebrated work have remained unclear.[3] Paredes never wrote formally on *Ballad*, but numerous anecdotes reveal that he had strong negative feelings about the movie. Recent archival findings at the University of Texas at Austin's Nettie Lee Benson Latin American Collection, where the Américo Paredes Papers are housed, indicate that Paredes's critical response may be tied to his conceptualization of a proper Mexican masculinity as expressed in folkloric forms such as the corrido. His personal papers and correspondence, when examined in conjunction with his scholarly writings on the corrido and machismo, reveal that Paredes was troubled less by the silencing of Cortez and the Mexican community than by the film's lack of a strong and proper heroic element, most tellingly lacking in the acting choices made by the lead actor in the film.

Although Paredes never published on the subject of ethnic representation in film, this is not to say that he was unaware of the growing importance of the film medium as a mode of popular culture and entertainment, as well as a disseminator of stereotypical images and ideology about the ethnic subject. In *"With His Pistol,"* for instance, Paredes discusses idealizations and stereotypes about Texas lawmen at the turn of the twentieth century, and he comments that the "'shoot first and ask questions later' method of the rangers has been romanticized into something dashing and daring, in technicolor, on a wide screen, and with Gary Cooper in the title role" (28). This statement reveals an understanding about film's iconic power to render certain subjects—the cowboy, the ranger, the Anglo hero—as mythically heroic. Paredes's novel *George Washington Gómez* (1990) provides a telling instance of film's ambivalent attraction in Don Pancho, a Mexican worker who goes to "the picture show, and for fifteen cents you went in and watched the cowboys. They had sound now. These Gringos! They could do anything. Yes, they had sound now, and you could hear the shots and the smacks when the cowboy hit the badman. It was nice going to the picture show. And when you came out you walked the aisle to the door with a cowboyish swagger you couldn't control, though you felt ashamed and tried to break your step" (181). Don Pancho is a Mexican, yet he derives pleasure from watching the Anglo-American hero defeat the "badman," a film character who was often a Mexican. In this passage, Paredes draws our attention to the powerful process of interpellation: the movie-watching experience encourages Don Pancho to root for the Anglo cowboy against his better judgment, and he feels torn between acceptance and rejection. The passage also shows Paredes's cognizance of the cinema's successful transfer of literary and historical stereotypes—the 'good' Anglo cowboy, the Mexican badman—into an image medium, and the medium's ability to make these stereotypes seem like accepted reality.

Paredes had much to say about the creation of stereotypical images about Mexicans, but not in the language of the film critic. *"With His Pistol"* contains a well-developed and oft-cited analysis of the "Anglo-Texan legend," a set of beliefs about the Mexican used to justify his wanton mistreatment.[4] The Anglo-Texan legend states that the Mexican is cruel, cowardly, and prone to thievery, and that his degeneracy is due to racial miscegenation (16). Against these characterizations, the legend places the Anglo Texan as the Mexican's superior. In noting the oppositionality between the "good" Texan and the "bad" Mexican, Paredes is establishing a relation that applies to the working of stereotypes, cinematic or otherwise, for stereotypical construction often relies upon the simple binary relation of good/bad, as I have earlier discussed. Unlike in the cinema, however, the Anglo-Texan legend was initially employed with real rather than symbolic effects, as in "the war propaganda works of the 1830's and 1840's about Mexican 'atrocities' in Texas, a principal aim of which was to overcome Northern antipathy toward the approaching war with Mexico" (16). To create the antinomial relationships necessary to lead a people to war, the Mexican must occupy the category of evil. And as Paredes notes, long after the U.S.-Mexico War, into "the 1870's, when the Indian danger was past, it was possible to ideal-ize the Plains savage. But the 'Mexican problem' remained. A distinction was drawn between the noble Plains Indian and the degenerate ancestor of the Mexican" (21). As evidenced in dime novels of the late 1800s and subsequently in early American film, the Mexican continued to be a favorite subject of negative stereotyping in Anglo-American cultural production.

In terms of the cinematic adaptation of *"With His Pistol in His Hand,"* stories told by Paredes's colleagues at the University of Texas, where he spent most of his career, have always indicated that he did not look favorably upon *The Ballad of Gregorio Cortez.*[5] Chicano/a film scholars have generally commended Robert Young's sincere attempt to portray the Mexican character positively, but it is clear that the attempt was a failure. In spite of the participation of Moctezuma Esparza as producer and Victor Villaseñor as screenwriter (the screenplay was subsequently adapted by Young), Chicano/a critics have followed a "stereotypes and distortions" model of criticism "devoted to demonstrating that certain films, in some respect or other, 'got something wrong' on historical, biographical, or other grounds of accuracy" (Shohat and Stam, 178). While critics have acknowledged Young's even-handedness in portraying the "true" story of Gregorio Cortez, most have faulted the film for silencing Cortez and the Mexican American community as active protagonists in the story. Rosa Linda Fregoso, for instance, notes that Cortez's "character hardly speaks on screen. . . . Cortez's silence is moreover significant because the film privileges Anglo-Texans as the subjects of verbal discourse, thus relegating Cortez to the status of a mute-silent Other. . . . Cortez's marginality from the verbal part of cinematic discourse directly corresponds to the elision of the Chicano point of view in the film" (*Bronze Screen*, 70). At the time of the film's release, the most prominent review of the film appeared in an essay written by Tatcho Mindiola in *La Red/The Net*, a Chicano/a educa-tion newsletter. Mindiola's review is paradigmatic of the contemporaneous Chicano/a response: the film "does not develop a perspective which puts the viewer within the Mexican community looking out. The audience is not given a sense of how Mexicans lived and how they were involved with Gregorio Cortez individually or collectively, nor of his importance as a symbol" (14). Mindiola's critique agrees with Fregoso's in calling attention to the Anglo-centric perspective of the film, despite its good intentions.

Not all responses to the film have been negative, as I have noted in men-tioning Chon Noriega's assessment of the film's revisionary stance vis-à-vis the Western. At the time of *Ballad's* release, Tomás Rivera, one of the leading Chicano/a public intellectuals of his generation, wrote a glowing review of the film in San Diego's *Voz Fronteriza*. Rivera was particularly impressed with Edward James Olmos's interpretation of Gregorio Cortez—unlike Parades, as we will see shortly. Recognizing that Cortez speaks but a few words throughout the film, Rivera states, "Olmos excellently portrays the accumulation of his cultural background by his actions, by his facial and body language." Rivera also exhorts, "the film is not a replica of the book on which it is based. It shouldn't be. The excellent study by Paredes *creates* the myth and adds to the legend. The film . . . recreates a spiritual history and allows Gregorio Cortez to converse silently throughout history. The film is not a study nor a true interpretation but a different metaphor, as human as the one wrought by the book. The film is clear and true poetry. Endless. With the stuff of humans" (7). In his review, Rivera disagrees with Fregoso on the issue of a "silent" Cortez, and he suggests that the film's importance is precisely in its ability to render Cortez's actions with great humanity. For Rivera, the film's power was in opening a new phase in the historical dialogue about the meaning of Cortez's actions.

While not entirely consistent, then, the Chicano/a response to *The Ballad of Gregorio Cortez* has been generally critical, especially in scholarly works. Yet almost twenty-five years after its release, one still wonders what Paredes himself thought about the movie. The documents collected at the Paredes Papers, including unpublished articles, class notes, and correspondence, reveal that Paredes perceived in the film a limited understanding of Mexican masculine identity—evidenced by a recapitulation of tired Mexican stereotypes—but he does not attribute this limited understanding to the Anglo-American director, as much of the criticism seems to do. Instead, Paredes looks disapprovingly upon Olmos's inability to portray Cortez with appropriate heroism and dignity onscreen.

The archives contain, for instance, a copy of *La Red/The Net*, the education journal in which Tatcho Mindiola's critical essay appeared. In a short, handwritten note attached to the article, Paredes commented that this was "the only critique of the film that is worth a damn." He elaborates no further here, but we get a fuller sense of Paredes's dissatisfaction in letters written to colleagues at the time of the film's premiere on PBS in June 1982.[6] In a response to a congratulatory letter from Carlos E. Cortés, who was at the time chair of the history department at UC Riverside, Paredes expressed a strong sense that the characterization of Cortez by Olmos reproduced harmful stereotypes about Mexicans. In his letter, Paredes acknowledges that "[a]rtistically, it was a superior piece of work; Robert Young deserves a great deal of credit for that." He laments, however, that it "is too bad that the actor playing Cortez chose to portray his character as a cross between

Chaplin and the racist stereotype of the Mexican as a timid little peon. Is Olmos a Chicano, really?" And in a letter written to Carolyn Osborn during the same period, Paredes remarks that the movie "is a good job, with most of the credit going to Robert Young, the director, who rewrote a trite script by Villaseñor. The woman translator was Young's idea, and a good idea it was. I was not as happy with the 'teatro' scene, which was added by one of the Chicanos. It was strictly 1960s–1970s stuff, and the hobby horse was just a little too much for me." Paredes then concludes that the "thing that bothered me most . . . was Eddie Olmos' interpretation of Cortez. He took a character noted for his coolness, dignity, and courage and turned him into a scared little peon, a kind of Tex-Mex Charlie Chaplin." Paredes's displeasure with the movie, moreover, grew into genuine antipathy as the years passed. In a 1990 handwritten note to a student requesting information on the film, Paredes writes: "I do not own a video of 'The Ballad of Gregorio Cortez' nor would I want to own one. Nor do I know who ultimately retained the rights to this travesty made out of a book of mine."

Paredes's negative response to the film centers on his vision of what the real Cortez was like, based on his interviews of people who knew him, as well as newspaper accounts. Cortez was said to possess great "presence" and "coolness" under duress (qtd. in R. Saldívar, *Borderlands*, 112). Olmos's portrayal, by contrast, was judged to be overly passive and submissive. Paredes also deemed Villaseñor's original script to have been weak, and his letters imply that he saw the insertion of contemporary Chicano/a politics— notable in the *teatro* scene he references—as anachronistic and over the top. Paredes, therefore, stood ironically at odds with critics who concentrated their analyses upon the Anglo director's failings rather than on any of the Chicano/a participants' choices over acting or storytelling techniques.

In none of his letters does Paredes specify the cinematic moment that led him to call Olmos's Cortez a "scared little peon," and, at least initially, it is difficult to find one because the movie begins at mid-chase, with Cortez on the run from a well-armed posse of lawmen. The film narrative then elliptically returns—again and again—to the moment of misunderstanding between Cortez and Sheriff Brack Morris that leads to the sheriff's death. Because the encounter between Cortez and the sheriff is retold from multiple perspectives, and because this is one of the rare scenes in which Cortez speaks, we may speculate that it is upon this instance that Paredes based his critique of Olmos's acting miscalculation.

Let us look, then, at the encounter between Cortez and Sheriff Morris. The scene is presented as a flashback, initially from the perspective of Boone Choate, the interpreter who was at least partially responsible for the misunderstanding and mistranslation between Cortez and the sheriff. It is crucial to understand that although the flashback begins from the subjective viewpoint of Choate, in cinematic practice a flashback achieves objective narration (Bordwell and Thompson, 106); the narrative viewpoint, therefore, agrees with the omniscient narrative voice of the film, which is sympathetic with Cortez. The scene opens with Cortez, his brother Romaldo, and the rest of the family at their small farm. As Sheriff Morris and Boone Choate approach, Gregorio sends his family inside the house while Romaldo stands at the gate. Gregorio also hides a revolver behind his back. Morris and Choate step off their buggy and ask to speak with Gregorio Cortez. Cortez steps forward and speaks to the sheriff in Spanish, as he does throughout the film. We begin to see in this scene the source of Paredes's objections to the character as developed by Olmos. Through the translator, the sheriff speaks first to Romaldo, and Romaldo relates to Cortez that the sheriff is looking for him. Cortez responds, "Gregorio Cortez, *a sus ordenes* [at your service]." This salutation is not unusual, but its manner of delivery is overly obsequious, and the rhythm of the words is delivered in the singsong of the Mexican Indian stereotype—seen most famously in the Mexican comedies starring Mario Moreno "Cantinflas." This mischaracterization, by a Mexican American actor hailed for his powerful role as "El Pachuco" in *Zoot Suit* (1981), is likely what caused Paredes to reject the film. According to the chapter entitled "The Legend" in *"With His Pistol in His Hand,"* Gregorio Cortez was a respectful, quiet man, but one who always stood with dignity and self-control (34–36). The obsequiousness of the Mexican peon that Paredes complains about is out of character here.

As the scene unfolds, Olmos's portrayal of Cortez is plagued by further inconsistencies and contradictions. In the moment when Cortez thinks he is about to be unjustly arrested, he speaks with some urgency, *"No nos puede arrestar* [You cannot arrest us]." His tone in this instance is pleading. In the next moment, when his brother is shot in the face, Cortez responds with a fury of bullets, shooting the sheriff in the chest, and as the sheriff goes down, Cortez seems terror stricken and out of control as he shoots at the fallen sheriff several more times. The scene ends with Cortez sobbing as he holds Romaldo in his arms. The characterization thus shifts radically: in one moment Cortez acts submissively, in the next he is pleading, and finally he is violently out of control. We can see, then, why for Paredes, this portrayal lacked the "coolness, dignity, and courage" for which the real and legendary Cortez was apparently known.

The inconsistencies in Olmos's acting notwithstanding, his portrayal of the physical and psychological responses to the shock of witnessing one's brother shot is not in and of itself unusual, and Olmos's performance appears realistic and against the conventions of a typical Western with its unassailable hero. Commenting on the movie's interrogation of the "limitations of the epic hero figure," Fregoso comments that a "departure from the male-hero concept of a previous era of Chicano cultural politics weighed heavily in Edward James Olmos's motives for portraying Cortez. . . . Olmos stated that in his characterization he 'intended to portray Gregorio Cortez as a 'human being' rather than a 'macho'" (qtd. in *Bronze Screen*, 80–81). As I discuss below, however, for Paredes, acting heroically was not a question of being a "macho."

A second instance that depicts a peon-like Cortez occurs during his meeting with an Anglo-American cowboy when Cortez is nearing the end of his journey across South Texas. In the scene, Cortez comes upon the lone cowboy sitting by his campfire, eating his dinner. Desperate, hungry, and exhausted, Cortez approaches the cowboy, and the cowboy offers him food, at which point Cortez devours the food in the animalistic fashion of a man who has not eaten in days. The two men talk a while, although it is the cowboy who is doing most of the talking. Cortez listens, seeming to understand but showing no evidence that he can speak English. As a show of gratitude, Cortez offers the cowboy what appears to be his only belonging, his knife. Cortez utters the words, "*Señor, gracias. Gracias por todo*," and his tone is subservient and he is almost in tears.

The Gregorio Cortez of the corrido and legend, as is well known, would not have been so obsequious. Paredes would have seen the distinction between a proper display of gratitude and the stereotypic groveling of the peon. The revised script that Robert Young delivered to Paredes contains this scene, but it contains none of the obsequiousness characteristic of the acting itself. Instead, the script emphasizes the camaraderie the two men achieve despite their language barrier. "The cowboy begins to eat and talk. It is apparent that he is lonely for companionship. He quickly learns that Gregorio speaks but little English, although it seems he understands some of what the cowboy is saying, for he nods his head as he listens" (Young, 18). The cowboy tells Cortez a funny story, and the written scene ends in laughter. "He begins to laugh and laugh at his story. Cortez begins to laugh too. Soon they are both laughing heartily, caught up infectiously in their laughter and in the absurdity of the situation. The cowboy then shakes his head. 'Damn, but it's real good to have someone to talk to.' (Cortez has not said a word.)" (19). While the scene with Cortez and the cowboy ends with a sense of equality and camaraderie in the screenplay, the same scene in the movie ends with Cortez in a more compromising position. Whether or not Olmos was truly attempting to avoid a "macho" stance, this scene not only eviscerates the masculine heroics of the corrido, but Cortez's humanity as well.

The question of an appropriate male response is central to Paredes's perception of *The Ballad of Gregorio Cortez*, and this same question appears to have been on Olmos's mind in his portrayal, but with a wholly different response. Was Paredes expecting Cortez to be a boastful macho who would respond to the sheriff, "I am Gregorio Cortez," as he does in the many versions of the ballad? While the corrido contains such language as, "Ah, so many mounted Rangers / Just to take one Mexican!" Paredes makes clear in "The Legend" that Cortez was "[n]ot a gunman, no, not a bravo. . . . He was a peaceful man." Still, Paredes emphasizes that Cortez "was a man, very much of a man" (34), and by this Paredes means that Cortez was a man who would stand up for his rights. For Paredes, Cortez represented what Renato Rosaldo calls the "Chicano warrior hero," a symbol of "an updated version of the ancient ideal of manhood" (154). While Rosaldo believes that the warrior hero "should be understood more poetically than literally," he also argues that in the contemporary moment, "changing Chicano narratives have dismantled these masculine heroics" (155). The question remains, then: Did Paredes nostalgically cling to a "primordial pastoral patriarchy" (155), and did such a stance influence his view that Olmos had completely misplayed his role as Gregorio Cortez?

Put another way, did Paredes reject one stereotype—that of the submissive Mexican peon—in favor of another one—that of the Mexican macho? I have suggested in the previous chapter that Paredes cannot so simply be reduced to the position of an essentialist Chicano patriarchy, that his conception of Chicano/a cultural identity is based on the understanding that cultural formations are characterized not by static traditions, but by the constant renovation of those traditions. The real Gregorio Cortez, as near as Paredes was able to determine, had a calm demeanor, was self-possessed, and could be persuasive, even charismatic, in his interactions with Mexicans and Anglos alike (*"With His Pistol,"* 55–58). He was not a macho in the way we understand the term today. In fact, Paredes saw the formation of the concept of machismo as an ersatz byproduct of late nineteenth- and early twentieth-century popular culture in the United States and Mexico.[7] Cortez's masculine stance was neither an idealized throwback to a time gone by nor a harbinger of the boastful representations that would later appear in American Westerns and Mexican popular songs. Rather, his masculinity was very much a consequence of ongoing, community-developed codes of conduct tied to patriarchal traditions in which one understood one's place in the social order. Under these codes, for instance, a man showed deference to his elders, but he also knew when he was in the right, and he could therefore act according to principle in the defense of his rights. In the corrido, *"La defensa es permitida* [A man must defend himself]" is not a macho declaration, but a statement of unambiguous masculine action made assertively because one is in the right.

Looking at Paredes's anthropological work, we can see that his expectations of Olmos were not centered on notions of an idealized masculine hero or even about cinematic verisimilitude. Instead, Paredes's writings suggest that he was often concerned with the ways in which Mexicans were objectified and rendered passively in American-produced ideas and images about them. Among his unpublished work, the Paredes archive contains a working paper entitled "Some Stereotypes About the Mexican American," which sheds light on Paredes's understanding of stereotypes, both negative and positive.[8] This working paper critiques the production of stereotypes about Mexicans and argues that some of these stereotypes are based on psychological projections, on a lack of factual evidence, and on a mistaking of universal human traits for cultural specificity. The paper lists several stereotypes of the Mexican, such as his supposed fatalism, his inability to think for himself, his laziness, and his excessive machismo. Significantly, these stereotypes are usually gender specific, applying mostly to men. When the Mexican woman appears, she is an object of erotic attraction, while the male consistently remains an object of derision.

The distinction in the depiction of Mexican men and women appears most prominently in "visual stereotypes": "The Mexican woman in the majority of cases is portrayed in Spanish dress. . . . The Mexican man . . . is most often portrayed as an Indian peon sleeping against an adobe wall; a ragged, unshaven bandit. . . . Needless to say, the man is portrayed in a decidedly negative (or 'Mexican') stereotype that reflects attitudes developed by Anglos during generations of conflict. . . . On the other hand, the 'Spanish' stereotype in which the woman is portrayed is romantic and idealized" (3). Paredes concludes that the *"señorita,* then, not only is desirable but acceptable as a prospective mate, since in terms of Anglo prejudices she can be considered 'white.' The Mexican man—who is a potential competitor for the *señorita's* attentions—is shown to have nothing but negative traits" (3). Paredes's analysis of stereotypes speaks to his understanding of the processes of domination and desire, especially as these fall along gender lines. Insofar as the Mexican male is conceptualized in a negative light, his depictions objectify him and strip him of his dignity and agency.

Analyzing the provenance of the stereotype of the Mexican American's fatalism, Paredes notes that this has been transferred from liberal social scientists' preconceived notions of the "village Indian." Ethnographers, too, are liable to produce beliefs about the Mexican's character based on assumptions rather than facts.

> It may be that the 'village Indian' himself is a projection of the American social scientist's own political and social views. Most often liberal in his outlook . . . the Anglo-American social scientist has sought new ideals of peace and cooperation among men, and he has projected them into the objects of his research. Thus the humble Mexican is seen as idyllically happy and integrated into his environment because the Mexican has defeated no one in the world wars or taken away anybody's national territory. The stereotype, in effect, has been turned inside out. But it still limits the observer's vision in many ways. (5)

Rather than the negative stereotype of the violent Mexican, some ethnographers produce the positive stereotype of the happy Mexican Indian or peon. Of course, neither figuration adequately describes the "village Indian," much less a contemporary U.S. Chicano/a. The common strand that assignations of fatalism, idyll happiness, sleepiness, and even banditry share is their association with passivity, with a lack of purpose, and ultimately with a loss of agency and humanity.

Paredes's analysis of the "village Indian" allows us to return to the subject of effective male action. Turning back to *The Ballad of Gregorio Cortez* and Paredes's vision of the appropriate representation of Mexican masculinity, it is important to note that, while it is not widely known, at least one other film treatment of *"With His Pistol in His Hand"* was proposed to Paredes before the 1982 adaptation—namely, one by Charles W. Smith in 1976. Smith sent Paredes a copy of the film treatment and Paredes read and commented upon it extensively. Paredes's response reveals a sense of nuance for verisimilitude, as well as an aversion to stereotypes or exaggerations of Mexican masculinity and heroics that simply reverse good/evil polarities. In the opening scene of the proposed movie, the main antagonist, Ranger Captain John Scully, is "snake-eyed . . . a coward without his two large goon-sidekicks" (Smith, 1). Paredes writes that he is "bothered by the rendering of Scully; believe it or not, because he is made a bit too villainous and too cowardly. . . . Border Mexican folklore shows the Ranger as a coward when the shooting starts; otherwise he is overbearing" ("Comments," 1). Paredes also criticizes the representation of Captain Scully as a sexual degenerate, specifically in the rape of Cortez's wife, named Leonor in Smith's screenplay: "It adds a bit of sensationalism that, in my opinion, does more harm than good. . . . Too much attention is focused on Scully . . . rather than on Cortez being pursued like a hunted animal because he stood up for very elemental rights as a citizen. The rape scene will get very negative reactions. . . . The apologists of the Texas Rangers could make a case that the whole film was an exaggerated libel on the Rangers, since raping Mexican women was not really their forte" ("Comments," 2). Paredes's comment on the characterization of Scully evidences his sense that to make the story believable and palatable, neither the Anglo-American nor the Mexican characters could be wildly stereotyped. Finally, we see yet again Paredes's concern for Cortez as an American citizen with fundamental rights.

In one of the final sequences, which narrates Cortez's lynching and its prevention by a newspaper reporter, Paredes demonstrates his sense that the depiction of Mexican heroism, while unavoidably linked with the depiction of Anglos, should not be idealized. With regard to this particular scene, Paredes felt it lacked realism, for why would a reporter hold sway over a mob? Paredes suggested "this might be a good place to give some credit to Sheriff F. M. Fly of Gonzales, who did save Cortez from lynching at the Gonzales jail." And he adds: "There is no reason to show all Anglos as blood-thirsty monsters; some of them were quite decent in the Cortez affair, and even the most partisan Chicanos admit that" ("Comments," 3). In a final observation to the screenwriter, Paredes states: "I think even Chicanos would not find an extremely exaggerated Ranger villain plausible. I would guard against making Cortez too much like an Anglo cowboy hero, on the other hand. Again, I believe that the sympathies of Anglo audiences, which will be in the majority, will be reached by showing that some Anglos were sympathetic toward Cortez in his situation, as they actually were" (3). These passages clearly suggest that Paredes had no patience for stereotypes or idealizations of any kind. As a good ethnographer, he sought to represent his subjects with a sense of their particular humanity, even within a fictional framework. In the previous statement, Paredes pointedly cautions against reversing the discourses of domination: Cortez should not follow the idealized heroism of the Anglo cowboy, and the Anglo cowboy should not follow the stereotyped cowardice of the Mexican peon. The quoted passage is also remarkable for its understanding of the relational quality of Anglo and Mexican constructions of masculinity.

Interestingly, Smith's treatment contains a scene in which Cortez must actually adopt a subservient role in order to escape the Ranger posse. Trapped in a thicket and needing water, Cortez rounds up some cattle "and begins to herd them toward the water tank, singing loudly, playing a drunken *vaquero*[.] He does a Tío Taco number on the two posse members waiting at the water tank, and thus successfully eludes the entire posse" (Smith, 3).

"Tío Taco" in this case is a derogatory term for a Mexican who is subservient or a sell-out to Anglo authority, a Mexican "Uncle Tom." Paredes read this scene and responded positively. "This might be a good scene to use some stereotyped dialogue, as a sort of take-off on the use of this type of dialogue in usual westerns, when you have Cortez doing 'a Tío Taco number'" ("Comments," 2). Paredes was known for his subtle sense of irony, and this comment shows him suggesting a critical use of the stereotypical Mexican of the Western in order to trick the Ranger posse. Such a suggestion would require the conscious performance of the subservient peon character, the same "scared little peon" that he objected to in Olmos's acting style, but in this case performed subversively to gain the upper hand.

The comments Paredes provided to Smith bear directly on the pivotal encounter between Cortez and Sheriff Morris in *The Ballad of Gregorio Cortez*. The scene, as I have mentioned, shows Olmos's performance veering between extreme submissiveness—Cortez meekly saying *"a sus ordenes* [at your service]"—and exaggerated heroics—Cortez standing over the fallen sheriff, emptying his revolver into the sheriff's inert body. Paredes could not have approved of either aspect of the performance, and he did object most vociferously to the portrayal of Cortez as a cowardly peon. Unlike the scene at the water tank written by Smith, the scene in *Ballad* when Cortez first meets Sheriff Morris contains different motivations. At the time of his first encounter with Morris, Cortez is still a peaceful man who should have no fear of the authorities because he has done nothing wrong—thus for him to show subservience and to then lose control of his emotions is beneath his "cool" character. The water-tank scene written by Smith, on the other hand, would carry a different level of urgency; Cortez is now a hunted man and every move is an act of survival. His coolness is shown precisely in performing the subservient Mexican as a way of escaping dire straits. Thus, while we cannot finally be certain of the reasons Paredes appears to have rejected the filmic adaptation of *"With His Pistol,"* his correspondence, unpublished essays, working papers, and the source text itself suggest that the movie failed at the level of the performance of a heroic masculinity consonant with the historical Gregorio Cortez and with the values of the Mexican community.

Elmer Kelton's Manhunters: Gregorio Cortez as Accidental Hero

The Austin premier of *The Ballad of Gregorio Cortez* on June 18, 1982, was certainly disappointing for Paredes—so disappointing that he regretted having given away the rights to the adaptation of the source text.[9] Around the same time, he learned of a literary adaptation of *"With His Pistol in His Hand"*: Elmer Kelton's *Manhunters*, a short Western novel originally published by Ballantine in 1974. Richard Bauman, a colleague and friend of Paredes, called the novel to his attention and on June 21 sent him a copy of the novel. Included with the book was a short note, which ironically stated, "Américo—Here is the unbiased and fair-handed work that balances your 'vivid though one-sided' one" (Paredes Papers). Bauman's short message referenced Kelton's "Author's Note" that accompanied later editions of *Manhunters*, in which Kelton writes that his novel is based on "the true story of Gregorio Cortez. . . . My version is fictional and makes no claim to following the actual Cortez story except in broadest terms." Acknowledging the corridos inspired by Cortez's deeds, Kelton adds, "professor Américo Paredes gathered many of these verses in a remarkable though one-sided book" (vi).[10] This final quote is the passage Bauman paraphrased in his note, and he probably intended to tweak his good friend's sensitivity to the uses that his most famous book was enduring.

To have his book be labeled "one-sided" could not have sat well with Paredes, for, after all, one of the aims of *"With His Pistol"* had been to respond— by way of historical inquiry, ethnographic analysis, and the collecting of folktales and songs as well as eyewitness accounts—to the prejudicial history that had already been written about the Mexican American people. If, as Bauman recalls, Paredes was not so much angry as let down by the film adaptation of his work,[11] then *Manhunters* rekindled his disappointment and transformed it into ire. Below Bauman's note, Paredes wrote,

> [w]ith a copy of *Manhunters* by one Elmer Keaton [sic], supposedly based on THE STORY of Gregorio Cortez. In truth it is lifted from *WHPistol* [sic] and fictionalized. First published in 1974, and supposedly corrects my "biased" account. In *Manhunters* Cortez is a harmless little man who helps a sheriff kill himself with his own gun. Period. Eddie Olmos must have read Kelton's book. He certainly did not read mine." (Paredes Papers)

Behind Bauman's ironic message and in Paredes's caustic response lies the sense that neither *Manhunters* nor *Ballad* correctly assesses the importance of Cortez as a figure of resistance and agential power. To call *"With His Pistol"* "one-sided" reduces its efficacy as an expression of Mexican American cultural critique and self-definition. Further, to make Gregorio Cortez a reactive figure rather than a proactive one, as both Kelton and Olmos's characterizations implied for Paredes, is to reduce the Mexican American heroic stance. In Kelton's novel, the Cortez character kills the sheriff accidentally rather than purposefully and in self-defense, which for Paredes made all the difference between timidity and valor. Finally, Paredes indicted *Manhunters* for practically plagiarizing *"With His Pistol,"* notwithstanding its watering down of Cortez's heroism.

Kelton's novel, however, is in fact only inspired by Paredes's study; it is not meant as a faithful rewriting. Kelton takes the basic elements of Gregorio Cortez's story—the horse trade gone bad, the botched translation, and the chase across South Texas—and transforms these into an entertaining adventure story about an innocent man unjustly accused. To give it its due, *Manhunters* is a Western imbued with an ostensibly progressive message of cultural tolerance. Kelton consciously avoids a "one-sided" representation of social relations in Texas at the turn of the twentieth century by showing that all groups were capable of racial intolerance. With this end in mind, the novel is filled with character types, from the callously racist Anglo lawman to the cunning Mexican politico interested in fomenting unrest. Significantly, the ethical center of the novel is occupied not by the Cortez character— who is nonetheless sympathetically rendered—but by a young Texas Ranger who only seeks justice.

Manhunters opens with the Cortez character, Chacho Fernandez, completing the breaking of a dozen broncs for an American rancher, Barnhill, in exchange for which he will receive a sorrel mare he has selected in advance. Felix, Chacho's brother, has already warned him to be careful because a *"gringo will always cheat you"* (4). Chacho, however, is a more trusting and reasonable man, and believes he will prove himself to the American through his skillful work. Chacho's naïveté ultimately proves fatal for his brother. When Chacho attempts to claim his sorrel mare, Barnhill verbally abuses him and rewards him with a lesser horse. Chacho, who knows he is in the right, punches Barnhill and returns to his ranch with the sorrel mare he was promised.

The local sheriff, Griffin Holliday, who has a "reputation among the Mexican people that he was firm but not unfair" (10), comes to question Chacho. The encounter turns violent when the sheriff's translator, Albert Stout, misunderstands Chacho's intentions. When Chacho tells the sheriff, in Spanish, "You can't arrest me for nothing," Stout understands differently and makes "a fatal mistake in translation. Chacho used the Spanish word *nada* for 'nothing.' But Stout mistook it for *nadie*, which meant 'nobody' . . . . 'He says he ain't goin' to let nobody arrest him!'" (28) With these words, Holliday raises his gun at Chacho, and when Felix tries to intervene, Holliday shoots him in the face, mortally wounding Felix. Chacho attempts to disarm the sheriff, and Holliday's gun goes off during their struggle, killing him. Chacho immediately sees that he must take flight, for if he stays he will certainly be lynched.

The narrative that follows is a classic chase story in which a young Texas Ranger captain, Kelly Sadler, and an older former Ranger, Joe Florey, try to catch Chacho before he reaches the Mexican border. They must also capture Chacho before Odom Willcox, the vengeful new sheriff, can get to Chacho and lynch him. Sadler is also the son-in-law of the dead sheriff and must overcome his own inclinations for revenge and see that proper justice is carried out. As the story unfolds, Sadler becomes the narrative and ethical center of the novel, as he witnesses several instances of Wilcox's indiscriminate violence upon innocent Mexicans and as he discovers Barnhill's culpability in the horse trade gone bad. With the help of Florey, who is an expert tracker, Sadler also comes to admire Chacho's abilities as a horseman and his powers of evasion. Eventually, Florey also helps Sadler realize that Chacho is an innocent man, and the two Anglos are able to safely deliver the Mexican to a fair trial in San Antonio.

In the best Western adventure tradition, the novel is fast paced, full of thrilling plot twists and narrow escapes, and peopled with strong characters. While the novel relies on the Western's penchant for simple character types and stereotypes—the crooked horse trader (Barnhill), the malevolent sheriff (Willcox), the resourceful tracker (Florey), the silent and righteous Ranger (Sadler)—it departs from traditional Westerns in two significant respects. First, the most important Mexican character is not simply presented as inferior to his Anglo counterparts. Although Chacho occupies less narrative space than Sadler, he is still a strong character, possessing desirable qualities of Western manhood, such as physical strength, mental acuity, his knowledge of horses and the environment, and an inner sense of justice. Chacho is a far cry from the villainous Mexican of an older generation of Westerns. In addition to Chacho, the novel represents a variety of character types within the Mexican population, from the scheming politician to the stoic and loyal friend to the beautiful señorita. While these characters are simple and undeveloped, the fact that there is a range of Mexican characters makes *Manhunters* distinctive among popular Westerns.

Additionally, like Kelton's other work, *Manhunters* is a Western rooted in history—though the history that it bases its story upon is subject to dispute, as we shall see. Unlike most of the popular Western's canonical writers—from Zane Gray to Louis L'Amour to Elmore Leonard—Kelton is recognized for his nontraditional Westerns, stories that challenge the myths of a timeless frontier in favor of historical realism and verisimilitude. In recent years, Kelton has become celebrated among critics for not giving in to nostalgia, for presenting the problems of common folk—working cowboys and small ranchers—and he has also participated in a minor culture war surrounding the proper depiction of the West. He sees himself as neither an apologist for a time of larger-than-life heroes that never was nor as a revisionist attempting to reframe history.[12] In this vein, *Manhunters* interweaves the history of conflict between Anglos and Mexicans in Texas, and it includes such issues as territorial wars and the dispossession of lands, as well as the mistreatment of Mexicans by the Texas Rangers.

Yet despite Kelton's cultural sensitivity and attention to historical detail, the novel reads like an apologia for Anglo dominance, masking the real cultural and historical conflicts in Texas and the West. Rather than exploring the unequal power relations that created conflict between cultures, Kelton seemingly explains them away as differences of individual opinion. And instead of exposing underlying notions of racial supremacy in the bigoted attitudes of some of his characters, Kelton flattens causes of conflict into differences among social equals, as if the novel's conflicts existed outside real racial/cultural hierarchies. There is, of course, no requirement that *Manhunters* should conform to contemporary ideas of historical realism or social justice, yet the "Author's Note" gestures toward just such an intent. After his comments on Paredes's "remarkable though one-sided book," Kelton opines that in "real life, all the fault, all the bigotry, were not on one side. In a time of unreasoning racial antipathies, there was blame enough to go around" (vi). This statement is not incorrect, but neither does it make possible an acknowledgement that Texas Mexicans during the early twentieth century were victims of systemic racial intolerance. Instead, the narrator explains the tensions between the Mexicans and Anglos as "a state of mutual antagonism [that] still remained between *la raza* and the *gringo*, and an angry heritage going back through all the border wars to the fall of the Alamo and even before. There had been provocation enough on both sides to justify a lifetime of hostility" (36). That cultural conflict existed between the two groups is not in dispute, but Kelton ascribes it to a distant, vague origin, and accounts for neither the supremacist racial views nor the power relations that ratified Anglo violence upon the Mexican.

It is at times when Kelton is drawing out what he perceives to be different points of view among individual men that one gets a sense that there may be something to Paredes's accusation that the novel is simply "lifted" from *"With His Pistol."* In brief moments, *Manhunters* reads as if it is responding defensively to Paredes's work. For instance, the theme of Texas Ranger atrocities, which made *"With His Pistol"* controversial among some Texas historians, is also taken up by the novel. But while Paredes works to demythologize the Rangers by showing their systematically unjust tactics against Mexicans, Kelton reifies their heroism and minimizes their questionable deeds. We see Kelton's apologist attitude early in the novel, when Chacho encounters a groups of Rangers while he is working some horses.

> Mexican people from San Antonio to the Rio Grande dreaded the Texas *rinches*. Chacho had heard many stories. He could not recall that he had ever been harmed by a Ranger or had ever seen anybody harmed by one. He could not think of anyone he personally knew who ever had been. . . . Nevertheless it was an article of faith among the people of the lower country that the Rangers were an oppressive force whose chief dedication it was to keep them in a position of servitude, somewhere a few steps above the black but several steps beneath the *gringo*. Chacho had long since decided there must be some truth to it, otherwise so many people would not declare it to be so. (6)

Initially, this passage would seem to take a fair-handed approach to the Mexican view of the Rangers: most Mexicans feared them because many Mexicans had been harmed by them. As Chacho mulls over these thoughts, the Rangers give him a suspicious look. He considers that maybe they think his horses are stolen. But rather than indignation, Chacho shows understanding: "Many horses *were* regularly stolen from ranches in this section of the country. It was no secret that some of the Mexican cowboys were among the most skillful thieves" (6). Incredibly, the narrative would have the reader believe that Ranger suspicion and its accompanying violence are excusable because "some" Mexicans are thieves. Thus, the passage unwittingly confirms Paredes's analysis of the "Texas legend," the set of widely held beliefs that Anglos held about Mexicans. One of these beliefs involves thievery, which "is second nature in the Mexican, especially horse and cattle rustling" (*"With His Pistol,"* 16). *Manhunters*, therefore, corroborates one part of this legend and takes it one step further: the novel makes the Mexican character internalize the idea of his own thieving nature.

Kelton deflects Ranger culpability at other times also. Even though the bad guy of the novel is an Anglo Texan, Kelton makes him a non-Ranger. Odom Willcox, the new sheriff, is an unsavory character, and the narration silently condemns his actions by making them utterly inhuman. During the manhunt for Chacho, Willcox murders several innocent Mexicans, and he unreflexively explains his methods. *"I'll shoot the son of a bitch first and then ask questions later. High time them damn people know who the boss is, anyway!"* (121). In *"With His Pistol,"* the shoot-first-and-ask-questions-later tactics are attributed not to sheriffs but to the Texas Rangers, while in *Manhunters*, the Rangers are actually agents of justice, as can be seen when Sadler and Florey finally capture Chacho Fernandez.

"If you are going to kill me," he [Chacho] said, his voice quavering, "do it now. Do not make me die a minute at a time."

The two *gringos* looked at each other, then back at Chacho. The younger one said, "We are not going to kill you, although those others [Willcox and his men] might."

"You are Rangers, are you not?" Chacho asked. "Rangers always kill a Mexican when they can."

Kelly Sadler shook his head, glancing at Joe Florey. "Where do they get that kind of a notion?"

Florey shrugged. "I guess there's always been a few Rangers who liked killin' a man, just as there's always been a few Mexicans who liked to a cut a throat." (147)

The two men who capture Chacho are Rangers, and they embody what is supposed to be the best of their breed. The notion that Rangers indiscriminately kill Mexicans is minimized as something that happens rarely, not as a matter of course. Further, we are reminded yet again that the killing of Mexicans is understandable because some of them are cutthroats. Systemic violence—namely, the well-documented Ranger atrocities that almost led to their disbandment—is rationalized into isolated instances with comparable Mexican analogues.[13]

While *Manhunters* tends to homogenize the sources of conflict in its treatment of social relations between Mexicans and Anglos, the novel is commendable for giving its main Mexican character admirable features and putting on display the remarkable similarities between aspirations of different culture groups. Although Chacho does not occupy the narrative's center—and neither is he its hero—he possesses the traits of a cowboy hero. Chacho is fast with a gun, good with horses, knows the land, and understands the difference between right and wrong. He performs selfless deeds, such as risking his life to save a young boy who has been gored by a bull. In the long hunt after their quarry, Sadler and Florey grow not only to respect his elusiveness, but they also judge by his actions that he cannot possibly be guilty of stealing horses and murdering sheriffs. In giving Chacho heroic qualities and in having Sadler and Florey identify with him, Kelton makes a powerful statement about the possibility of true equality among men in the West, regardless of their ethnic and cultural background. In the waning moments of the narrative, Florey says it best: "Look at them eyes. You see a killer's eyes? No you just see a poor unlucky Mexican who got himself pushed in a jam. . . . If he wasn't a Mexican, damn near any judge in the country would turn him loose" (148). The moment expresses empathy and an understanding of the unfair treatment Mexicans were receiving.

We return, finally, to the question of agency and the elements of a proper heroic stance for the Mexican. *Manhunters* closes with Chacho's safe transport to San Antonio, where he will stand trial. In order to get him on a train, Sadler and Florey must avoid Willcox's posse, and with these actions they ratify the honor and goodness of the Texas Rangers. Unlike the original Gregorio Cortez, who turned himself in willingly to authorities, Chacho is caught and must depend on the benevolence of his captors. Like the accidental killing of the sheriff that opens the book, Chacho's final capture preempts the possibility of heroic action and diminishes the story of Gregorio Cortez. Therefore, although the portrayal of Chacho in *Manhunters* is generally admirable, this main Mexican character affronts the reader for the same reason *The Ballad of Gregorio Cortez* affronted Paredes: both works portray a passive victim rather than an agential hero.

The distinctions between "*With His Pistol*" and its successors, particularly *Manhunters*, map out a struggle for the representation of Gregorio Cortez and Mexicans in popular culture and the public sphere. Provocatively, Paredes and Kelton, notwithstanding their different approaches to the story of Gregorio Cortez—particularly the degree to which each author examines the social conditions that go into the production of the story—are remarkably similar in their personal backgrounds and commitment to retelling the folkloric dimensions of Texas and the West. Both men were born in the early part of the twentieth century, Paredes in 1915 and Kelton in 1926. Both men attended the University of Texas at Austin; Kelton attended in the 1940s and studied journalism and English, while Paredes studied English and folklore and earned three degrees at the university—in 1951, 1953, and 1956. Both men served in World War II, and both men met their foreign-born wives while on their tours of duty. But what joins Paredes and Kelton more than their personal histories is their abiding passion for recording the stories of the common folk, Kelton in West Texas and Paredes in South Texas. Kelton recalls that he "heard a wealth of stories as a boy. . . . I guess knowing so many of those stories, told by the people who lived them, has helped color the kind of fiction I write" (*My Kind of Heroes*, 26). Paredes also grew up hearing stories of common people, namely of people living and working together and forming communities and cultural traditions, often under duress. Paredes was compelled to write about the stories of his folk in ethnographic studies, fiction, and poetry. And he was pressed to write about one man in particular, Gregorio Cortez, a peaceful man forced to take heroic action in the face of Anglo injustice.

Yet while Kelton and Paredes share a commitment to retelling the stories of their individual communities, Paredes's responses to the different interpretations of the Cortez story instantiate the need within the Mexican American community to participate in the representation of their own stories and in the preservation of their identity. In the foregoing discussion, I have focused on issues of masculinity, heroism, and agency, but questions of representation touch upon every aspect of Mexican American identity. If, in 1958, *"With His Pistol in His Hand"* performed a necessary counter-discursive act in the wake of the dominant culture's damaging historiographies of Mexican Americans, its cogency is no less apparent today. Paredes's study continues to make the case for the importance of telling the story from the Mexican community's point of view, as well as for taking a stand when one is in the right, without excuses and without passivity—and without needing some other person or group to do the talking for the Mexican.

Reformulating Hybrid Identities and Re-inscribing History in Contemporary Chicano/a Literature and Film

> How to start. . . . Well, okay, I guess it all started that first day of summer—the movie got that part right, at least.
> —Nena (Maria Candelaria), in *Come and Take It Day* (2002)

How to start? And how to end? These are always important questions, for beginnings and endings exert a strong influence upon a reader's relationship to any narrative, including a study such as my own. If my examination of Mexican male identity representation necessarily begins with early twentieth-century film and literature produced by Anglo-Americans, then it must conclude with late twentieth- and twenty-first-century Chicano/a self-representation, for this historical moment sees an opening of expressive possibilities for Mexican Americans, particularly in the realms of poetry and independent film. I close my project with a discussion of a contemporary Chicano/a filmmaker, Jim Mendiola, and a Chicana poet, Evangelina Vigil. Together, these artists explore notions of representation, history-making, and constructions of Mexican masculinity. Mendiola's *Come and Take It Day* (2002) reveals the contingent and hybrid quality of Mexican American cultural identity at the same time that it critiques continuing representations of Mexican American male deviance in the dominant media. Vigil's *Thirty an' Seen A Lot* (1985) is concerned with, among other topics, preserving the Mexican presence in postmodern American society, as well as with examining and revising—from a woman's perspective—definitions of Mexican masculinity. Significantly, Mendiola and Vigil continue the Chicano/a dialogue with the culturalist interventions of Américo Paredes, as both artists intertextualize "With His Pistol in His Hand" as a way of interrogating Chicano/a identity in the late twentieth- and early twenty-first centuries.

Unlike Chicano/a cinema during the sixties and seventies, with its concerns for defining an essential subject in resistance to Anglo-American stereotyping, and unlike much of the eighties and nineties cinema, with its interest in participating in mainstream culture, Come and Take It Day proposes contingency and hybridity as the defining elements of Chicano/a identity. The film scrutinizes contemporary media images of ethnic deviance—the present-day equivalents of the bandido stereotype—but it does not posit the transcendent Chicano/a hero as antidote. Instead, Day intertextualizes Paredes's "With His Pistol in His Hand"—and several other texts—and imagines a Chicano/a unburdened by the demand to uphold cultural essence but still capable of contesting historical and popular cultural discourses that deprecatorily define Mexican Americans. Come and Take It Day exemplifies the importance of seeing beyond a perceived fixity in the representation of race, ethnicity, and masculinity. Thirty an' Seen A Lot is also concerned with historical matters, and like Come and Take It Day, its geographical focus is San Antonio and the Mexican presence in that city's downtown. Vigil proposes that the transformation of San Antonio into a tourist mecca threatens to erase its Mexican presence, even as San Antonio's Mexican character becomes a selling point for the tourist industry. Ultimately, both Vigil and Mendiola reinscribe Mexican American identity and history in ways that are self-reflective and empowering in the face of historical, media, and popular cultural erasure.

A Brief and Argumentative History of Chicano/a Cinema

Chicano cinema emerged during the late sixties as part of the Chicano/a Movement for civil rights and, from its beginnings, stood in opposition to dominant Anglo-American culture. In my analysis, the developmental trajectory of Chicano/a cinema exhibits four distinctly identifiable and sometimes overlapping phases, with Come and Take It Day signaling a recent move toward a contingent cultural expression that nevertheless continues the practices of oppositionality and critique so important within the tradition. Rosa Linda Fregoso broadly defines Chicano cinema's chief function as "the documentation of social reality through oppositional forms of knowledge about

Chicanos" (*Bronze Screen*, xxiv–xv). From its inception, Chicano/a cinema has engaged the politics of identity formation, expressed opposition to forms of oppression, and sought solidarity with other revolutionary cinemas, mainly Latin American New Cinema. While the notion that Chicano/a cinema embodies "oppositional forms of knowledge" provides a basic understanding of Chicano/a filmic practice, it can also be misleading, for oppositionality assumes that Chicano/a culture is ideologically opposed to dominant Anglo-American culture in every instance. Still, the Chicano/a Movement, with its revolutionary calls for a transformation in U.S. society's treatment of Mexican Americans, certainly influenced an oppositional perspective. During the 1970s, a series of critical essays of Hollywood stereotypes about Chicanos/as and Latinos/as set the tone for the emerging Chicano/a cinema.[1] The resulting cinematic expression therefore often contains a binary quality that negates all things Anglo-American, despite its engagement with American culture. Chon Noriega identifies the "anxiety over 'Gringo' influences as the force that led Chicanos to seek models in the Mexican and Cuban revolutions" (145).

A character of oppositionality, then, describes one dimension of Chicano/a cinema. Because of its location in the U.S. economic frame, and because of Chicano/a culture's interaction and interchange with American culture, Chicano/a cinema expresses oppositionality *and* rapprochement. "From the start . . . Chicano cinema has had to mark out a space for itself between a weapon and a formula, between the political weapon of New Latin American Cinema and the economic formula of Hollywood. Too often, however, these two practices are seen as mutually exclusive, rather than as the thesis and antithesis of a cinematic dialectic at work in the Americas" (Noriega, 149). Critics and filmmakers, because of the need to maintain solidarity with the Chicano/a Movement, have often elided the relationship with a broader American culture that Chicano/a artistic production—cinematic or otherwise—expresses. The Chicano/a elision of the engagement with American culture is understandable—Mexican Americans have long suffered discrimination in U.S. society and continue to experience denied entry in the American culture industry[2]—but contemporarily, we are beginning to understand that Chicano/a artistic production in the United States articulates hybridity rather than purity, contingency rather than essentialism.

Mexican American culture translates the notion of hybridity as *mestizaje*, the term for the historical blending of indigenous and Spanish cultural elements that were initiated more than five hundred years ago at the time of the Spanish conquest of the Americas. During the 1960s and 1970s, the "end result of the concept [of mestizaje] was a neoindigenism that sought an alternative to European and Anglo American influences" (Noriega, "Between a Weapon," 150). Consequently, critical accounts of Chicano/a culture that emphasized resistance to American culture tended to do so at the cost of fixing Chicano/a identity within a timeless and unchanging indigenous matrix. To be sure, the identification with indigeneity was due to a complex set of circumstances that began as a response to the original Spanish conquest and denigration of Mesoamerican peoples. Taking their cue from the indigenous ideologies of the Mexican Revolution—including the declaration that to be *mexicano* was to be a *mestizo*, with an emphasis on the Indian side—Chicano/a activists and artists declared their Indianness in response to the Euro-American erasure of their native ethnicity.[3]

Contemporarily, perhaps because of gains made to secure civil rights and full citizenship, Chicanos/as are more confident in acknowledging the diverse blendings that occur when cultures meet, including Mexican-Anglo mixings. Of course, the mestizaje of Mexican and Anglo cultures goes back to their first contacts, but during the twentieth century we see examples of it from the big-band sounds embraced by Zoot-suiters during the 1940s to the punk and heavy metal beats adapted in the 1980s.[4] These twentieth-century meldings are not the signs of an assimilationist impulse, but evidence of an acquisitive and adaptive culture, ready to use the tools at its disposal to forge new Chicano/a identities.[5] Most recently, films such as *Come and Take It Day* express hybridity as a way to critique monological cultural attitudes and as a way of claiming a rightful space for Chicanos/as in contemporary society. For Chicanos/as, mestizaje/hybridity becomes a strategy for expressing cultural change without losing cultural specificity.

We may witness these more inclusive transformations in Chicano/a self-conception—a move from essentialism to contingency—by briefly examining two films from the first phase of Chicano/a cinema, Luis Valdez's *I Am Joaquin* (Teatro Campesino, 1969), which is regarded as the first Chicano/a film, and Sylvia Morales's *Chicana* (1979), the feminist response to *Joaquin*. These films "frame the cultural and national period and together delineate its historical, political and aesthetic vision" while they "set forth a worker-based ideology and cultural identity that are rooted in a pre-Columbian mythopoetics and the 500-year history of *mestizo* resistance" (Noriega, 156). In other words, these films fix identity within essentialist conceptions of culture.

In *I Am Joaquin*, Luis Valdez adapts and visually narrates Corky Gonzalez's Chicano/a Movement poem of the same title. In 1967, when Gonzalez wrote "I Am Joaquin," the poem instantly became an emblem of Chicano/a Movement politics, with its defiant call to revolution and urgent exploration of Chicano/a identity. While the poem's message ultimately puts the Chicano/a in an either/or bind vis-à-vis the culture's relation to Anglo-American society—Joaquin must choose "Between the paradox of / Victory of the spirit" and "to exist in the grasp / of American social neurosis" (3)—the poem's importance lies, in the assessment of Rafael Pérez-Torres, in that it points to "the discontinuities that will mark the procession of Chicano culture . . . over the course of the next quarter century" (77).[6] In other words, the paradoxical bind the poem instantiates is paradigmatic of the continuing debates over cultural assimilation versus preservation within dominant society. Somehow, the film version of the poem is less indeterminate, and far more dogmatic than the poem, in its expression of cultural nationalism, and this is perhaps due to *I Am Joaquin*'s visual emphasis. The film uses camera movement to bring still photographs to life and combines music with Valdez's reading of "I Am Joaquin." Valdez chooses journalistic photographs of the Chicano/a Movement, stock photography of urban plight and pollution, and historical images from Mexican history and culture (mural art, ancient artifacts, Mexican revolutionary photographs) to tell an agonistic story of the Chicano/a experience in the United States. Because Valdez reads the poem in a defiant monotone, the viewer is left with a sense that Mexican American culture is statically resistant to Anglo-American culture. In Noriega's analysis, Valdez's "stentorian voice overpowers the poem's occasional irony and ambiguity" (157). *Joaquin*, therefore, marks an early insistence on fixity in the construction of Chicano/a identity.

Sylvia Morales's *Chicana* attempts to debunk the overvaluation of the Chicano warrior hero instantiated by Valdez's masculinist aesthetics, but it simultaneously relies on a mythic construction of Chicana identity. I agree with Rosa Linda Fregoso that *Chicana* is critical of culturally hegemonic practices within as well as outside of Chicano/a culture, but her claim that the film's "epic account refuses the tendency to idealize the Aztecs and offers instead a critical revision of our lineage" is belied by *Chicana*'s romantic invocation of the matrilineality of indigenous Mesoamerican cultures ("Chicana Film Practices," 172). Compared to *Joaquin*, the film makes a stronger argument for Chicanas' vital contributions to the Chicano/a Movement and for their work in preserving Chicano/a culture. *Chicana* critiques masculine expectations of woman's place in the domestic sphere, and in this respect it de-essentializes woman's subjectivity. And while Valdez's film is often tendentious in its approach to Chicano/a identity, Morales uses humor, irony, and understatement to subtly stretch the possibilities of Chicana self-conception. Yet while *Chicana* unhinges the Movement's strict masculine/feminine axis, it troublingly re-essentializes Chicana identity with its reliance on originary notions about Aztec matrilineal society. In effect, *Chicana* takes too many liberties with pre-Columbian history, shaping it to the film's admittedly laudable political ends.

We should not, of course, lose sight of *Chicana*'s significant contribution to Chicano/a cinema. It establishes a Chicana cinematic discourse that is "markedly counter-aesthetic" because it critiques "two kinds of discourses: the dominant culture's, which has distorted the Chicana subject; and the aesthetic discourse of Chicano males," which has often refused to give Chicanas a voice (171). Nevertheless, any counter-aesthetics must be watchful of not reversing and re-inscribing its object of critique. While *Chicana* offers a critique of Chicano masculinity, it too closely mirrors *I Am Joaquin*'s mystification of Chicano/a subjectivity.

As I have noted, films made at the height of the Chicano/a Movement attempt to present an essentialized culture because one of the Movement's greatest concerns was to affirm Chicano/a culture in the wake of Anglo domination. By the 1980s, with the Movement losing momentum, Chicano/a cinema moved more and more toward the mainstream, engaging in increasingly high degrees of professionalization and taking on increasingly close connections with Hollywood (Noriega, 145). The 1980s mark another important milestone in Chicano/a cultural production, for it is arguable that at this moment film begins to articulate a more contingent Chicano/a identity. In 1981, Luis Valdez released *Zoot Suit*, the first Chicano/a-directed Hollywood film. *Zoot Suit* begins the second period of Chicano/a cinema, and it stands at a midpoint between the essentialism of the Chicano/a Movement and the contingency that is to characterize later cultural productions. Thus Valdez, who has directed independently as well as within Hollywood, bridges the transformation between essentialist and contingent expressions of identity.

Narrated in musical form, *Zoot Suit* is the story of the 1942 Sleepy Lagoon trial, in which several Mexican American youths were convicted of the murder of one of their own. The story is told against the backdrop of the Zoot Suit riots in Los Angeles, when American sailors violently attacked Mexican American youth for what was perceived as an un-American fashion statement—the wearing of the colorful and excessive zoot suit.[7] In both form and content, *Zoot Suit* embodies a hybrid cultural formation: it takes a Chicano/a play and adapts it to the American musical, and it explores the contours of an emergent Mexican American youth culture during the 1940s. Yet not all critics have labeled *Zoot Suit* a hybrid production. Fregoso, for instance, argues that the film's "production of cultural identity is grounded in an 'archaeology'" (*Bronze Screen*, 36), a term she borrows from Stuart Hall. In "Cultural Identity and Cinematic Representation," Hall delineates two modes in the formation of cultural identity: the first, based on an "archaeology," unproblematically recovers identity based on static and past configurations; the second formation, which Hall privileges, is based on an "imaginative rediscovery" of identity, which is grounded in the present circumstances of culture even as it acknowledges the influence of past traditions on the formation of identity (Hall, 220–36). Fregoso argues that *Zoot Suit* recapitulates an outmoded and over-masculinized Chicano identity.

Although the film tends to essentialize Mexican masculinity, its representation of Chicano/a identity cannot be relegated to a reductive "archaeology." The subject of *Zoot Suit* is, after all, Chicano/a youth culture in rebellion against the Mexican nationalism and traditionalism of a previous generation. Additionally, the film depicts a cultural moment dominated not so much by "originary" inclinations as by hybrid articulations: the *pachuco* protagonist borrows the zoot suit fashion from African American youth culture, while he blends American big-band swing—with its own cultural antecedents in African American jazz—with Latin rhythms. Therefore, if *Zoot Suit* explores, for instance, Aztec mythology, it does so not to recapture an unattainable past, but to acknowledge the residual influence of this mythology on cultural formation. Furthermore, the film's purposefully uncertain ending—we are left, in the final sequence, to ponder the protagonist's fate—reveals that the future of Chicano/a identity is always open and waiting to be written. These cinematic moves characterize identity formations that gesture toward de-essentialism rather than fixity.

Robert M. Young's *The Ballad of Gregorio Cortez* (1982), discussed in the previous chapter, is the first motion picture to tell the story of Gregorio Cortez's legendary resistance to the Anglo-Texan authority at the turn of the century. Although Américo Paredes's *"With His Pistol in His Hand"* (1958) serves as textual inspiration, the film itself weakly presents Cortez's heroism. Nevertheless, *Ballad* deserves a measure of recognition for bringing together a multiethnic collaborative spirit to the making of independent features that deal with these kinds of subjects. The original screenplay, while finally used, was written by a notable Chicano/a novelist, Victor Villaseñor, and the film was produced by Moctezuma Esparza, the most prominent Chicano/a producer of his time. When it aired on PBS in 1982, it was the first Chicano/a-produced movie in the American Playhouse series, so it paved the way for future Hispanic filmmakers, including Jimmy Mendiola.

American Me (1991), directed by Edward James Olmos, closes the second phase of Chicano/a film history, and its importance lies in being the first Chicano/a-directed film to explore notions of hybridity from the perspective of a cultural formation rather than an ethnic formation. *American Me* confronts the possibility that a non-Mexican may participate in lived Chicano/a culture. In the film, J.D. (William Forsythe) is a gang member living in East Los Angeles who, despite his perceived white ethnic identity, calls himself a Chicano/a because he inhabits the particular social and cultural space of a Mexican American neighborhood. In a moment that tellingly expresses the complexity of his hybrid cultural formation, a member of an opposing white gang is confused about the fact that J.D. "talks like a Chicone." J.D.'s response, "La Primera, ese [The First, man]"—his gang neighborhood identification—demonstrates that cultural identity is neither transcendent nor pure, for his affiliation is cultural rather than ethnic/racial.

The third phase of Chicano/a cinema begins in the mid-nineties when, due to very limited opportunity within Hollywood, the most visible films exploring Chicano/a identity simply regurgitate a congratulatory and apolitical multiculturalist ideology. Such is the case with Gregory Nava's *Mi Familia/My Family* (1995), *Selena* (1997), and the recent PBS-produced series, *American Family* (2002). The Chicano/a identity these films express is premised on the initial proclamation of the culture's "unique" features (superstitious practices, boisterous family dynamics), on the commemoration of the culture's suffering in its acculturation to U.S. society, and on the conclusion that Chicanos/as are, in the end, "American" (they value family, they want success). These films' celebrations of the Chicano/a culture's distinctiveness are reminiscent of the Texas folklorists that Américo Paredes long ago criticized for carrying a "romantic point of view [that] deals not with living things but with idealizations of them" ("Folklore," 17). The films' tendency to romanticize and to emphasize unusual cultural elements—what Paredes called "local color"—eviscerates Chicano/a cinema's historically critical relation to mainstream culture. The result of these films' celebration of Chicanos/as' Americanness is a loss of the distinctiveness of Chicano/a culture.

In the foregoing, I have provided a schematic overview of the first three phases of Chicano/a cinema because my greatest interest is with what is, in my estimation, a fourth phase in Chicano/a filmmaking. This final period, which overlaps with phases two and three, is characterized by contingency, playfulness, and a critique of American modernity; it evokes Chicano/a Movement films, but without the Movement's complete denial of a monolithic Anglo-American culture. Fourth-phase cinema self-reflexively appropriates Hollywood's generic conventions and transforms them in a critical fashion; it is an independent cinema because its expressive concerns deal with localized subjects outside the ken of Hollywood's marketing imperatives; it is internationalist, drawing upon hemispheric filmmaking traditions. And finally, fourth-phase films are often shot on video and may be short format.

Chicano/a film critics have recognized some of these stylistic and thematic elements in the work of Mexican, Chicano/a, and Latino/a artists, but this latest moment in independent filmmaking is as yet unrecognized as a new movement proper. Perhaps this new phase does not need to be called a movement—perhaps we need to only recognize its loose constellation of common representational strategies. Nonetheless, film critics have taken notice of such filmmakers as Lourdes Portillo, whom Chon Noriega notes has contributed to "the development of an alternative Chicana/Latina film practice, challenging assumptions about an essential subject, style, and genre for the female, ethnic, and bicultural filmmaker" (Noriega, *Shot in America*, 187). Films that fit the fourth-phase aesthetic include Sylvia Morales's *Esperanza* (1985), Carlos Avila's *Distant Water* (1990), Jim Mendiola's *Pretty Vacant* (1996), Guillermo Gómez Peña's *Border Brujo* (1990) and *The Great Mojado Invasion, Part 2* (2001), Sergio Arau's *A Day Without a Mexican* (2004), and Hector Galan's *Los Lonely Boys: Cottonfields and Crossroads* (2006).

In a critical move similar to that of Noriega and others, Charles Ramírez Berg has identified a "resistant form of postmodern" cultural expression in recent Chicano/a documentaries. Ramírez Berg calls this a Mexican American postmodernism, characterized by "fragmentation, heterogeneity, hybridity, an ironic relation to the past, and a healthy skepticism about the master narratives of progress, liberation, and science" ("El Genio," 75–76). He avers, additionally, that "nearly all Chicano filmmakers—whether they work in fiction or film—are border documentarians in that their films almost always refer back to their Mexican roots, directly or indirectly juxtaposing their heritage with their current U.S. existence" (76). In the following discussion, I argue that *Come and Take It Day* exemplifies fourth-phase Chicano/a cinema, for it explores a specific aspect of Chicano/a identity in a manner that is self-reflexive, intertextually nuanced, and critical of the continually changing relation between Chicanos/as and U.S. modernity.

Contingency and Hybridity in Come and Take It Day

Jim Mendiola's *Come and Take It Day* first appeared as a work in progress in the spring of 2001, when it debuted at the Américo Paredes Annual Conference at the University of Texas at Austin. Its presentation at a conference dedicated to Paredes was a strategic move, for the film is heavily indebted to Paredes's contributions to our understanding of Mexican American culture and identity. Even in rough form, the movie's ironic and humorous explorations of contemporary Mexican American identity struck a chord with the audience. *Come and Take It Day* is the story of two cousins, Jesse and Miguel, who believe they are descendants of Gregorio Cortez. Jesse in particular feels that he and Miguel are the rightful heirs to the lost treasure of Gregorio Cortez, the $1,000 in silver that was supposedly given to Jesús González, "El Teco," for leading the authorities to Cortez. In their complicated quest for the lost treasure, the cousins make a painful realization about their identities, and Miguel is tragically shot by a Texas Ranger.

The film, which is told from multiple perspectives as first-person interviews by several characters, is divided into three titled sections—"First Day," "Discovery Day," and "Come and Take It Day"—but it begins with an untitled prologue that provides a tight synopsis of the film's narrative and thematic concerns. The film's prologue, which is almost three minutes long, initially follows the conventional style of an investigative documentary film, with Jesse (Jesse Borrego) providing an unseen interviewer with information about the death of Miguel (Jacob Vargas). The film's first shot frames Jesse's head and shoulders and maintains the camera in a fixed position. About one minute in duration, this relatively long opening shot establishes that Jesse blames himself for Miguel's death. At this point, the viewer expects a run-of-the-mill mystery, told in the slow, methodical style of an investigative documentary. But then the movie launches into a montage sequence in which technical proficiency is only eclipsed by thematic richness. Employing an extremely fast-paced editing technique and a heavy metal soundtrack, the remaining two minutes of prologue—composed of almost ninety separate shots—introduce the film's dominant themes: the hybrid and contingent character of Chicano/a identity; the critique of the U.S. media's construction of Latino males as deviant; the commodification of Mexican American culture in San Antonio; the fragmentation of Chicanos/as along class lines; and the constructed and ideological nature of "history" and "truth."

One of Day's central concerns is to investigate the constituents of contemporary Chicano/a hybridity and contingency. We see this in the initial scene of "First Day," when Miguel and Nena (Maria Candelaria) first meet. Miguel wears the typical heavy metal outfit that defines many young working-class San Antonians—blue jeans, a black Black Sabbath T-shirt, biker boots, and a studded leather bracelet. Additionally, because he enjoys flowers, he earlier placed a Texas bluebonnet over his right ear. Nena, who is a savvy future graduate student (on her way to Berkeley), notices these juxtapositions and comments, "[t]hat's an interesting neo-hippie-*pachuco* thing you've got going there." The remark, which confuses Miguel because he is not as well educated as Nena, reveals that hybridity is a notion that is both constantly articulated and always questioned within Chicano/a culture. (The disjunction between Nena's high academic analysis and Miguel's blank expression also exposes the dangers of mystifying culture in academic jargon, as well as the rarely acknowledged class differences within Chicano/a communities.)

That Chicano/a culture is defined by hybridity or mestizaje may be a foregone conclusion for some, but this should not lead us to surmise that the film invokes hybridity in a merely celebratory fashion. Instead, *Come and Take It Day* articulates a critical Chicano/a hybridity. We see this critical stance during Miguel and Jesse's visit to the "Come and Take It Day" celebrations at Fort Walker in Gonzales, Texas. Miguel walks into a local convenience store looking for, among other things, rolling papers, and while he is browsing through various Texas tourist store knickknacks, an Anglo family enters the shop. As they happily handle and try on the merchandise, a twangy country song plays in the background. For Miguel, the experience is momentarily unnerving. The Chicano *metalero* looks uncomfortable and out of place in the tourist shop. He turns to a mirror in the store, as if comparing himself to the family. As he studies himself from head to toe, he straightens his posture and smiles mischievously. He then picks up a Davy Crockett coonskin cap, a disposable camera, and, incongruously, a sticker of Emiliano Zapata from a bubblegum pack. Sticking the image of Zapata to the coonskin cap, he puts on the hat and, walking over to Jesse, declares himself a "neo-*turista* hybrid," echoing Nena's earlier remark. The scene critiques the unconscious acceptance and mass consumption of Texas myths by cutting between Miguel's rebellious appropriation and the family's innocent usage of the cap, and it shows the oppositional and playful potential of hybrid expressions of identity.[8]

If, as I have noted, Chicano/a cinema of the sixties and seventies affirmed Chicano/a identity through essentialist notions of culture, *Come and Take It Day* affirms identity by asserting identity's contingent status. Much of the Movement's discursive practices were predicated on invocations of a reclamation of Chicanos'/as' Aztec origins, and Norma Alarcón recollects the "quest for a true self and identity which was the initial desire of many writers involved in the Chicano movement of the late 1960s and early 1970s." Contemporarily, Chicano/a expressive culture gives way "to the realization that there is no fixed identity" ("Chicana Feminism," 250). Chicano/a contingency acknowledges "the complex and multiple ways in which the subject . . . is constituted," as well as the "discourses that transverse consciousness and which the subject must struggle with constantly" ("Theoretical Subject[s]," 34, 38). Contemporary Chicano/a identity, therefore, does not emerge from a fixed past formation, but from the particular socio-cultural spaces and discourses the subject inhabits.

In *Come and Take It Day*, the concept of contingency revises the two protagonists' vision of an unassailable and essential self-identity. Jesse and Miguel believe that they are the great-great-grandsons of none other than Gregorio Cortez, the Tejano folk hero. Thus, their vision of themselves is alloyed by an assumption of implicit masculine agency, and perhaps this assumption has led them, ironically, to a degree of laxity in the affirmation of their culture. While doing genealogical research, however, Jesse discovers that his heroic lineage is false. A cynical self-taught intellectual, Jesse narrates that his family's "Cortez myth always bothered me; [it was] a bit too convenient in its brown nobility." What Jesse discovers is that the narrative of his family's heroic pedigree is an essentialist myth. Yet more shockingly, he learns that he and Miguel are actually the great-great-grandsons not of Gregorio Cortez, but of Jesús González, "El Teco"—the man who, according to the Cortez legend, turned Cortez in to the Texas Rangers for one thousand dollars in silver. The scene in which Jesse delivers the news to Miguel is both humorous and unsettling, un uncanny moment of (mis)recognition (fig. 10).

> JESSE: El Teco, the *vendido* Judas narc? The dude's our great grandfather.
>
> MIGUEL: Shut up, no he's not.
>
> JESSE: *En serio.*
>
> MIGUEL: He's not!

A sustained pause follows this exchange as Miguel struggles to come to terms with his imagined self-conception. Fortunately, it does not take long for either Miguel or Jesse to incorporate this new interpretation of their lineage, since their day-to-day existence as Chicanos/as is already defined by a cultural formation that is hybrid rather than pure, contingent rather than essential.

The representation of hybridity and contingency are instantiated within a filmic discourse that maintains a critical stance vis-à-vis a dominant culture that, in ambivalent fashion, simultaneously construes Chicano males as stereotypically deviant and commodifies Mexican American culture as part of San Antonio's tourist industry. In the film, Miguel's mistaken killing by a Texas Ranger is justified because he was a metalero who happened to be fascinated by an infamous serial killer, Richard Ramírez. As a working-class Chicano/a practicing an alternative lifestyle, Miguel lives on the margins of society. In Nena's version of the story, she tells her audience—a graduate class at Berkeley—that "they [the authorities and the media] painted him as this drug-dealing, heavy metal-loving social deviant." Yet as Jesse makes clear, Miguel's life choices expressed an oppositional stance: "It was Richard Ramírez the media figure that Miguel was into, rather than Richard Ramírez the serial killer. . . . It was political, man! The night-stalker's transgressive

FIGURE 10. Jesse (Jesse Borrego) and Miguel (Jacob Vargas) in *Come and Take It Day* (CTD Pictures, 2002) (DVD frame enlargement).

Latino presence in the *gringo* media? Miguel dug that. Plus, you know they were both big AC/DC fans." *Day*'s critique of the media's construction and conflation of negative stereotypes about Latinos/as takes place from the very space of imputed deviance: Jesse and Miguel embrace their marginal status and use it oppositionally. By refusing to conform to mainstream American or middle-class Mexican American norms, the characters are doubly transgressive.

Come and Take It Day shows, furthermore, that the marginalization of Chicanos/as—especially working-class Chicanos/as—occurs even as San Antonio's Mexican American heritage undergoes a process of Disney-fication. Jesse, Miguel, and Nena work at a café on San Antonio's River Walk. The movie's opening sequence shows Miguel walking to work as a tour boat glides along in the river next to him. As the tour guide narrates the river's history and related trivia—we hear the tour guide ask, "Did anyone see the movie *Selena?*"—a gawking tourist photographs Miguel. Though he looks somewhat out of place in his backwards cap and heavy metal clothes, he obliges her by posing and waving the "Ozzy" sign.[9] The scene succinctly establishes the relation between Mexican Americans and tourism in San Antonio: they are either part of the scenery or part of the infrastructure that supports the industry, yet they are not allowed to narrate their own history—the tour guide tells their story for them. Provocatively, Miguel's dress and actions in this scene subvert the act of culture-collecting that the tourist attempts, for Miguel does not quite fit within the tour guide's tidy narrative.

In several other instances, *Day* mocks the concept of San Antonio as a tourist destination. While arguing with Nena about his plans to move to Thailand, Jesse tells her that at least that country "has never been colonized, which is more than I can say for this remember-the-Alamo, Sea World, buy-a-sombrero tourist attraction of a town." Jesse's derisive comment implies that San Antonio's Mexican heritage has been so commercialized that its cultural significance has weakened for many Mexican Americans. Further, the film's instantiation of the commodification of the Mexican heritage against the backdrop of Chicano/a deviance signals the dominant culture's ambivalent relation to Chicanos/as: it desires the economic benefit of marketing the Mexican heritage, but it attempts to contain Mexicans' presence and agency.

The commodification of Mexican American culture and the construction of Chicano/a deviance are accompanied by a fragmentation of the Chicano/a community. This deterioration occurs along class lines as they are defined by levels of education, and it also happens through implied racial hierarchies. In an interview, Mendiola specifically discusses class conflict within the Chicano/a community: "I used to work in a tourist restaurant. . . . Mainly Mexican Americans worked there. It was an interesting dynamic that happened when these educated brown college people would come and work for the summer among the working-class and some really poor people, who were the dishwashers. There was a certain hierarchy based on class" ("Pedal"). We see Mendiola's class analysis in the representation of the relationship between Jesse and Miguel and their boss, Carlos (Rick Delgado), on Nena's first day at work. Carlos gives Nena a tour of the restaurant and warns her to watch out for the cooks and the busboys, whom he labels "oversensitive *vatos*" and "drug-dealing punks." When Nena asks to see the dish room, Carlos quickly turns her away with the words, "third world, forget it." Class divisions among Chicanos/as—which also reflect, in this last example, the reproduction of racialized neocolonial relations between first and third worlds—is evidenced in other ways. For instance, Miguel recounts to Nena that while Jesse and Carlos were once good friends, Carlos's family eventually "moved to the north side [of San Antonio] to get away from the negative influence—us."[10] By "us," Miguel means Jesse and himself, but also working-class Mexican Americans, some of whom are given the label of "deviant."

As I have suggested, *Come and Take It Day* also represents the fragmentation of the Chicano/a community along levels of educational achievement that usually accompany class divisions. In the film, Nena is a college-educated, graduate school–bound Chicana who purports to understand Chicano/a culture better than Jesse and Miguel. For instance, after being caught snooping in Jesse's journal, Nena sheepishly explains, "I was fascinated by your words. . . . The ones suggesting a postcolonial critique." She makes a reference to Américo Paredes and other cultural theorists as a way of proving her cultural capital. Though Jesse perfectly understands her and is intimately familiar with the work of Paredes, Nena uses academic language as a way to demonstrate her superiority. Jesse and Miguel, however, make clear that they are not taken in by her fancy words. In another scene, Miguel turns the tables on her by exposing her unexamined elitism.

MIGUEL: Why do you talk like that?

NENA: Talk like what?

MIGUEL: You know, "Gauguin," "Sahiba colors," show-off words.

NENA: Do I sound condescending?

MIGUEL: You mean, do you make me feel stupid?

NENA: [Silence.]

MIGUEL: Sometimes. But I know you don't mean it.

In this scene, *Day* once again uses humor to point out that while education is certainly a worthwhile goal, it can often divide Chicanos/as.

Perhaps *Day*'s most important contribution to contemporary Chicano/a cinema is its playful exposing of the constructed and ideological nature of discourses, in whatever form those discourses may appear—whether as documentary or narrative films; as "historical," "truthful," or "fictional" accounts of events; or as cultural symbols, such as the Alamo. In its prologue, *Day* explores the truth-making tendencies of the documentary form by couching its narrative as a series of documentary interviews investigating the reasons for Miguel's death. It also makes references, through Nena's commentary, to the narrative film adaptation of the events associated with Miguel's death: "it all started that first day of summer—the movie got that part right, at least." Throughout its narrative, *Day* leads the viewer to question and revise the veracity/fictiveness of the discourses within which it participates and upon which it comments.

While Chicanos/as' artistic expression has always challenged the notion of "history" as written by the dominant culture, *Day* radically turns the question inward. Chon Noriega writes that Chicano/a film asks, "How can Chicanos depict history when historians, journalists, and Hollywood have either distorted, censored, or repressed the history of the Chicano experience?"

(Noriega, "Between a Weapon and a Formula," 153). Chicano/a cinema has responded by producing a "historical discourse [that] operates within a bicultural logic that informs, undercuts, or otherwise engages 'History.' Films may draw upon culture-based, alternative forms of history telling, as in the *corrido*" (153). *Come and Take It Day* takes particular questions of history and confronts Chicanos/as with them. For instance, in the account of Gregorio Cortez's resistance to the Texas Rangers, what heterogeneous interpretations has Cortez's story taken in the Chicano/a community? Nena's version of the story assumes a critical historicism and places it within the academic discourse of postcolonial studies: "June, 1901. Gregorio and his brother sharecropped a small ranch in Gonzales, Texas. . . . [Cortez's actions against the sheriff were a case of the] subaltern's challenge to the colonial power." Jesse's retelling, meanwhile, is far more politically fraught: "For the *raza*, it was a rare instance of sticking it to the *gringo*." Carlos's revision of the story demonstrates contemporary forgetfulness: "You know, [Cortez was] the dude who evaded the Texas Rangers. . . . [He] fled to Mother Mexico." Not knowing that Cortez was a Tejano, Carlos assumes he was an immigrant.

Mendiola's marshalling of different interpretations of an event recalls such classic films as Akira Kurosawa's *Rashomon* (1950), but rather than commenting on the undecideability of truth, *Day* argues that the construction of history depends on the discursive communities within which one participates, as well as the power relations within these communities. In terms of its own engagement with Gregorio Cortez's story, *Come and Take It Day* suggests that Chicanos/as must actively participate in the story's preservation and dissemination, for Cortez is a crucial part of Chicano/a self-identity. The presence of Cortez in Chicanos/as' self-identity does not imply an essentialist abstraction like Jesse and Miguel's during the first half of the story; rather, the account of Cortez's resistance informs contemporary understandings of community and history. The film cautions against Jesse's early romanticism, but it also warns against Carlos's historical amnesia. If, in the days of Gregorio Cortez, the corrido was a dominant narrative form, then *Day* makes a space for contemporary forms such as film—and in Miguel's version of the story, the graphic novel—to produce knowledge about Mexican American history.

Come and Take It Day's inward emphasis on questions of history accompanies a broader critique of dominant culture's interpretation of history and truth about Chicanos/as. Like the Movement films before it, *Day* "sustain[s] an intertextual dialogue with previous Hollywood representation," but it does not limit its critique to the film medium (Noriega, 153). I have already referenced the film's questioning of the documentary's truth-making tendencies, as well as its assessment of the media's construction of Chicano male deviancy. *Day* also humorously comments on the proliferation of "real-life" book exposés and sensationalistic journalism. Nena refers to a made-for-TV movie and calls the written account of Miguel's death, *Sex, Silver & Sin!* a "constructed mythology." Carlos has cashed in on the "option" to his version of the events, written by "the dude who did the JonBenet Ramsey movie rewrite." Jesse, meanwhile, has written a memoir, *Notes of a 'Beatnick Spic'*. Finally, the Spanish-language Mexican tabloid *¡Alarma!* has published a huge exposé on the events surrounding Miguel's death. The reproduction of these humorous intertexts within the movie suggests a media establishment out of control in its appropriation of Chicano/a history.

The most powerful symbol—both mythic and historical—of Anglo-Texan dominance in San Antonio and the rest of Texas is the Alamo, and in *Come and Take It Day* the shrine to Texas liberty becomes fodder for hilarious critique. During a day off work, Jesse and Miguel decide to take in some sights in the San Antonio area, and they playfully discuss some possible destinations.

MIGUEL: So let's be *turistas* today.

JESSE: *Órale*, we're on vacation, right?

MIGUEL: Yeah, vacation.

JESSE: Where do you want to go, the Alamo?

MIGUEL: *Chale*, forget the Alamo!

The expression "forget the Alamo" may or may not be an intertextual wink at the well-known line from John Sayles's *Lone Star* (1995).[11] In any case, the phrase criticizes the Alamo's ideologically heavy-handed uses to remind Mexicans of Anglo-Texas's domination. This ideological critique of the Alamo is one of the many ways in which, per Charles Ramírez Berg's assessment of postmodern Chicano/a cinema, *Come and Take It Day* "questions not only the past but also . . . dominant political structures" (85).

While *Come and Take It Day* contests dominant culture's interpretations of history and truth, the film nevertheless embraces Chicano/a participation in and dialogue with Anglo-American culture. Unlike Chicano/a Movement films, which reject the dominant culture and deny Hollywood's influences, *Day* confidently appropriates non-Chicano/a cultural forms as part of its aesthetic. For instance, rather than adhering to a Mexican-derived musical tradition for its soundtrack, *Day* employs heavy metal music to give the narrative a gritty, pulsating feel and a contemporary Chicano/a flavor. The use of this musical genre may hint at cultural assimilation, but within the film's context, heavy metal signals the distinctive and oppositional character of San Antonio's working-class Chicano/a culture. Heavy metal does not, however, displace the corrido as the valued form of musical expression.[12] Consistent with its concern for preserving the story of Gregorio Cortez, *Day* ends with a corrido about Miguel's death.

As stated previously, first- through third-phase Chicano/a films often express anxiety vis-à-vis their relation to Hollywood. Fourth-phase films such as *Day*, on the other hand, self-consciously and playfully exploit the film industry's formal conventions. *Day* structures its narrative using classical Hollywood cinema's three-act structure. Like Hollywood's narrative style, *Day*'s narrative "depends on the assumption that the action will spring primarily from *individual characters as causal agents*. . . . the narrative invariably centers on personal psychological causes: decisions, choices, and traits of character" (Bordwell and Thompson, 108). Although *Come and Take It Day* obviously engages broader cultural and political themes, all the action in the narrative emerges from individual desires. As Jesse admits, it was his desire for revenge (against Carlos) that caused Miguel's demise. Desire foregrounds the film's investigation of cinematic narrative conventions. Without desire, there is no story, yet desire—for legitimacy, money, love—is the very element that causes the story to go horribly wrong for Jesse, Miguel, Nena, and Carlos. Ultimately, the film posits that desire is unavoidable, making stories possible and binding narratives across cultures.

While *Day*'s narrative follows a classic three-act structure, it also emulates the documentary form by replicating its investigative techniques, blurring the distinctions between fiction and reality. The film opens with talking heads of Jesse, Nena, and Carlos, each of whom has a different interpretation of events. Like a documentary in the tradition of *The Thin Blue Line* (Morris, 1988), the film builds tension and viewer interest by showing the different facets of the mystery. The documentary form, however, is not *Day*'s ultimate stylistic signature. As I have earlier pointed out, the film begins in the slow and methodical style of a documentary, but suddenly accelerates the narrative by using the quick editing style of a music video—and by adding a driving heavy metal soundtrack. In the space of two minutes during the prologue, the film makes almost ninety editing cuts, or about one per second. Clearly, then, *Day* is completely at ease in appropriating various narrative and formal techniques derived from classic Hollywood, independent documentary film, and even the highly stylized contemporary music video.

Furthermore, *Day* intertextualizes a broad array of films, especially its ethnic forebears. In the prologue, we overhear a tour guide ask, "Did anyone see the film *Selena*?" Miguel, meanwhile, makes reference to "Eddie Olmos" in *Zoot Suit* (Luis Valdez, 1981), repeating the pachuco's cool-cat expression,

"Órale!" And Nena provides a comparative analysis of *The Ballad of Gregorio Cortez* and the classic Blaxploitation film, *Sweet Sweetback's Baadasssss Song* (Van Peebles, 1971), stating that while both films deal with an ethnic subject on the run from white authority, "*Ballad* has this real passive [protagonist]. . . ." Obviously, she agrees with *Ballad's* critical reception. These allusions demonstrate *Day's* conscious dialogue with various American filmmaking traditions, particularly with other ethnic and politically conscious filmmakers.

While the most recent period in Chicano/a cinema expresses hybridity and contingency, the closing sequence of *Come and Take It Day* suggests that hybridity, contingency, and oppositionality cannot be restricted to cinematic representation. In the final sequence, Jesse makes his way along San Antonio's River Walk when he is photographed by a tourist, creating a parallel with the opening sequence with Miguel. As he is photographed, Jesse makes the "Ozzy" sign and angrily screams, "Remember Miguel, *cabrones* [assholes]!" Thus, we are asked to keep Miguel—and not the Alamo—in our memory of San Antonio's cultural history. Disturbingly, however, the film closes with Jesse's picture being placed in a photo album by the tourist who took it. As the album is closed, we glimpse its first page, which contains a photo of the Alamo. The scene fades to a shot of suburban idyll as the soundtrack plays the corrido about Miguel's death. What are we to make of this final, disquieting moment? Jesse's scream of protest signals Chicano/a culture's continued oppositionality to dominant narratives, but his circumscription within the photo album portends the ultimate victory of American capitalist modernity: the tourist succeeds in collecting the culture, and we are left in the safety and cultural homogeneity of the suburb. Yet the power of *Come and Take It Day's* troubling conclusion lies in taking the Chicano/a spectator out of the comfortable tendency to celebrate the culture's critical stance. In the final analysis, Jesse's confinement within the photo album suggests that while hybridity and contingency may open routes for critiquing dominant culture, only Chicanos/as' self-conscious, lived relation to American modernity and postmodernity carries the possibility of maintaining cultural specificity.

Evangelina Vigil: Recovering the Mexican American Presence

Evangelina Vigil, a poet who like Mendiola was born and raised in San Antonio, provides yet another avenue for remembering Miguel and other members of the Mexican American community who may otherwise go unnoticed in dominant histories and mainstream popular culture. Through her poetry, which contains an ethnographic quality for its ability to describe the details of daily life in San Antonio, Vigil reminds us of the important presence of Chicanos/as in the city's downtown. Vigil's poetry collection, *Thirty an' Seen a Lot* (1985), records the presence of the Mexican American population in a downtown area that, at the time of the collection's publication, was experiencing a transition from a somewhat sleepy shopping zone with mixed businesses to an increasingly sanitized tourist hotspot where large hotels and franchise restaurants could cater to middle-class tourists. Vigil's poems exist as simple recollections of places and people in a moment before they vanish in the wake of the booming tourist industry, whose only use for Mexicans is as dishwashers and bellhops for the downtown restaurants and hotels. In a way, the poems recount downtown as it existed before the characters who inhabit *Come and Take It Day* come to experience the postmodern city.

Thirty an' Seen a Lot has been praised for capturing the sounds and rhythms of the working-class, Mexican American population of the city during the late seventies and early eighties.[13] This period coincides with a moment in San Antonio's economic history when the downtown area was quickly growing and its planners were constructing the city's image—arguably ersatz—as a historically Mexican American, visitor-friendly town, a destination for conventioneers and honeymooners alike.[14] Vigil's poems are as much about seeing as they are about hearing. The poetic persona of *Thirty* is eyewitness to dramatic economic changes that slowly push the Mexican American population to the margins of the city's downtown, even as the city's Mexican American roots are celebrated and homogenized. Vigil takes the poetry right to the streets of downtown San Antonio and its environs to shape a vision of the fading-away of Mexican customs as they give way to the transformation of the city into a tourist magnet.

Yet even as Vigil records a certain cultural dissolution, her accounting for the Mexican presence in the heart of San Antonio also allows for the rememorizing and memorializing of the people pushed to the margins. One of the opening poems of the collection, "Spinning on Solid Ground," speaks to the feeling that everything solid—all the cultural forms, people, and places that a Mexican American woman growing up in San Antonio once knew—is melting into air.

No, ya no es como antes   No, it's not like before
todo ha cambiado   everything has changed
dice mi abuela   my grandmother says
suspirando   sighing
viendo   watching
marvelling [*sic*] at la   marveling at the

transformación	transformation
del centro, del Mercado—	of downtown, of the Marketplace—
cosas concretas y seguras	concrete and sure things
en mi espacio hueco	in my hollow space (4)[15]

In this poem, as in others, the poet borrows the voice of the older generation to aid in accounting for the changes taking place and in giving these historical texture. The changes in question occur in the traditionally Mexican American marketplace, *el mercado*, located downtown. In this and other poems, Mexican cultural forms and places are disappearing, giving way to a new and uncertain future. The marketplace is part of the cultural institutions that once felt "concretas y seguras [concrete and sure]," but that are now giving way to a sense of an "espacio hueco [hollow space]" in the narrator's imagination.

Several of Vigil's poems give us a visual tour of downtown, and in the spirit of Ralph Waldo Emerson's universal eye, Walt Whitman's wandering through New York City in "Walking to Brooklyn Fairy," William Carlos Williams's *Paterson*, or, most recently, Raul R. Salinas's remembrances of Austin in "Trip Through the Mindjail" and *East of the Freeway*, the reader is able to experience the sights and changes of downtown San Antonio as if walking with the narrator of the poems. In another poem, called "el mercado en San Antonio," "where the tourists trot," we see a particularly apt example of this roving witness to change, as the narrator relates that

el otro día	the other day
me levanté bien temprano	I woke up very early
y una buena caminada di	and took a good walk
por la plaza y el mercado	through the plaza and the
	marketplace (21)

The poem has a documentary, quotidian quality, but it also contains a sense of uncertainty in the face of change, for as it unfolds, the narrator begins her keen observations of the transformations of the downtown cityscape.

y luego como casi media hora	then for nearly half an hour
me pasé entretenida	I passed the time absorbed
viendo por entre vidrieras	looking into display cases
aterradas y pañosas	dusty and hazy
de tiendillas y boticas	of little shops and pharmacies
ya abandonadas	already abandoned
pero nunca olvidadas	but never forgotten

donde en años del pasado	where in years past
se vendían comics	comics were sold
anillos importados	imported rings
y velitas y novellas	little candles and novels
santitos y rosarios	saints and rosaries (21)

In this, the poem's second stanza, the narrator links present and past, noting a transitional moment in the cultural and economic history of downtown. The dusty shop windows the narrator gazes at are circa 1980s, and they can no longer be found today in downtown San Antonio. During the late 1980s, the city experienced a new boom in hotel construction after the rehabilitation and expansion of its famed River Walk/Paseo del Rio, as well as the addition of the Rivercenter Mall in 1988. Both of these are within a short walk of the Alamo and not far from the subject of the poem, el mercado. A small shop like the one described in the poem would have no place in the renewed city center.

"El mercado en San Antonio" becomes a record of the Mexican presence in the center of a city that is too willing to forget its Mexican population. The objects encountered behind the shop windows are distinctly Mexican cultural items, such as Catholic saints and rosaries, and candles with popular saints embossed on the glass. The narrator is like a child, enthralled by looking at the relics in the shop windows. The shops are abandoned, soon to be replaced by new tourist shops and restaurants. Significantly, the poem presents these objects as images already existing in the past, "abandoned / but never forgotten." The narrator expresses the need to keep these objects present, but acknowledges that they exist "en años del pasado [in years past]," without a promise of return, other than in memory.

As the narrator of "el mercado en San Antonio" reminisces about the changes wrought by time and the economic reorganization of downtown, she is suddenly brought back to the present, reminded more powerfully than ever that Mexicans are not completely erased from the city. A voice interrupts her ponderings; it is the polite yet firm pleading of a beggar.

dice la voz artificial	the artificial voice says
oiga, señorita,	listen, young lady
perdone la molestia	pardon the interruption
pero por casualidad	but by any chance
¿no traerá usted un nicle	would you happen to have a nickel
que me pueda dar?	you might give me? (21)

The voice is described as artificial, but only because it is foreign to the poet lost in thought. In actuality, the voice's cadence is simple, unhurried, and authentic in its own right. Surprised and taken out of her reverie, the narrator looks upon him.

y veo al señor	and I see the man
barbudo, flaco, hambreado, y crudo	bearded, thin, hungry, and hungover
adicto al licor	addicted to liquor
vagabundo solitario	lonely vagabond
perdido al mirar	lost to seeing (22)

Rather than reproducing the distance that is often seen in the encounter between the assumed middle-class subject and the homeless Other—especially an encounter in an urban setting—the ensuing exchange occurs on the basis of respect and equality between two individuals. The first hint of this equal relationship is in the reference to the *señor* of the poem. The narrator could have just as easily used *hombre* or another generic noun to identify the man, but instead she uses a word whose connotation of respect more closely approximates "sir," which is one of the English equivalents of "señor."

The idea that the man is "perdido al mirar [lost to seeing]" is a commentary on the general social unease that a man such as this may cause, yet the poet's universal eye accepts him and the circumstances that may have created him. Surprised that he would only ask for a nickel, the narrator is charmed by the man's simple act of perseverance and by his humility, so she gives him a quarter. The result of the encounter is that "él comprende el respeto / y yo la claridad cristal [he understands the respect / and I the crystal clarity]" (22). In other words, the man no longer escapes notice, for he and the narrator have reached a mutual recognition and understanding based on their shared humanity. The poem ends with a return to the location that inspired the narrator's thoughts and made possible the chance meeting with the homeless man.

el mercado queda	the marketplace is located
por la calle Produce Row	on Produce Row Street
y la plaza queda	and the plaza is located
en el corazón del centro	in the heart of downtown
por la calle Comercio	on Commerce Street
de Comercio y Soledad	at Commerce and Soledad (22)

The location given is precise. One can still return today to the exact corner where the narrator observes the dusty shop windows and where the man asks for a nickel. While the particular shops are long gone—and the man, too—the names of the streets remain, some of them as they are known to the local Mexican population.

The poem's ending is significant because it signals the condition of Mexican Americans in the city that was once their own. The poem concludes at the intersection of Commerce Street—a street that announces its commercial nature in its name—with Soledad—a name that literally translates to "solitude," but that also implies aloneness, loneliness, bereftness. Are the narrator and the homeless man stuck between commerce and loneliness, between an ahistorical capitalist modernity and cultural isolation? The poem's existence as an act of writing and as a recording of a vanishing moment partially preclude such a conclusion. Vigil's strong sense of history and the seemingly photographic quality of her poetry preserve some of this presence.

While the mood of "el mercado en San Antonio" has a melancholy feel, Vigil does not settle for sad remembrances of times and people overtaken by the modern, capitalist world. The man's presence, and the lessons the narrator learns from him, are indicative of a will to survive and persevere. The man asks for only a nickel, and when the narrator wonders what good a nickel will do, he responds,

con ojos brillantes como espejos	with brilliant eyes like mirrors
me da una mirada penetrante	he gives me a penetrating look
y como entre sonrisa y dolor	and as if between a smile and sorrow
la voz artificial me informa:	the artificial voice informs me:
pues nunca sabe uno	well one never knows
un poquito aquí	a little here
un poquito acá	a little there
quién diga quizás junte	who knows maybe I'll gather
suficiente pa'—	enough for—(22)

The man's eyes are "like mirrors," literally reflecting back to the narrator and allowing her to see herself in them. Ultimately, the poem conveys a spirit of resilience in the face of great adversity, and the two characters are facing it together. The man may be an outcast, but he is no more an outcast than is the narrator, and together they must find a way to endure, "un poquito aquí / un poquito acá."

Norma Alarcón has observed that the poems in the collection, including "el mercado en San Antonio," resemble, "both formally and thematically, the traditional *corridos* that treat us to narrative portraiture" (122). This is particularly the case for what is perhaps the collection's most important poem, "with his polka in his hand," which Vigil dedicates to Américo Paredes, for reasons made immediately obvious in the poem's title and theme. In "with his polka in his hand," the narrator once again finds herself in the mercado of downtown San Antonio, this time sitting in a bar, "tired out *de todo el día* [from the whole day]." And yet again, the poet's eye takes in the minute details of the scene, seeing in them evidence of inexorable change. The narrator half-ironically notes that she is

in a classy joint
with delicately leaved green plants
blossoming in all directions
and picturesque windows
brilliant mirrors
and a polished wooden antique bar (25)

This is certainly a well-tended bar, made attractive to the tourists who come in for a drink and a break from the South Texas heat in the summer. The objects in the scene are described as "picturesque," "brilliant," and "polished," as if framed within the walls of a museum.

Yet not unlike "el mercado en San Antonio," "with his polka in his hand" introduces a character who unexpectedly enters and destabilizes the scene. This time it is a *viejito*, a little old man, appearing like a ghostly presence from the past. His entrance signals a nostalgic look backward, but also the avowal of a residual presence.

and I gazed out
through elongated window structures
framing like a picture
el patio en el mercado: [the patio in the marketplace:]
whereupon
just one drink ago
troteaban los pies indios [trotted the Indian feet]
clad in dusty shoes
de aquel viejito [of that little old man]

The idea of "framing," as in a photograph or painting, is again brought to the fore. The reader gets a feeling of stasis, as if looking at an object long gone that is romanticized and idealized. Vigil presents an idealized vision, but it is not her own; instead, it is the city's vision of its own downtown, designed for tourists. And it takes the narrator some moments to recognize that something in the scene has changed, "just one drink ago." This is both an instance of surprise and a sudden realization that the temporality of this very event is itself now in the past, existing as a continually constructed memory. The present thus exists as a palimpsest, layered and ruptured as the past—in the figure of the old man—makes a return. The drink gives the narrator a moment of clarity and shortly leads to cultural affirmation. Again and again, the poem presents frames within frames, as the old man gone past is being framed by the constantly changing present. The viejito, "que se atravesaba en frente de la puerta / de la cantina cara y gringa [who crossed in front of the door / of the expensive and white bar]," exists within this framing, yet he is not immobilized by it. The patio that the narrator looks at is framed by the windows, and the old man himself just a moment ago walked in front of the doorframe, into the narrator's field of vision, then stepped out of the frame.

The viejito also inspires the narrator to reflect about herself and her culture in a way that breaks the poem's original static opening.

Yo	I
por un instante	for an instant
esperando que él pasará	waiting for him to pass
y él	and he
contenido	self-contained
en sus pensamientos claros	in his clear thoughts
pushing with a strong weathered	pushing with a strong weathered
brown arm	brown arm
an ancient wooden cart	an ancient wooden cart
y en su mano izquierda	and in his left hand
un radio de transistor	a transistor radio
sí, un radio de transistor	yes, a transistor radio
aventando acordeón	blaring out accordion (25)

The viejito is outside, and with his wooden cart he remains a class and cultural Other to the denizens of the "cantina cara y gringa." The narrator sits "esperando que él pasara," as if expecting him to quietly disappear. Yet he does not oblige, as he is possessed by his "pensamientos claros." He interrupts and challenges the picturesque framing, a figure of admiration as he pushes the cart with one strong arm while holding the transistor radio with the other. This last detail is significant enough that the narrator repeats it, "sí, un radio de transistor / aventando acordeón." The verb *aventando* literally means "throwing," but in this contexts it signifies "projecting" or "blaring." In Spanish, aventando also carries the sense that the person engaged in the action is showing off, displaying a skill, expressing self-confidence, or even

FIGURE 11. Graciela Iturbide's *Mujer ángel* (1979) (photo courtesy of the Wittliff Collections, Texas State University–San Marcos).

daring fate. In his complete self-possession, the viejito declares his Mexican American cultural identity as he holds the transistor radio that is playing the accordion-driven *conjunto* music so popular among South Texas Mexicans.

The very juxtaposition between the old man as a class/cultural Other and the picturesque and touristic scene inspires the poetic narrative into being. The old man possibly represents a Mexican past, a former moment that has been overtaken by the modern. Yet this Mexican element is not fully gone, for the old man adapts a thoroughly modern object of the present—the portable radio—to his cultural past. And this throws the narrator into an existential spin. This moment of cultural recognition, along with its attendant juxtaposition of the past with the present, remarkably recalls Graciela Iturbide's *Mujer ángel* [Angel Woman] (1979), a photograph of an indigenous Mexican woman in the Sonoran Desert walking down a road with a large boom box in her hand (fig. 11). Both the scene in the photograph and the scene in Vigil's poem are discordant, but they effectively merge a cultural past with the irrevocably modern present. In *Mujer ángel* and "with his polka," cultural elements thought to exist merely residually make a stronger claim on the present than previously imagined.

The narrator's response to what she sees causes amazement, an almost giddy joy, and a series of associations that lead, finally, to cultural reclamation.

I utter to myself out loud
"He's carrying a polka in his hand!"
and the anglo client seated next to me
glances over uncomprehendingly
and I think of Gregorio Cortez
and Américo Paredes
y en que la defensa cultural es permitida
[and that the defense of one's culture is justified]
and that calls for a drink
and another toast (26)

The old man and the radio stand at opposite ends of a long temporal shift that has seemingly overtaken Mexican American culture in downtown San Antonio. Yet paradoxically, the old man proves the endurance of Mexican culture by its near absence, hinted at in the picturesque quality of his surroundings. In actuality, the culture is present and ever adaptive. The old man carries not a weapon, like the famous Gregorio Cortez, but a radio that literally transmits culture. In all likelihood, the old man is listening to one of San Antonio's long-running radio stations—KCOR-AM 1350, or the ever popular KEDA-AM 1540, known among its Mexican American audience as "Radio Jalapeño." These are among the oldest radio stations in San Antonio dedicated to playing traditional Mexican and Tex-Mex music, and their airwaves know no class boundaries, attracting recent Mexican immigrants as well as Chicanos/as whose roots go way back. In the case of the poem, Mexican radio is even heard in a ritzy downtown bar.[16]

While Vigil's poems explore a seemingly evanescent Mexican American culture in downtown San Antonio, they also explore issues that lie at the forefront of Chicano/a cultural politics. Like other Chicana writers before and after her—Gloria Anzaldúa, Ana Castillo, Lorna Dee Cervantes, and Sandra Cisneros, to name a few—Vigil investigates the construction of the masculine subject within her culture. While "with his polka" implicitly investigates one aspect of masculinity, her poetry can also overtly and acidly critique macho tendencies, and in the process it proposes new masculine formations. We see Vigil's critique of modes of Mexican masculinity in "me caes sura, ese, descuéntate [You disgust me, man, beat it]." This poem is a mocking reproduction of the voice of the male. It is written in the first person and is seemingly addressed to a single individual, but because the subject is unnamed, it is clear that the narrator is criticizing, more generally, the machismo present in Mexican American culture. The opening stanza addresses the unnamed subject of the poem's diatribe.

eres el tipo	you're the type
de motherfucker	of motherfucker
bien chingón	a real badass
who likes to throw his weight	who likes to throw his weight
around	around
y aventar empujones	and hurl shoves
y tirar chingazos	and throw punches

The tone of the poem consciously imitates the macho male who is the subject of its critique. Further, the poem lays bare the threat for real violence and abuse embodied in the macho stance. Unlike the viejito of "with his polka," who blares or throws his music, the *chingón* of "me caes sura" hurls, shoves, and throws punches.

By the second stanza, the voice of the narrator acquires a second level of vehemence that is all the more cutting for its cold distancing and rejection.

y precisamente por esa razón [and precisely for that reason]
whereas ordinarily
out of common courtesy or stubbornness
the ground I'd stand and argue principles—
esta vez que no [this time, no]
porque esa clase de pendejadas [because those kinds of idiocies]
mi tiempo fino no merece [my finite time does not deserve]
y mucho menos me energia [and much less my energy]
solo que ahí se acaba el [so that's where that shit ends]
    pinche pedo

The use of the male voice effectively mimics and ultimately subverts its power. The tone is derisive and finally dismissive. Vigil ends the poem abruptly, showing that the female narrator is in control of the discourse.

Yet Vigil is not unwilling to open a dialogue with her male readers. She specifically addresses a male audience in "para los que piensan con la verga [for those who think with their dick]," which carries the parenthetical subtitle, *"with due apologies to those who do not"* (57). This poem appears on the page facing "me caes sura," and although its tone is similarly irate, its acerbity excepts men who do not share sexist or macho values, and it invites those men who would agree with the narrator to read further. Both of these poems also share a sense of humor that strikes a balance between wryness and ribaldry, delivered in the accessible argot of working-class Chicanos/as. In other poems, Vigil praises José Montoya and Arturo Valdez, men whom she believes have positively contributed to Chicano/a cultural politics through their art, intellect, and activism. In the poems dedicated to these men, Vigil sees each as examples of what a Chicano man may become—someone who is progressive, "really walking forward" (55), and someone who struggles to "recrear balance / igualdad / respeto [recreate balance / equality / respect]" (60). Inasmuch as Vigil's poems look back upon the disappearing past, they also look to the future, to a moment when Chicano/a men and women can live in balance, equality, and respect with one another and within the larger social structures in which they participate.

Sharing concerns for the preservation of cultural memory among Chicanos/as and seeking to interrogate the underlying assumptions and constructions of the contemporary masculine subject, Evangelina Vigil and Jim Mendiola exemplify an artistic sensibility characterized by contingency and hybridity. For her part, Vigil well understands the tenuous quality of living in the modern city, where the drive for economic progress and urban renewal preempts the urgent need of ethnic communities to preserve their history as a people, in opposition to the "official" history tailored for tourism. Similarly, Mendiola interrupts the insidious process of cultural amnesia that sometimes occurs within the Chicano/a community, and he deploys a thoroughly modern medium—digital video—to sing a new "corrido" for his people. In the examination of masculine identity, Vigil looks within her culture to question the production of Mexican machismo, while Mendiola looks beyond it to critique constructions of ethnic deviance in the dominant media and popular culture. Ultimately, both artists lay claim to the writing of a Chicano/a cultural history while acknowledging the transformations wrought by the postmodern condition and advocating the adaptations required for the culture to not only survive but to thrive. Vigil and Mendiola are but two contemporary artists who have successfully intervened in historical and popular cultural discourses about Chicanos/as. There are many more twenty-first-century writers, filmmakers, musicians, painters, sculptors, and performers working in other diverse media who are questioning, critiquing, and revising the deterministic ways in which Chicano/a male identity in particular and Mexican American identity in general may be conceived. In small and large presses, performance venues, film and arts festivals, galleries and museums, Chicanos/as continue to take the reins of self-representation to define themselves in particular ways, often using past negative representations ironically to subvert their original meanings.

Epilogue

The Return of the Stereotypical Repressed: Why Stereotypes Still Matter

Throughout *Badmen, Bandits, and Folk Heroes,* one of my goals has been to demonstrate the potentially subversive instability of representational forms in the depiction of Mexican male identity in American culture, from production to reception. I have used the concept of ambivalence in my discussion of Anglo-American representation of ethnic identity, and it has made possible the deconstructing of the often contradictory messages that representations of Mexican identity produce. Through my methods, I have sought to destabilize the monological discourses instantiated by the stereotypical representation of Mexican male identity. By necessity, it was important to begin with the pivotal moment in which U.S. cinema emerged, for it was also at this moment that stereotypes of Mexican masculine identity began to proliferate widely in the public sphere. It should not surprise us, given the long history of fascination with the Mexican Other, that Mexicans first appear in American movies at almost the same time that narrative movies make their debut in the United States (although when I teach early American movies, my students are nonetheless surprised). We have also seen that the dialogue between narrative film and written texts—whether those texts be popular novels or high literature, newspapers, or scholarly works—provides crucial insights into the adaptation of certain kinds of stereotypical depictions, and that interaction also sheds light on the subsequent debates over the exact nature of Mexican identity at particular historical moments. The "greaser," the Mexican "badman," the revolutionary, the social deviant—these figures emerged at different historical junctures and articulated the ambivalent relation between American culture and Mexican masculinity.

I have used two other terms, contingency and hybridity, to discuss the Mexican American relation to the dominant Anglo-American society, as well as the subsequent Chicano/a expressions of identity in literary and cinematic texts. In my analysis, cultures are contingent because the world is ever-changing, and because social, political, and economic forces create the necessity for continual adaptation to new material circumstances. Notwithstanding the nationalist/essentialist formations of identity produced during the 1960s and 1970s—themselves also emerging out of an ideological necessity of countering damaging stereotypes—Chicano/a cultural production expresses a contingent character because Chicano/a culture has been in constant flux, first as a result of the dramatic changes in citizenship status that occurred after 1848, and subsequently because of the difficult acceptance and integration of Chicanos/as into U.S. society. Yet as we move inexorably into the twenty-first century in postmodern America, we may feel all too comfortable in claiming contingency and hybridity as the *modi operandi* of daily life. Thus, we must caution that the easy feelings of freedom in our interactions with contemporary cultural forms can be deceptive, for we are still subject to being contained within structures of power and representation over which we have no control, much as Jesse is in the final moments of *Come and Take It Day*, when his image is "collected" and then "trapped" within the pages of a travel album by the tourist who has taken his photograph.

Keeping this precaution in mind, allow me to close my study with two examples that may help us better understand our inscription within structures of power and representation. Examining the issues from the perspectives of class and racial formation, we see that some Mexicans and Chicanos/as may not have the same access to the forms of agency others may imagine for themselves, and the current debates over Mexican immigration exemplify the tenuous hold on freedom that people of Mexican descent are experiencing. While most Mexican Americans may feel untouched by the controversies over immigration, dominant representational forms do not always distinguish between Chicanos/as and Mexican nationals, legal citizens and illegal immigrants. Too many Chicanos/as and legal Mexican immigrants have had their status questioned or have been subjected to unlawful deportation as a consequence of the unfounded fear that the United States is being overrun by an invading horde from south of the border. There is a way in which the most recent backlash against immigrants is a reaction to the greater presence of Mexicanness in American culture. Put another way, the dominant Anglo-American culture is going through an identity crisis in the wake of growing multiculturalism in American society, and this anxiety is manifested as fear of the Mexican immigrant.

If Chicano/a critiques and subsequent subversive refashionings of stereotypes have weakened the power of these types of representations, this weakening does not mean that derogatory stereotypes do not remain at the deeply sublimated levels of our cultural imaginary. In certain reactionary circles today, we are witnessing what I call the return of the stereotypical repressed, as old stereotypes—once thought outmoded—are reinvigorated with new denigrating messages. One such example of the stereotypical repressed can be seen in the campaign by an anti-immigrant group that has posted its hate messages on the World Wide Web. Protesting the issuance of driver's licenses to immigrants in California, the organization posted a mock-up of a license for the fictional state of "Mexifornia." Pictured on the license is "Gold Hat" (Alfonso Bedoya, from *The Treasure of the Sierra Madre*, see fig. 1). In the license, his name is "Jose Gomez Jr.," his sex is "Mucho," his weight "Too Much," and he is "Entitled to: / Drive / Attend College / Purchase Guns / Vote." Clearly an instance of hate speech, the fake license relies on the most well-worn and negative stereotypes of Mexicans to propagate fear and loathing not only of illegal Mexican immigrants, but also of Mexicans and Chicanos/as.[1] Ironically, the use of this image to sell hatred reveals a misapprehension of the image's subversive possibilities, revealing that the anti-Mexican purveyors of this image are trafficking not so much in the monologics of hate, but in the dialogics of ambivalence.

Indeed, Gold Hat's image and famous speech contain other, more positive intertexts, including Luis Valdez's 1986 play "I Don't Have to Show You No Stinking Badges." The play comments on the difficulties experienced by Chicano/a and Latino/a actors in Hollywood, where the few available roles are for stereotyped characters. More recently, Gold Hat's rebellious line has also been applied in an empowering manner by immigrant rights groups, which use it to voice their protests against strictures requiring immigrants to always carry identification or else be deported. According to anecdotes, pro-immigration protesters in the 2006 demonstrations in Los Angeles carried signs reading, "We don't need no stinkin' badges!" In 2007, when Valdez's play was performed by El Centro Su Teatro in Denver, the theatre's artistic director Anthony J. Garcia acknowledged the line's central message in connection with immigration issues: "We [Mexicans and Chicanos/as] have a right to be here . . . and I don't have to prove to you that I belong here."[2] Gold Hat's image and words, derived from an original context that carried derisive implications, have been molded by different groups to produce markedly different meanings and for diametrically opposite goals. Gold

Hat embodies an unambiguous example of the ambivalence of stereotypical representation, as well as of the multiple and sometimes nefarious uses to which images may be put.

A second instance of the stereotypical repressed may be observed in the transference of negative stereotypical categories to other peoples who may also be seen as a threat to the American way of life. If, at the beginning of the twentieth century, Mexicans (and sometimes other groups, including the Irish) constituted the greatest threat to Anglo-American values, then at the beginning of the twenty-first century, Muslims and Muslim Americans have come to occupy the place of greatest menace. Soon after the attacks of September 11, 2001, I was witness to an occurrence of hate speech directed against Muslims, specifically Arabs. I overheard two men talking of "those people" who invade cities by taking over ownership of convenience stores, who are "dirty" and "greasy" in their ways. Before my eyes, I saw Arab identity maligned using the same inflammatory language reserved for Mexicans a century earlier. More shocking still was that the two men participating in this exchange were an Anglo-American and a Mexican American. Standing together, they seemed to have found common ground by identifying a common threat in the Arab Other.

Today, more than ever, it is crucial that spectators reflect critically on the real-world effects of images produced by popular culture across media. The analysis of ambivalence strongly suggests that if derision and desire have the potential to reside in every image we encounter, then this will only be the case if we actively work through the meanings implicit in these images. Subversion and transformation require yet another step, one in which we stop being merely spectators and become creators within the discourses we inescapably inhabit. With new threats upon Chicanos/as', Latinos/as', and other marginalized groups' rightful claim to their place in American culture, we need to critique, revise, and participate within representational structures to more wholly define an agential identity.

Notes

Introduction

1. A classic poem of the Chicano/a Movement, "El Louie" has a long history of critical inquiry and debate, as Renato Rosaldo has noted in his discussion of José Montoya's poetics. In *Culture and Truth*, Rosaldo is among the first Chicano/a critics to depart from the nationalist, "classic norms" of Chicano/a criticism, "which asked him [Louie], on the one hand, to be a more elevated figure and, on the other, to embody the values of the pristine, authentic culture" (215). For Rosaldo, Louie is a "playful persona whose whimsical fantasies join together old things in new ways. His distinctive cultural practices personify a certain Chicano gift for improvisation and recombination. . . . The result is not identity confusion but play that operates within, even as it remarks, a diverse cultural repertoire" (215–16). Other writers who, with different perspectives, concentrate on notions of hybridity in "El Louie" include José Limón in *Chicano Poems, Mexican Ballads*, and José David Saldívar in *The Dialectics of Our America*.

2. See Raymund Paredes's *The Image of the Mexican in American Literature* (Diss. UT 1973), Blaine P. Lamb's "The Convenient Villain: The Early Cinema Views of the Mexican American" (1975), and Arthur Pettit's *Images of the Mexican American in Fiction and Film* (1980) for examples of analyses that read the representation of Mexican identity in binary terms of negative and positive.

3. Throughout my analysis, I will follow Mario T. García's assessment that the Chicano/a Movement ended around 1980—ironically, the beginning of the "decade of the Hispanic"—with the ascendance of conservative governments and the waning of activism in the United States. See García, *Mexican Americans: Leadership, Ideology, and Identity, 1930–1960* (1991).

4. Limón calls the social relations existing in the U.S. Southwest in the early part of the twentieth century a "quasi-colonialism" (*American Encounters*, 111). Other Chicano/a scholars, most notably Rodolfo Acuña in *Occupied America* (1981), have compared the Mexican American social condition in the United

States to colonialism, calling the Mexican population an "internal colony." In my analysis of Mexican American representation throughout my study, I draw comparisons with the post-colonial from a theoretical position expressive of ideas of dominance, desire, and ultimately the ambivalence of social relations.

5. It is also usually the case that the stereotype is read as "truth" by those for whom its distortions are already considered "facts." Note, however, that I am not here indicating a dichotomy between the "mainstream" and the "marginal" spectator, wherein the latter possesses a critical knowledge that the former cannot access; neither spectator has a monopoly on oppositional reading, and both are susceptible to passive acceptance.

6. Among the earliest critical works to respond to negative stereotypical representation was Limón's 1973 "Stereotyping and Chicano Resistance," featured in Chon Noriega's *Chicanos and Film*.

7. In a discussion concerning the stereotype's endurance, Ramírez Berg wonders "whether *any* use of such an oft-repeated and well-known stereotype can exist without in some ways serving to reinforce it" (*Latino Images*, 86).

8. Shohat and Stam acknowledge Donald Bogle's analysis of African American actors' resistant performances in *Toms, Coons, Mulattoes, Mammies and Bucks*. Bogle "emphasizes the resilient imagination of black performers obliged to play against script and studio intentions, the capacity to turn demeaning roles into resistant performance" (*Unthinking Eurocentricism*, 196).

9. Like so many stereotypical images, Bedoya's bandit revolutionary has also been used to reinforce preconceived negative ideas about Mexicans, such as those perpetuated by reactionary groups in California intent on demonizing Mexican immigrants. See my discussion of the return of the stereotypical repressed in the Epilogue.

10. Américo Paredes develops the term "Greater Mexico" in *A Texas-Mexican "Cancionero,"* where he defines it as "all the areas inhabited by people of a Mexican culture—not only within the present limits of the Republic of Mexico but in the United States as well—in a cultural rather than a political sense" (qtd. in Limón, *American Encounters*, 215). I expand the meaning of the term "Greater Mexican literature" by including Anglo-American texts that significantly engage with Mexican culture in the United States and Mexico.

Chapter 1

1. In *Anglos and Mexicans in the Making of Texas, 1836–1986*, David Montejano documents that between 1915 and 1917, at the height of tensions between Anglos and Mexicans, the lynching of Mexicans rose markedly (122).

2. Cecil Robinson's *With the Ears of Strangers* (1963, revised as *Mexico and the Hispanic Southwest in American Literature* in 1977) and Raymund Paredes's "The Image of the Mexican in American Literature" (Diss. UT 1973) are among the first literary studies to take up the representation of the Mexican in American cultural production. Arthur Pettit's *Images of the Mexican American in Fiction and Film* (1980)

adds film analysis. Among the works these writers examine, we find *Francis Berian, or the Mexican Patriot* (1826), the tellingly titled *Mexico Versus Texas* (1838), and *The Lone Star: A Tale of Texas* (1845). These titles predate what is understood as the beginning of the dime novel (1859), but may be classed more generally as western adventure stories.

3. To one degree or another, Robinson, R. Paredes, and Pettit indict Crane for his supposedly derogatory representation of the Mexican. In "Stephen Crane and the Mexican" (1971), Paredes argues that in Crane's stories about the violent relationship between the Anglo and Mexican, the Mexican is the troublemaker and always the vanquished. "He reeks of violence and brutality—qualities which are very much a part of his way of life" (32). Paredes adds that the Mexican's fate is to be a coward: the "surest proof of how cheaply Crane values the Mexican is that in his stories, the Mexican never 'holds steady,' but collapses and disintegrates, his doom assured" (37).

4. In "Unraveling the Humanist," Stanley Wertheim criticizes Crane for depicting the Mexican as "degenerate, menacing, and violent, yet ultimately cowardly" (70).

5. I visited the Library of Congress in the fall of 2001. I would like to thank Charles Ramírez Berg, professor of Film Studies at the University of Texas at Austin, for helping me acquire copies of these films.

6. Once again, Pettit's and R. Paredes's early works on ethnic representation in film prove foundational and themselves establish a pattern for future critiques.

7. Unlike the "José" of "One Dash-Horses," the "Jose" of *The Greaser's Gauntlet* carries no accent in his name. I have not explored to what extent Crane insisted on "José," but evidently the writers of the *Biograph Bulletin* saw no need to include the customary accent over the final syllable.

8. See Catherine E. Kerr, "Incorporating the Star: The Intersection of Business and Aesthetic Strategies in Early American Film."

Chapter 2

1. See Mark Anderson's *Pancho Villa's Revolution by Headlines* for an analysis of how Villa attempted to manipulate newspaper headlines to turn American opinion in his favor, as well as how American newspapers framed the Mexican Revolution to fit the political and business interests of the corporations that were tied to these newspapers.

2. Alfred Charles Richard's *The Hispanic Image on the Silver Screen: An Interpretive Filmography from Silents to Sound, 1898–1935*, provides an extensive compendium of movies made during the opening years of the American film industry. While his compilation is certainly exhaustive, Richard does not indicate which, if any, of these films he viewed, although he does put together selected excerpts from reviews and playbills that provide ample descriptions of the movies in question. A high percentage of the films discussed in Richards' book are no longer available or are unviewable because they are in states of deterioration.

3. There is no indication as to how close *Barbarous Mexico* followed Turner's text, save for having the same title.

4. Several other overlapping and mutually reinforcing factors very likely influenced the stereotypical discourse during the years 1910–20: the onset of the revolution impelled a dramatic movement of refugees into the United States; the consequent U.S. response to this mass migration was broadly xenophobic, and included exclusionary laws and discriminatory attitudes (Vélez-Ibáñez, 57–87). Some of the revolution's refugees did in fact look "to spread their revolutionary ideologies," and were a thorn on the side of American businesses in the West (Pike, 238). The beginning, in 1915, of the *Tejano*-led seditionist movement in South Texas augmented American fears that revolution would spread from Mexico into the United States. While the increase in the Mexican population and the threat of renewed warfare on Texas soil were no doubt cause for Anglo alarm, these factors were very likely subsumed by the broader threat of revolution and chaos in Mexico. In my research, I have found no films that directly register immigration or internal revolution as threats, although we can guess that a film such as *Martyrs of the Alamo* (1915) unconsciously registered these fears, as it served to reinforce the sense that Texas was rightfully and irrevocably Anglo land.

5. The bandoleers across the chest are so iconically menacing that they are unconsciously integrated in the characterization of contemporary Mexican villains. In Robert Rodriguez's *Desperado* (1995), Navajas (Danny Trejo) wears a bandoleer of throwing knives across his midriff. The character sports a heavy mustache and displays a constant snarl; on his chest he prominently displays a tattoo of a woman—perhaps a *soldadera*—wearing a *charro* hat. These icons of the revolution project the bandit revolutionary threat in a contemporary setting.

6. My assessment of the importance of Mexican identity to the formation of Anglo-American identity in Hart's Anglo cowboy is at variance with Slotkin's view, which recognizes the Mexican only as one among many of Hart's adversaries. According to Slotkin, Hart's adversaries are "reminiscent of the dangerous classes and human 'scum' of the metropolis: cardsharks, brothel-keepers, and racketeers, many of them half-breeds or 'Mexicans'" (245).

7. The *Treasures from the American Film Archives* series is made possible by the National Film Preservation Foundation, a congressionally created organization entrusted with preserving historically significant American films.

8. Slotkin sees the representation of Whiteness in a similar vein when he recognizes the "racial overtones" in the script, as well as "Blaze" Tracy's "intensely 'masculine' . . . and White" persona (250). While Slotkin emphasizes the hero's Whiteness, he does not fully acknowledge the extent to which the Anglo-American attains myth-hero status through the degradation of a subject who is specifically Mexican.

9. Another American writer, John Steinbeck, also saw Mexicans as primitive and close to the earth. See Phillip D. Ortega, "Fables of Identity: Stereotypes and

Caricature of Chicanos in Steinbeck's *Tortilla Flat*," Robert Gentry, "Nonteleo-logical Thinking in Steinbeck's *Tortilla Flat*," and Joseph R. Millichap, *Steinbeck and Film* for discussions of Mexicans and primitivism in the work of Steinbeck.

10. This passage is strikingly similar to Américo Paredes's utopian vision of a border uprising in the closing pages of *George Washington Gómez*, in which the title character imagines, in a more ethnic embodiment, "an enormous, well-trained army that included Irishmen and escaped American Negro slaves" that would "defeat not only the army of the United States but its navy as well" (282).

11. See J. Lawrence Mitchell's "Jack London and Boxing" for an analysis of London's writings on the sport of boxing, including his novels, *The Game* (1905) and *The Abysmal Brute* (1913). Mitchell also notes that in "The Mexican," London's "socialist sympathies clearly trump his unreflective racism" (240).

Chapter 3

1. *Rio Grande* suggests the wholly different treatment the Mexican female receives in American film, as compared with the Mexican male. She signifies exoticism and sexual allure; as a "figure of forbidden sexuality," she constitutes a different form of ambivalence, as José Limón elaborates in *American Encounters* (111).

2. The Western's ambivalence toward the Mexican is so deep that it extends to the scholarship on the Western itself. With the possible exception of Slotkin, the Western's scholars refuse to see the presence of the Mexican subject. Kitses, for instance, mentions only the Native American as the Anglo hero's antithesis in his discussion of "the charged racial and sexual dynamics of the genre" (13). Further, the index to the new edition of *Horizons West* contains no references to Mexico or Mexicans. In Michael Coyne's *The Crowded Prairie*, a similar lack of vision holds true. Recognizing that "the strand of American identity Westerns addressed and constructed was white and male," Coyne comments on the Western's failure to address ethnicity: "Westerns marginalized the Indian because they were only marginally *about* the Indian. Equally, there are very few Blacks in the Westerns, and fewer Black heroes" (4–5). Though he is prepared to argue that the Western only "marginally" takes up Native American and African American identity, Coyne elides the possibility that the Western has often been about Anglo-American identity *in relation* to Mexican identity.

3. As I elaborate later in the chapter, the Mexican government's threatened boycott of derogatory American movies in 1922 is one other factor that may have influenced the positive portrayal of the Mexican in the 1923 version of *The Bad Man*, although perhaps it was not as significant as the revolution. See Helen Delpar's "Goodbye to the 'Greaser': Mexico, the MPPDA, and Derogatory Films, 1922–1926."

4. According to the Internet Movie Database, Spanish- and French-language versions of *The Bad Man*, with different casts and intended for foreign markets, were also produced in Hollywood. In 1947, the film appeared again as a tele-play.

5. Note that the Spanish, as written by Browne, is mostly incorrect. The appropriate phrase would be, "*Señoras y señores*," but Browne apparently saw no need to write the Spanish language lines in their correct form, perhaps because this was a light comedy. Browne is consistently inconsistent throughout the play, often inventing nonsense words to draw out the humor in Pancho Lopez's speaking parts.

6. The name "Trampas" itself is curious, for as any reader fluent in Spanish can confirm, it is impossible not to think of this name associated with its Spanish meanings—the acts of cheating, treachery, tricking, or trapping. Neither *The Virginian* nor its film adaptations make reference to the origin of this name, but one cannot but connect Trampas with the well-established Mexican badmen who appeared in dime novels and Westerns of the same era.

Chapter 4

1. The best-known meditation on Mexico's pathological character is Octavio Paz's *The Labyrinth of Solitude*, which posits that Mexico's pathologies go back to the primal rape of the Indian woman, and thus to the moment of the mestizo nation's birth.

2. Paredes wrote *The Shadow* around the fifties, and he notes in the preface that he attempted to publish it on several occasions, without success. In 1998, Arte Público Press published the novel as part of its *Pioneers of Modern U.S. Hispanic Literature* series.

3. The causal links the novel examines include: the reorganization and displacement of the Mexican labor force on both sides of the border; conflict and contradiction between exploited workers in the country and the city; and world-capital's attenuation of agrarian reform and communitarian movements in the wake of the bourgeoisie's consolidation of power. For a complete discussion of the novel's social analysis, see my article "Américo Paredes's *The Shadow*: Social and Subjective Transformation in Greater Mexico."

4. "La defensa es permitida" is, ironically, quoted from "The Ballad of Gregorio Cortez," the *corrido* that forms the basis of Paredes's classic study *"With His Pistol in His Hand"* (1958).

5. My argument in this section is inspired by Delueze and Guattari's vision, in *Anti-Oedipus: Capitalism and Schizophrenia*, of capitalism's deterritorializations and reterritorializations of subject peoples. As Robert J. Young notes in *Colonial Desire*, Deleuze and Guattari's description of "the operations of capitalism as a territorial writing machine seems not only especially suited to the historical development of industrialization, but also describes rather exactly the violent physical and ideological procedures of colonization, deculturation and acculturation, by which the territory and cultural space of an indigenous society must be disrupted, dissolved and then reinscribed according to the needs of the apparatus of the occupying power" (169–70).

Chapter 5

1. See Paredes's *"With His Pistol in His Hand"* for a full analysis of the historical events, legends, and ballads related to Gregorio Cortez.

2. In his own way, Paredes was a modern-day Cortez. With his study, he single-handedly challenged the combined history- and myth-making of Texas's luminary historians, Walter Prescott Webb and J. Frank Dobie. Paredes's exposure of deep-seated cultural biases in the works of these scholars stirred controversy, but Paredes stood by his views and he was ultimately recognized for his contribution to the untold history and cultural ways of Mexicans in Texas and Greater Mexico.

3. For significant analyses of *The Ballad of Gregorio Cortez*, see Tatcho Mindiola, "The Ballad of Gregorio Cortez"; Guillermo Hernández, *"The Ballad of Gregorio Cortez"*; Carl Gutierrez-Jones, "Legislating Languages: *The Ballad of Gregorio Cortez* and the English Language Amendment"; and Rosa Linda Fregoso, *The Bronze Screen: Chicana and Chicano Film Culture*.

4. For a discussion of the "Anglo-Texan legend" and Paredes's revisionary and critical poetics, see Renato Rosaldo, *Culture and Truth*; Ramón Saldívar, *Chicano Narrative: The Dialectics of Difference*; and José E. Limón, *Mexican Ballads, Chicano Poems: History and Influence in Mexican American Social Poetry*, and *Dancing With the Devil: Society and Cultural Poetics in Mexican American South Texas*.

5. This information is based on informal conversations with José E. Limón, who was a student and colleague of Paredes's. Subsequently, I have interviewed Richard Bauman, who was also a close friend and colleague. Bauman recalls Paredes's disappointment with the characterization of Cortez as "a weepy, stumbling figure at places."

6. Interestingly, Paredes received numerous positive letters immediately after the television premiere of the film. Friends and colleagues were for the most part happy that Paredes was receiving broader public recognition for his accomplishments, and they felt the film accurately portrayed the plight of Gregorio Cortez.

7. See "The United States, Mexico, and *Machismo*" for an in-depth discussion of the development of machismo in nineteenth- and twentieth-century U.S. and Mexican cultures.

8. On the top right-hand corner of this working paper, the words "Not for Publication" demonstrate that Paredes saw this as a work in progress. Notwithstanding this possibility, multiple copies of "Some Stereotypes About the Mexican" are found in different folders within the collection, indicating that Paredes's thoughts on the subject of the stereotype were well developed. (Multiple copies also indicate he used this paper as class lecture notes.) Some of the ideas in this working paper are encapsulated and amplified in "On Ethnographic Fieldwork Among Minorities" and "The United States, Mexico and *Machismo*."

9. See letter to Chuck Schwanitz, dated July 27, 1982. Paredes Papers, Box 15, Folder 11.

10. According to its publication history, *Manhunters* exists in three editions, the 1974 and 1983 editions published by Ballantine, and a 1994 edition by Texas Christian University Press. The first edition of the novel does not contain Kelton's "Author's Note," but it appears that by 1982, in Bauman's copy of the novel, the "Author's Note" was inserted. The quotes from Kelton's "Author's Note" are from the Texas Christian University edition; quotes from the actual novel are from the 1974 paperback edition.

11. Author interview with Richard Bauman, August 9, 2006.

12. For recent work on Kelton's importance among contemporary Western fiction writers, as well as discussions on his realistic aesthetic, see the essays by Kenneth W. Davis, John Wegner, and Ira Yates Blanton, Jr. Kelton has much to say about the role of history and the writer's relation to it in "Politically Correct or Historically Correct?" from his collection of essays, *My Kind of Heroes*.

13. See Samora, Bernal, and Peña's *Gunpowder Justice: A Reassessment of the Texas Rangers* for a study and critique of the Texas Rangers' role in law enforcement and politics.

Chapter 6

1. Several of the early critiques of cinematic stereotypes about Chicanos/as may be found in Chon Noriega's edited collection *Chicano/as and Film*. The late 1960s and early 1970s also saw the production of manifestos that defined the oppositional character of an emergent Chicano/a cinema, also contained in *Chicano/as and Film*.

2. For a lucid account of Chicano/a cinema's politically vexed relationship with Hollywood, see Noriega's *Shot in America: Television, the State, and the Rise of Chicano Cinema* (2000).

3. For an extended discussion of the identification with the indigenous heritage during the Chicano/a Movement, see Rafael Pérez-Torres's *Movements in Chicano Poetry*.

4. See Michelle Habell-Pallán, *Loca Motion: The Travels of Chicana and Latina Popular Culture*, for a lively analysis of the Chicana punk scene.

5. Although cultural exchange and mixing between the Mexican and Anglo has not traveled both ways equally—as this study hopefully attests—the deep influence of Chicanos/as on Anglo-American culture merits further study.

6. See Rafael Pérez-Torres, *Movements in Chicano Poetry*, Bruce-Novoa, "Dialogical Strategies, Monological Goals: Chicano Literature," and José Limón, *Mexican Ballads, Chicano Poems* for analyses of the importance of "I Am Joaquín" within Chicano/a cultural nationalism. While an in-depth examination of the poem is beyond the purview of my study, it is useful to note that the poem, once read as the sine qua non of Chicano/a cultural nationalism, may be interpreted, from the contemporary perspective, in a more expansive manner. For instance, its

closing lines could today be seen as a call to unity among Latinos/as of diverse backgrounds from throughout the Americas.

7. See Chon Noriega, "Fashion Crimes," in *Aztlán: A Journal of Chicano Studies* 26.1 (Spring 2001).

8. The image of Zapata as a trading card in a bubblegum pack, an object of consumption and collection, is disturbing in another way, as I will argue: Zapata as trading card presents the possibility that oppositionality may be contained and ultimately commodified.

9. Along with AC/DC and Metallica, one of the icons of heavy metal rock in San Antonio is Ozzy Osbourne and the group he fronted in the seventies, Black Sabbath. The "Ozzy" sign looks like a "Hook-em-Horns," but with the thumb extended; it is usually accompanied with a wagging tongue and demonic look. In the early eighties, Osbourne incurred the wrath of city leaders when he urinated from the roof of the Alamo. Perhaps this action resonated with working-class Mexicans in San Antonio, cementing his iconic status among them.

10. Like many cities in the United States, San Antonio is segregated along class and ethnic lines. The South and West sides are predominantly working class and Mexican, while the North Side is middle and upper class and white.

11. In *Lone Star*, the main character, Pilar (Elizabeth Peña), proposes a form of agency that masters history by "forgetting," i.e., rewriting, it.

12. The version of *Come and Take It Day* that first aired on PBS in 2002 (a mere twenty years after *The Ballad of Gregorio Cortez*) relied heavily on a soundtrack by the Australian heavy metal band AC/DC. The DVD release of the film, which appeared a year later, was stretched to feature length and employed a generic heavy metal soundtrack. It is unclear why this change occurred.

13. See Julián Olivares's "Seeing and Becoming: Evangelina Vigil, *Thirty an' Seen a Lot*" for the earliest and most significant assessment of the dominant themes in this collection.

14. The Greater San Antonio Chamber of Commerce Web site contains a brief history of the development of the downtown River Walk. The year 1980, when the city began the River Walk rehabilitation project, coincides with a building boom in downtown hotels and the development of a mall and other shopping, tourist, and convention attractions. See http://www.sachamber.org/visitor/riverwalk_history.php for a complete history of the River Walk and other downtown development. Significantly, the redevelopment and re-imagining of downtown San Antonio and the River Walk goes back the 1960s, when the city leaders staged Hemisfair '68 as part of San Antonio's 250th anniversary. In the process of constructing the fair's centerpiece structure, the Tower of the Americas, a downtown neighborhood and many historic structures were destroyed, making possible the future economic transformation of the city.

15. The translation of this and other poems are my own.

16. Ironically, the unnamed bar of the poem is likely Mi Tierra. A San Antonio institution, Mi Tierra is a bakery-bar-restaurant owned by a Mexican American

family. Over the years, its good food and drinks have made it a popular refueling stop for politicians, celebrities, and tourists alike. Like a Tex-Mex Hard Rock Café, it is a repository of Mexican American popular cultural kitsch, including one of Selena Quintanilla's outfits.

Epilogue

1. The Web site belongs to American Patrol, a virulently anti-immigrant and anti-Mexican organization headed by Glenn Spencer. The Southern Poverty Law Center (SPLC) has placed the American Patrol among anti-immigrant organizations who spread racism against Mexicans and other non-white groups; it has called Spencer's tactics "bigoted and vulgar." See http://www.splcenter. org/intel/intelreport/article.jsp?sid=175. The SPLC also notes, in quoted commentary by Spencer, that his hate message frequently extends to all Hispanics, including Chicanos/as.

2. A review of Valdez's "I Don't Need No Stinking Badges" was carried by the *Denver Post* on March 1, 2007. See http://www.denverpost.com/entertainment/ci_5323176 for the online version of the article, written by John Moore.

Bibliography

Acuña, Rodolfo F. *Occupied America: A History of Chicanos*. 1971. New York: Harper & Row, 1981.

Alarcón, Norma. "Chicana Feminism: In the Tracks of 'the' Native Woman." *Cultural Studies* 4 (1990): 248–56.

———. "The Theoretical Subject(s) of *This Bridge Called my Back* and Anglo-American Feminism." *Criticism in the Borderlands: Studies in Chicano Literature, Culture, and Ideology*. Ed. Hector Calderon and José David Saldívar. Durham, N.C.: Duke University Press, 1991. 28–39.

Allport, Gordon. *The Nature of Prejudice*. Reading: Addison-Wesley, 1954.

Alonzo, Juan J. "Américo Paredes's *The Shadow*: Social and Subjective Transformation in Greater Mexico." *Aztlán: A Journal of Chicano Studies* 27.1 (2002): 27–57.

———. "From Derision to Desire: The Greaser in Stephen Crane's Mexican Stories and D. W. Griffith's Early Westerns." *Western American Literature* 38 (Winter 2004): 374–401.

Anderson, Mark Cronlund. *Pancho Villa's Revolution by Headlines*. Norman: University of Oklahoma Press, 2000.

Arteaga, Alfred. "An Other Tongue." *An Other Tongue: Nation and Ethnicity in the Linguistic Borderlands*. Ed. Alfred Arteaga. Durham, N.C.: Duke University Press, 1994. 9–33.

Badger, Clarence G., dir. *The Bad Man*. Perf. Walter Huston. First National Pictures, 1930.

"The Bad Man." Review. *Chicago Daily Tribune*. November 25, 1930. 31.

"The Bad Man." Review. *Variety*. March 26, 1941.

Bauman, Richard. Telephone interview. August 9, 2006.

Bazant, Jan. *A Concise History of Mexico: From Hidalgo to Cárdenas, 1805–1940*. Cambridge: Cambridge University Press, 1986 [1977].

Berg, Charles Ramírez. "Stereotyping in Films in General and of the Hispanic in Particular." *Howard Journal of Communications* 2 (1990): 286–300.

———."El Genio del Género: Mexican American Border Documentaries and Postmodernism." *Reflexiones 1998*. Ed. Yolanda C. Padilla. Austin: CMAS Books, 1999.

———. *Latino Images in Film: Stereotypes, Subversion, and Resistance*. Austin: University of Texas Press, 2002.

Bhabha, Homi K. *The Location of Culture*. London: Routledge, 1994.

Blanton, Jr., Ira Yates. "The Triumph of Tradition in Six Novels by Elmer Kelton, 1971–1998." Diss. Texas Tech University, 1999.

Bogle, Donald. *Toms, Coons, Mulattoes, Mammies, and Bucks: An Interpretive History of Blacks in American Films*. New York: Continuum, 1989.

Bordwell, David, and Kristin Thompson. *Film Art: An Introduction*. Fifth ed. New York: McGraw-Hill, 1997.

Browne, Porter Emerson. *The Badman: A Play in Three Acts*. New York: Samuel French, 1920.

Brownlow, Kevin. *The War, the West, and the Wilderness*. New York: Knopf, 1979.

Bruce-Novoa, Juan. "Dialogical Strategies, Monological Goals: Chicano Literature." *An Other Tongue: Nation and Ethnicity in the Linguistic Borderlands*. Ed. Alfred Arteaga. Durham, N.C.: Duke University Press, 1994.

Buscombe, Edward, ed. *The BFI Companion to the Western*. New York: Atheneum, 1988.

Cabanne, Christy. *Martyrs of the Alamo*. Triangle Distributing Corp., 1915.

"Captured by Mexicans." Advertisement. *The Moving Picture World*. April 4, 1914. 98.

Carewe, Edwin, dir. *The Badman*. Perf. Holbrook Blinn. Edwin Carewe Productions, 1923.

Clemens, Jeremiah. *Bernard Lile, an Historical Romance*. Philadelphia: J. B. Lippincott & Co., 1856.

Clifford, James. *The Predicament of Culture: Twentieth-Century Ethnography, Literature, and Art*. Cambridge: Harvard University Press, 1988.

Cockcroft, James D. *Mexico: Class Formation, Capital Accumulation, and the State*. New York: Monthly Review Press, 1983.

Conway, Jack, dir. *Viva Villa!* Perf. Wallace Beery. 1934. VHS. MGM/UA Home Entertainment, 1993.

Coyne, Michael. *The Crowded Prairie: American National Identity in the Hollywood Western*. New York: I. B. Tauris, 1997.

Crane, Stephen. "The City of Mexico." 1895. Vol. 8 of *The University of Virginia Edition of the Works of Stephen Crane*. Ed. Fredson Bowers. Charlottesville, Va.: University Press of Virginia, 1975. 429–32.

―――. "The Mexican Lower Classes." 1895. Vol. 8 of *The University of Virginia Edition of the Works of Stephen Crane*. Ed. Fredson Bowers. Charlottesville, Va.: University Press of Virginia, 1975. 435–38.

―――. "The Five White Mice." 1895–96. Vol. 5 of *The University of Virginia Edition of the Works of Stephen Crane*. Ed. Fredson Bowers. Charlottesville, Va.: University Press of Virginia, 1975. 39–52.

―――. "One Dash-Horses." 1895–96. Vol. 5 of *The University of Virginia Edition of the Works of Stephen Crane*. Ed. Fredson Bowers. Charlottesville, Va.: University Press of Virginia, 1975. 13–25.

―――. *The University of Virginia Edition of the Works of Stephen Crane*. Ed. Fredson Bowers. 10 vols. Charlottesville, Va.: University Press of Virginia, 1975.

Crow, Charles L. "Ishi and Jack London's Primitives." *Rereading Jack London*. Ed. Leonard Cassuto. Stanford: Stanford University Press, 1996. 46–54.

Davis, Kenneth W. "Kelton's Clio: The Uses of History." *Southwestern American Literature* 27.2 (Spring 2002): 19–25.

De Leon, Arnoldo. *They Called Them Greasers: Anglo Attitudes Toward Mexicans in Texas, 1821–1900*. Austin: University of Texas Press, 1983.

Deleuze, Gilles, and Felix Guattari. *Anti-Oedipus: Capitalism and Schizophrenia*. Tr. Robert Hurley et al. Minneapolis: University of Minnesota Press, 2000 [1977].

Delpar, Helen. "Goodbye to the 'Greaser': Mexico, the MPPDA, and Derogatory Films, 1922–1926." *Journal of Popular Film & Television* 12.1 (1984): 34–41.

―――. *The Enormous Vogue of Things Mexican: Cultural Relations Between the United States and Mexico, 1920–1935*. Tuscaloosa: University of Alabama Press, 1992.

Flores, Richard R. *Remembering the Alamo: Memory, Modernity, and the Master Symbol*. Austin: University of Texas Press, 2002.

Friedman, Lester D., ed. *Unspeakable Images: Ethnicity and the American Cinema*. Urbana, Ill.: University of Illinois Press, 1991.

Fregoso, Rosa Linda. "Chicana Film Practices: Confronting the 'Many-Headed Demon of Oppression.'" *Chicanos and Film: Representation and Resistance*. Ed. Chon Noriega. Minneapolis: University of Minnesota Press, 1992. 168–82.

―――. *The Bronze Screen: Chicana and Chicano Film Culture*. Minneapolis: University of Minnesota Press, 1993.

―――. *meXicana Encounters: The Making of Social Identities on the Borderlands*. Berkeley: University of California Press, 2003.

Furer, Andrew J. "'Zone-Conquerors' and 'White Devils': The Contradictions of Race in the Works of Jack London." *Rereading Jack London*. Ed. Leonard Cassuto. Stanford: Stanford University Press, 1996. 158–71.

García Canclini, Néstor. *Hybrid Cultures: Strategies for Entering and Leaving Modernity*. Trans. Christopher L. Chiappari and Silvia L. López. Minneapolis: University of Minnesota Press, 1995.

García, Mario T. *Mexican Americans: Leadership, Ideology, and Identity, 1930–1960*. New Haven: Yale University Press, 1991.

Gentry, Robert. "Nonteleological Thinking in Steinbeck's *Tortilla Flat*." *The Short Novels of John Steinbeck: Critical Essays with A Checklist to Steinbeck Criticism*. Ed. Jackson J. Benson. Durham, N.C.: Duke University Press, 1990. 31—38.

Gilman, Sander. *Difference and Pathology: Stereotypes of Sexuality, Race, and Madness*. Ithaca: Cornell University Press, 1985.

Gilroy, Paul. *The Black Atlantic: Modernity and Double Consciousness*. Cambridge: Harvard University Press, 1993.

Gonzalez, Rodolfo "Corky." "I am Joaquin / Yo Soy Joaquin." 1967.

Griffith, D. W. *The Fight for Freedom*. 1908. Biograph. Library of Congress Motion Picture, Broadcasting and Recorded Sound Division.

———. *The Greaser's Gauntlet*. 1908. Biograph. Library of Congress Motion Picture, Broadcasting and Recorded Sound Division.

———. *The Red Girl*. 1908. Biograph. Library of Congress Motion Picture, Broadcasting and Recorded Sound Division.

———. *The Tavern Keeper's Daughter*. 1908. Biograph. Library of Congress Motion Picture, Broadcasting and Recorded Sound Division.

———. *The Vaquero's Vow*. 1908. Biograph. Library of Congress Motion Picture, Broadcasting and Recorded Sound Division.

———. *The Thread of Destiny*. 1910. Biograph. Library of Congress Motion Picture, Broadcasting and Recorded Sound Division.

———. *The Birth of a Nation*. 1915. DVD. Kino Video, 2002.

Gunning, Tom. *D. W. Griffith and the Origins of American Narrative Cinema*. Urbana, Ill.: University of Illinois Press, 1991.

Gutiérrez-Jones, Carl. "Legislating Languages: *The Ballad of Gregorio Cortez* and the English Language Amendment." *Chicanos and Film: Representation and Resistance*. Ed. Chon Noriega. Minneapolis: University of Minnesota Press, 1992. 168–82.

———. *Rethinking the Borderlands: Between Chicano Cultural and Legal Discourse*. Berkeley: University of California Press, 1995.

Habell-Pallán, Michelle. *Loca Motion: The Travels of Chicana and Latina Popular Culture*. New York: York University Press, 2005.

Hall, Stuart. "Cultural Identity and Cinematic Representation." *Ex-Iles: Essays on Caribbean Cinema*. Ed. Mbye B. Cham. Trenton: Africa World Press, Inc., 1992. 220–36.

Hart, William S., dir. and perf. *The Aryan.* Triangle Distributing Corporation, 1916.

———, dir. and perf. *The Patriot.* Triangle Distributing Corporation, 1916.

———, dir. and perf. *Hell's Hinges.* Kay-Bee Pictures,1916. *Treasures from the American Film Archives.* Vol. 1. DVD. Image Entertainment, 2000.

Hernández, Guillermo. "The Ballad of Gregorio Cortez." *Critica* 1.3 (Spring 1985): 122–31.

"Highly amusing comedy. . . ." Advertisement. *New York Times.* September 2, 1920. 7.

Huston, John, dir. *The Treasure of the Sierra Madre.* Perf. Humphrey Bogart, Walter Huston, and Alfonso Bedoya. 1948. DVD. Warner Home Video, 2006.

Jay, Gregory S. "'White Man's Book No Good': D. W. Griffith and the American Indian." *Cinema Journal* 39.4 (Summer 2000): 3–26.

Katz, Friedrich. *The Life and Times of Pancho Villa.* Stanford: Stanford University Press, 1998.

Kazan, Elia, dir. *Viva Zapata!* Screenplay by John Steinbeck. Perf. Marlon Brando and Anthony Quinn. 1952. VHS. Fox Video, 1993.

Keller, Gary D. "The Image of the Chicano in Mexican, United States, and Chicano Cinema: An Overview." *Chicano Cinema: Research, Reviews, and Resources.* Ed. Gary D. Keller. Binghamton: Bilingual Review/Press, 1985. 13—58.

Kelton, Elmer. *Manhunters.* New York: Ballantine Books, 1978.

———. *Manhunters: A Novel.* Fort Worth: Texas Christian University Press, 1994.

———. *My Kind of Heroes: Selected Speeches.* 1995. Abilene, Texas: State House Press, 2004.

Kerr, Catherine E. "Incorporating the Star: The Intersection of Business and Aesthetic Strategies in Early American Film." *Business History Review* 64.3 (Autumn 1990): 383–410.

Kitses, Jim. *Horizons West: Directing the Western from John Ford to Clint Eastwood.* New edition. London: British Film Institute, 2004.

Knight, Alan. *The Mexican Revolution.* Vol. 1, *Porfirians, Liberals and Peasants.* Cambridge: Cambridge University Press, 1986.

Lamb, Blaine P. "The Convenient Villain: The Early Cinema Views the Mexican American." *Journal of the West* 14.4 (1975): 75–81.

Langman, Larry. *A Guide to Silent Westerns.* Westport, Conn.: Greenwood Press, 1992.

Limón, José E. *Mexican Ballads, Chicano Poems: History and Influence in Mexican American Social Poetry.* Berkeley: University of California Press, 1992.

————. "Stereotyping and Chicano Resistance: An Historical Dimension (1973)." *Chicanos and Film: Representation and Resistance*. Ed. Chon Noriega. Minneapolis: University of Minnesota Press, 1992. 3–17.

————. *Dancing with the Devil: Society and Cultural Poetics in Mexican American South Texas*. Madison: University of Wisconsin Press, 1994.

————. "Tex-Sex-Mex: American Identities, Lone Stars and the Politics of Racialized Sexuality." *American Literary History* 10 (1997): 598–616.

————. *American Encounters: Greater Mexico, the United States, and the Erotics of Culture*. Boston: Beacon, 1998.

London, Jack. "The Mexican." 1913. *Five Great Short Stories*. New York: Dover Publications, Inc., 1992.

MacGowan, Kenneth. "The New Season." *Theatre Arts Magazine* 5.1 (January 1921): 4–9.

Mantle, Burns, ed. *The Best Plays of 1920–21 and the Year Book of the Drama in America*. Boston: Small, Maynard & Company, 1921.

Mendiola, Jim. "Pedal to the Metal: AC/DC Meets Gregorio Cortez in Jim Mendiola's New Video Corrido." Interview with Camille T. Taiara. *San Francisco Bay Guardian*. November 7, 2001. http://www.sfbg.com/AandE/36/06/film3.html.

————, dir. *Come and Take It Day*. CTD Pictures, 2002.

"Mexico's Ban on Mexican Movie Villains Forbids all Pictures it Considers Propaganda." *New York Times*. February 11, 1922. 15.

Millichap, Joseph R. *Steinbeck and Film*. New York: Frederick Ungar Publishing Co., 1983.

Mindiola, Tatcho. "The Ballad of Gregorio Cortez." *La Red/The Net: Newsletter of the National Chicano Council on Higher Education* 80 (May 1984): 11–17.

Mitchell, J. Lawrence. "Jack London and Boxing." *American Literary Realism* 36.3 (Spring 2004): 225–42.

Mitchell, W. J. T. "Translator Translated (Interview with Cultural Theorist Homi Bhabha)." *Artforum* 33.7 (1995): 80–84.

Montejano, David. *Anglos and Mexicans in the Making of Texas, 1836–1986*. Austin: University of Texas Press, 1987.

Montoya, José. "El Louie." *Aztlan: An Anthology of Mexican American Literature*. Ed. Luis Valdez and Stan Steiner. New York: Alfred A. Knopf, 1972. 333–37.

Moore, John. "Review: 'I Don't Have to Show you No Stinking Badges.'" *Denver Post*. March 1, 2007. http://www.denverpost.com/entertainment/ci_5323176.

Morales, Sylvia. *Chicana*. 1979. VHS. Ruiz Productions, 1992.

Morsberger, Robert E. "Steinbeck on Screen." *A Study Guide to Steinbeck: A Handbook to His Major Works*. Ed. Tetsamuro Hayashi. Metuchen, N.J.: The Scarecrow Press, Inc., 1974. 258–98.

———. "Steinbeck's Zapata: Rebel Versus Revolutionary." *Zapata*. By John Steinbeck. Ed. Morsberger. New York: Penguin Books, 1991. 203–23.

Neale, Steve. "The Same Old Story: Stereotypes and Difference." *Screen Education* 32/33 (1979/80): 33–37.

Noriega, Chon. "Between a Weapon and a Formula: Chicano Cinema and its Contexts." *Chicanos and Film: Representation and Resistance*. Ed. Chon Noriega. Minneapolis: University of Minnesota Press, 1992. 141–67.

———, ed. *Chicanos and Film: Representation and Resistance*. Minneapolis: University of Minnesota Press, 1992.

———. "Internal 'Others': Hollywood Narratives 'About' Mexican Americans." *Mediating Two Worlds: Cinematic Encounters in the Americas*. Ed. John King, Ana M. López, and Manuel Alvarado. London: British Film Institute, 1993.

———. "Birth of the Southwest: Social Protest, Tourism, and D. W. Griffith's *Ramona*." *The Birth of Whiteness: Race and the Emergence of U.S. Cinema*. Ed. Daniel Bernardi. New Brunswick, N.J.: Rutgers University Press, 1996. 203–26.

———. *Shot in America: Television, the State, and the Rise of Chicano Cinema*. Minneapolis: University of Minnesota Press, 2000.

———. "Fashion Crimes." *Aztlán: A Journal of Chicano Studies* 26.1 (Spring 2001): 1–13.

Olmos, Edward James, dir. *American Me*. 1992. DVD. Universal Pictures, 2003.

Olivares, Julián. "Seeing and Becoming: Evangelina Vigil, *Thirty an' Seen a Lot*." *The Chicano Struggle: Analyses of Past and Present Efforts*. National Association for Chicano Studies. Binghampton: Bilingual Press/Editorial Bilingüe, 1984. 152–65.

Ortega, Philip D. "Fables of Identity: Stereotypes and Caricature of Chicanos in Steinbeck's *Tortilla Flat*." *Journal of Ethnic Studies* 1.1 (1973): 39–43.

Paredes, Américo. *"With His Pistol in His Hand": A Border Ballad and its Hero*. 1958. Austin: University of Texas Press, 1986.

———. *A Texas-Mexican "Cancionero": Folksongs of the Lower Border*. Urbana, Ill.: University of Illinois Press, 1976.

———. Letter to Carolyn Osborn. July 15, 1982. Américo Paredes Papers. Nettie Lee Benson Latin American Collection. University of Texas at Austin. Box 15, Folder 11.

————. Letter to Carlos E. Cortés. July 27, 1982. Américo Paredes Papers. Nettie Lee Benson Latin American Collection. University of Texas at Austin. Box 15, Folder 11.

————. Letter to Chuck Schwanitz. July 27, 1982. Américo Paredes Papers. Nettie Lee Benson Latin American Collection. University of Texas at Austin. Box 15, Folder 11.

————. Letter to Mary Lou Hornbuckle. May 13, 1990. Américo Paredes Papers. Nettie Lee Benson Latin American Collection. University of Texas at Austin. Box 15, Folder 8.

————. *Between Two Worlds*. Houston: Arte Público Press, 1991.

————. "The Folklore of Groups of Mexican Origin in the United States." *Folklore and Culture on the Texas-Mexican Border*. Ed. Richard Bauman. Austin: CMAS Books, University of Texas at Austin, 1993. 3–18.

————. *George Washington Gómez: A Mexicotexan Novel*. 1990. Houston: Arte Público Press, 1993.

————. "On Ethnographic Fieldwork Among Minorities." *Folklore and Culture on the Texas-Mexican Border*. Ed. Richard Bauman. Austin: CMAS Books, University of Texas at Austin, 1993 [1977]. 73–110.

————. "The United States, Mexico, and Machismo." *Folklore and Culture on the Texas-Mexican Border*. Ed. Richard Bauman. Austin: CMAS Books, University of Texas at Austin, 1993 [1971]. 215–34.

————. *The Shadow*. Houston: Arte Público Press, 1998 [1955].

————. "Comments on 'The Ballad of Gregorio Cortez.'" n.d. Américo Paredes Papers. Nettie Lee Benson Latin American Collection. University of Texas at Austin. Box 15, Folder 7.

————. "Some Stereotypes About the Mexican American." n.d. Working paper. Américo Paredes Papers. Nettie Lee Benson Latin American Collection. University of Texas at Austin. Box 13, Folder 9.

Paredes, Raymund A. "Stephen Crane and the Mexican." *Western American Literature* 6 (1971): 31–38.

————. "The Image of the Mexican in American Literature." Diss. University of Texas at Austin, 1973.

Paz, Octavio. *The Labyrinth of Solitude*. 1961. New York: Grove Press, 1985.

Pérez-Torres, Rafael. *Movements in Chicano Poetry: Against Myths, Against Margins*. Cambridge: Cambridge University Press, 1995.

Pettit, Arthur G. *Images of the Mexican American in Fiction and Film*. College Station: Texas A&M University Press, 1980.

Pike, Fredrick B. *The United States and Latin America: Myths and Stereotypes of Civilization and Nature*. Austin: University of Texas Press, 1992.

Read, Alan, ed. *The Fact of Blackness: Frantz Fanon and Visual Representation.* Seattle: Bay Press, 1996.

Richard, Alfred Charles. *The Hispanic Image on the Silver Screen: An Interpretive Filmography from Silents into Sound, 1898–1935.* New York: Greenwood Press, 1992.

Rivera, Tomás. "The Ballad of Gregorio Cortez." *Voz Fronteriza* 9.1 (September/October 1983): 5–7.

Robertson, Jamie. "Stephen Crane, Eastern Outsider in the West and Mexico." *Western American Literature* 13 (1978): 243–57.

Robinson, Cecil. *Mexico and the Hispanic Southwest in American Literature.* Tucson, Ariz.: University of Arizona Press, 1977. Rev. from *With the Ears of Strangers.* 1963.

Rodriguez, Robert. *Desperado.* 1995. DVD. Columbia TriStar Home Video, 1997.

Rosaldo, Renato. *Culture and Truth: The Remaking of Social Analysis.* 1989. Boston: Beacon Press, 1993.

Saldívar, José David. *The Dialectics of Our America: Genealogy, Cultural Critique, and Literary History.* Durham, N.C.: Duke University Press, 1991.

———. *Border Matters: Remapping American Cultural Studies.* Berkeley: University of California Press, 1997.

Saldívar, Ramón. *Chicano Narrative: The Dialectics of Difference.* Madison: University of Wisconsin Press, 1990.

———. *The Borderlands of Culture: Américo Paredes and the Transnational Imaginary.* Durham, N.C.: Duke University Press, 2006.

Samora, Julian, Joe Bernal, and Albert Peña. *Gunpowder Justice: A Reassessment of the Texas Rangers.* Notre Dame: University of Notre Dame Press, 1979.

Sherwood, Robert E. "The Bad Man." *Life.* November 1, 1923. 26.

Shohat, Ella. "Ethnicities-in-Relation: Toward a Multicultural Reading of American Cinema." *Unspeakable Images: Ethnicity and the American Cinema.* Ed. Lester D. Friedman. Urbana, Ill.: University of Illinois Press, 1991. 215–50.

Shohat, Ella, and Robert Stam. *Unthinking Eurocentrism: Multiculturalism and the Media.* London: Routledge, 1994.

Slotkin, Richard. *Gunfighter Nation: The Myth of the Frontier in Twentieth-Century America.* New York: Harper Perennial, 1992.

Smith, C. W. "'The Ballad of Gregorio Cortez': A Treatment for an Adaptation." Américo Paredes Papers. n.d. Nettie Lee Benson Latin American Collection. University of Texas at Austin. Box 15, Folder 7.

Southern Poverty Law Center. "Anti-Immigration Groups." *Intelligence Report,* Spring 2001. http://www.splcenter.org/intel/intelreport/article.jsp?sid=175.

Spivak, Gayatri Chakravorty. "Can the Subaltern Speak?" *The Post-Colonial Studies Reader*. Ed. Bill Ashcroft, et al. London: Routledge, 1995. 24–28.

Taylor, Clyde. "The Re-Birth of the Aesthetic in Cinema." *The Birth of Whiteness: Race and the Emergence of U.S. Cinema*. Ed. Daniel Bernardi. New Brunswick, N.J.: Rutgers University Press, 1996. 15–37.

Taylor, Mark C. *Altarity*. Chicago: University of Chicago Press, 1987.

Teatro Campesino. *I Am Joaquin*. Narr. Luis Valdez. El Centro Campesino Cultural, 1969.

Thorpe, Richard, dir. *The Bad Man*. Perf. Wallace Beery. Metro-Goldwyn-Meyer, 1941.

Treasures from the American Film Archives. Vol 1. DVD. Image Entertainment, 2000.

"A Trip Thru Barbarous Mexico." Advertisement. *The Moving Picture World*. March 15, 1913. 1142.

Usai, Paolo Cherchi, gen. ed. *The Griffith Project*. 5 vols. London: British Film Institute, 1999.

Valdez, Luis. "I Don't Need No Stinking Badges." 1986. *Zoot Suit and Other Plays*. Houston: Arte Público Press, 1992.

———. "Zoot Suit." 1978. *Zoot Suit and Other Plays*. Houston: Arte Público Press, 1992.

———, dir. *Zoot Suit*. Perf. Edward James Olmos. 1981. DVD. Universal Studios, 2003.

Vélez-Ibáñez, Carlos G. *Border Visions: Mexican Cultures of the Southwest United States*. Tucson, Ariz.: University of Arizona Press, 1997.

Vigil, Evangelina. *Thirty an' Seen a Lot*. Houston: Arte Público Press, 1985.

"Wallace Beery Plays in Capitol's 'Bad Man.'" *Eagle*. April 2, 1941.

Wallerstein, Immanuel. "Culture as the Ideological Battleground of the Modern World-System. *Geopolitics and Geoculture: Essays on the Changing World System*. Cambridge: Cambridge University Press, 1991. 158–83.

———. "The Rise and Future Demise of the World Capitalist System: Concepts for Comparative Analysis." *The Essential Wallerstein*. New York: The New Press, 2000. 71–105.

Watts, Jr., Richard. "The Bad Man." *New York Herald Tribune*. September 29, 1930.

Wegner, John. "Modes of Confrontation in Elmer Kelton's *The Time it Never Rained*." *Southwestern American Literature* 27.2 (Spring 2002): 69–74.

Wertheim, Stanley. "Unraveling the Humanist: Stephen Crane and Ethnic Minorities." *American Literary Realism, 1870–1910* 30.3 (Spring 1998): 65–75.

"The Whimsical Bandit." *New York Times*. October 9, 1923. 17.

Williams, Raymond. *Marxism and Literature*. Oxford: Oxford University Press, 1977.

Woollcott, Alexander. "A Mexican Robin Hood." *New York Times*. August 31, 1920. 16.

Young, Robert J. *White Mythologies: Writing History and the West*. London: Routledge, 1990.

———. *Colonial Desire: Hybridity in Theory, Culture and Race*. London: Routledge, 1995.

Young, Robert M., dir. *The Ballad of Gregorio Cortez*. Perf. Edward James Olmos. 1982. VHS. Metro-Goldwyn-Mayor (MGM), 1983.

———. "The Ballad of Gregorio Cortez." n.d. Screenplay. Américo Paredes Papers. Nettie Lee Benson Latin American Collection. University of Texas at Austin. Box 9, Folder 13.

Index

ghosts: symbolism of, 100–103, 107–8
Gold Hat: symbolism of, 15, 16,
17(fig.), 46, 167–68, 170n9
Gómez-Peña, Guillermo, 8
Gonzalez, Rodolfo "Corky," 138–39,
176n6
González, Jesús, 144, 146
greasers, 4, 22; as character, 15, 23, 25,
33–44, 52–53
Greaser's Gauntlet, The, 19, 22, 33, 42, 45,
52, 53, 171n7; cut-in, 39–41; hero
in, 66, 67; themes in, 35–36, 37–39
"Gregorio Cortez," 109
Griffith, D. W., 18, 58; racism of,
23–24, 32–33; Westerns, 19, 22,
33–44

Hart, William S., 19, 54, 55, 56–57,
66–67, 172n6
hate speech, 167, 168
Hearst, William Randolph, 48, 51
Hearst conglomerate, 19, 47, 48, 49
Hearst-Selig News Pictorial, 48
Hell's Hinges, 55–56
heroes, heroism, 29, 54, 96, 122;
Anglo-American, 24, 44, 55, 116;
good badmen, 66–67; Mexican
American, 30–31, 110–11, 114,
141; Texas Rangers as, 130–31;
Whiteness and, 56–57
history-making, 135, 149–50, 177n11
Hollingsworth, Alfred, 56(fig.)
Hottentot Venus: as Other, 11–12
Huston, John, 15–16
Huston, Walter, 69, 78, 79(fig.), 83
hybridity, 2, 21, 136, 137–38, 166;
in *Come and Take It Day*, 143–53

I Am Joaquin, 138–39, 176n6
identity, 93; American, 65–66, 67–68,
166–67; Chicano/a, 137–38, 142,
145–46, 150; contestation of, 20–21;
cultural, 3, 140–41; formation of,
12–13; male, 25–26; Mexican,
85–86, 96; Mexican American, 1–2;

Mexican male, 5, 118, 165–66;
popular culture and, 17–18
"I Don't Have to Show You No
Stinking Badges," 167
immigrant rights groups, 167–68
imperialism, 30, 105
Indianness: and identity, 138
individualism, 102, 103
Insurrection, The, 50
Iturbide, Graciela, 161

Juarez After the Siege, 48, 49

Kalem studios, 49
Kazan, Elia, 20, 94, 99
Kelton, Elmer: *Manhunters*, 20, 110–11,
127–29, 130–34, 176n10; nontraditional Westerns, 129–30

land disputes: as theme, 100–108
Latin American New Cinema, 137
legends: Anglo-Texan, 116–17
Liberty, 51
Life of General Villa, The, 50–51
literature, 8, 18, 47, 170n10; Mexicans
in, 58–63, 170–71n21; popular, 23,
24, 33
London, Jack, 173n11; "The Mexican,"
19, 59–63
"Louie, El," 2, 13, 169n1
lust: as theme, 35, 37, 70–71
lynching, 22, 170n1

Madero, Francisco, 48, 91, 92
Manhunters, 20, 110–11, 176n10;
Paredes on, 127–28; themes in,
128–29, 130–34
Martin, Chrispin, 81, 83(fig.)
Martyrs of the Alamo, 57–58, 172n4
masculinity, 20, 47, 64, 135, 141;
codes of conduct, 122–23; Gregorio
Cortez's, 121–22; Mexican, 4–5,
30–31, 115, 146, 165–66; Mexican
vs. Anglo-American, 25–26, 68–69;
Villa's, 91–92

Ramona, 33, 40
redemption, 37, 38–39, 67
Red Girl, The, 33, 42, 45
reform, 35–37
resistance, 16; to modernity, 105–6
revolutionaries, 4, 19, 20, 52, 106; dress, 53–54; portrayals of, 59–63, 85–99; Villa as, 50–51
Rio Grande, 65, 173n1
Rivera, Tomás, 117–18
Roland, Gilbert, 16
romance, 37–38, 40–41, 42–43

salvation: as Griffith theme, 36–37
San Antonio, 21, 177n9, 177n10; tourism in, 136, 147–48, 177n14; Vigil's poetry on, 154–64
satire: The Bad Man as, 69–74
scapegoats, 39, 42
Scully, John, 124
self-representation, 135–36
Selig newsreels, 49
sexuality, 25–26, 93; in Viva Villa!, 89–91; in Viva Zapata!, 97–98
Shadow, The, 20, 85, 86; themes in, 99–108
Smith, Charles W., 124–26
social mobility, 148–49
social movements: slogans, 16–17
Somewhere in Mexico, 49–50
Song of the Lark, 58–59
"Spinning on Solid Ground," 154–55
Starring Pancho Villa as Himself, And, 58
Steinbeck, John, 172–73n9; Viva Zapata!, 94, 96, 98–99
stereotypes, 6, 167, 170n5; ambivalence of, 45, 86–87; formation of, 3–4, 9–11; Mexican male, 2–3, 15–16, 22, 25, 33–34, 46–47, 122–23; as mode of representation, 8–9; of Native Americans, 13–14, 42; Paredes on, 123–24; of Texans, 115–16; in Viva Villa!, 87–91; in Viva Zapata!, 96–99
subjectification, 6–7, 10, 105

subjective splitting, 9–10, 11, 16
Sykes, Johnny, 89, 91, 92–93

Taint of Fear, 51
Tampico Incident, The, 48, 49
Tavern Keeper's Daughter, The, 33, 34, 35, 36–37, 66, 67, 90
Texas, 24, 58, 109–10, 116–17, 130, 172n4
Texas Rangers, 110, 111, 116, 124–25, 130–31, 144, 146
Thirty an' Seen a Lot, 21, 135–36; themes in, 154–64
Thread of Destiny, The, 33, 42–43
"Three White Mice, The," 26
tourism: in San Antonio, 136, 147–48, 156, 159–60, 177n14
Treasure of the Sierra Madre, 15–16, 17(fig.), 46, 84
Trip Through Barbarous Mexico, A, 48, 49
truth: in film making, 150–51
Turner, John Kenneth, 58

Under Fire in Mexico, 48, 50
U.S. Marines, 49
U.S.–Mexico War, 116–17

Valdez, Luis: works by, 138–41, 167
Vaquero's Vow, The, 33
Velez, Lupe, 16
Veracruz: U.S. Marines in, 49, 50
Vigil, Evangelina, 3; poetry of, 21, 135–16, 153–64, 177–78n16
Villa, Francisco "Pancho," 10, 19, 48, 52, 53, 57, 69, 97; film portrayals of, 85–91; masculinity of, 91–92; newsreels on, 50–51; United States and, 49–50
Villa—Dead or Alive, 48, 50
village Indians, 124–25
villains: in Griffith films, 34, 35, 42; in literature, 24–25; Mexicans as, 44, 55–56, 172n5; in Westerns, 19, 53, 54
Villaseñor, Victor, 117, 119, 141

About the Author

Juan J. Alonzo is currently an associate professor in the English department at Texas A & M University. He received his Ph.D. in American Literature and Cultural Studies from the University of Texas at Austin. His teaching and research interests include Mexican American literature and culture, American literature, film studies, and American studies. Alonzo's specialties include Chicano/a literature and cultural studies, the representation of ethnicity in the American Western, contemporary Chicano/a filmmaking, and the work of Américo Paredes. He has published essays in *Aztlán: A Journal of Chicano Studies*, *Western American Literature*, *A Companion to the American Novel* (Blackwell 2009), and *Recovering the U.S. Hispanic Literary Heritage*, volume 6 (Arte Público 2006). He has a forthcoming essay on the films of Jesús Salvador Treviño in *Born of Resistance: Cara a Cara Encounters with Chicano/a Visual Culture* (Arizona 2009). A native of San Antonio, professor Alonzo grew up watching Westerns with his father, to which he traces his fascination for the movies.

LaVergne, TN USA
11 January 2011
212079LV00001B/4/P